Neurobiology of Cognition

COGNITION Special Issues

The titles in this series are paperback, readily accessible editions of the Special Issues of *COGNITION: An International Journal of Cognitive Science*, edited by Jacques Mehler and produced by special agreement with Elsevier Science Publishers B.V.

VISUAL COGNITION, Steven Pinker, guest editor

THE ONSET OF LITERACY: Cognitive Processes in Reading Acquisition, Paul Bertelson, guest editor

SPOKEN WORD RECOGNITION, Uli H. Frauenfelder and Lorraine Komisarjevsky Tyler, guest editors

CONNECTIONS AND SYMBOLS, Steven Pinker and Jacques Mehler, guest editors

NEUROBIOLOGY OF COGNITION, Peter D. Eimas and Albert M. Galaburda, guest editors

Neurobiology of Cognition

edited by
PETER D. EIMAS

and
ALBERT M. GALABURDA

A Bradford Book
The MIT Press
Cambridge, Massachusetts
London, England

First MIT Press edition, 1990
© 1989 Elsevier Science Publishers B.V., Amsterdam, the Netherlands

Reprinted from *Cognition: International Journal of Cognitive Science*, Volume 33, numbers 1-2 (1989). The MIT Press has exclusive license to sell this English-language book edition throughout the world.

Printed and bound in the United States of America

Library of Congress Cataloging-in-Publication Data

Neurobiology of cognition / edited by Peter D. Eimas and Albert M. Galaburda. — 1st MIT Press ed.

  p. cm. — (Cognition special issues)
"Reprinted from Cognition: international journal of cognitive science, volume 33, numbers 1-2 (1989)"—T.p. verso.
"A Bradford book."
Includes bibliographical references.
ISBN 0-262-55019-9
1. Cognition. 2. Neurobiology. I. Eimas, Peter D.
II. Galaburda, Albert M., 1948–   . III. Series.
[DNLM: 1. Cognition—physiology. 2. Neurobiology. BF 311 N494]
QP395.N485   1990
612'.8—dc20
DNLM/DLC
for Library of Congress   90-5517
                                                              CIP

Contents

Some agenda items for a neurobiology of cognition:
An introduction*

PETER D. EIMAS

Brown University, Providence

ALBERT M. GALABURDA

*Beth Israel Hospital and Harvard Medical
School, Boston*

Eimas, P.D., and Galaburda, A.M. 1989. Some agenda items for a neurobiology of cognition:
An introduction. Cognition, 33:1–23.

Introduction

Professor Frank Schmitt has written "... theories of higher brain function
(learning, memory, perception, self-awareness, consciousness) ... in general
lack cogency with respect to established anatomical and physiological facts
and are without biophysical and biochemical plausibility" (Schmitt, 1978,
p. 1). Not surprising in light of this statement, we find that Schmitt has also
applauded efforts attempting to construct a "... detailed, self-consistent
theory ... that specifies the operational repertoires at the level of molecules,
individual neurons, or groups (circuits) of neurons, and that explicitly defines
the postulated information processing mechanism" (p. 1). This goal, obviously desirable to most cognitive scientists and neurobiologists, can be
achieved only if cognitive scientists and neurobiologists alike make concerted
efforts to know those aspects of neurobiology and cognitive science, respectively, that are most relevant to their own research, and to keep abreast of
updated accounts. Indeed, we foresee little hope of a theory that is a biologically consistent, realistic description of human cognition in the absence of
interdisciplinary knowledge. It is the purpose of this special issue of *Cognition*
to bring to its readership a sample of instances in which theory in neurobiology has begun to become explanatory of complex behavioral processes, or in

*Preparation of this discussion was supported by a Sabbatic Leave Award from Brown University to
P.D.E. and by grants HD 05331-19 to P.D.E. and HD 20806-3 to A.M.G. The order of authorship is alphabet-
ical. Requests for reprints should be sent to Peter D. Eimas, Department of Cognitive and Linguistic Sciences,
Brown University, Providence, RI 02912, U.S.A., or to Albert M. Galaburda, Beth Israel Hospital and
Harvard Medical School, Neurology Unit, 330 Brookline Ave., Boston, MA 02215, U.S.A.

which such theory seems possible in a reasonable, not-too-distant future. There is little doubt in the minds of cognitivists that there is an entity called "the brain", and there is likewise little uncertainty in the brains of most neuroscientists regarding the existence of "the mind". But there is certainly an absence of unanimity among cognitive scientists for the belief that "the brain" will provide the ultimate explanations for things cognitive in complex organisms, or among neuroscientists that current formulations of "the mind" by cognitive scientists represent realistic accounts of what the behaviors of brain actually are. Nevertheless, few cognitivists would hold to the beliefs of substance dualists; virtually all are materialists in the sense of believing that for each and every act of cognition, whether, for example, perceiving an object as a separate, three-dimensional entity among a myriad of entities or understanding passages of poetry, there is to be found a neuroanatomical structure and a neurophysiological correlate, that is, an instantiation in the workings of the brain. Nevertheless, there is sentiment among some that there are limits on materialism, that is, on the extent to which explanations of the cognitive may be found in the physical. Thus, for example, Fodor (1975) argues that the natural kinds of the science of cognition, for instance intentions and the constituents of human language as exemplified by phrases, clauses, and sentences, will not be captured by the natural kinds constituting brain science. The latter include, for example, the anatomical constructs of DNA, neurotransmitters, peptides, ion channels, synapses, axons and dendrites, small neural nets, larger neural maps, larger distributed neural systems, or whole nervous systems. The constructs of neurobiology also include the physiological processes that these structures support, such as transcription, synaptic transmission, enzymatic activity, ionic transport, axonal and dendritic depolarization, neuronal group firing, event-related potentials, or hemispheric glucose consumption.

There is an interesting (and to some maddening) direct counter to the contention that the natural kinds of cognition cannot be reduced to the natural kinds of neuroscience. This is the argument of eliminative materialism, recently presented in an articulate and comprehensive treatise by Patricia Churchland (1986). While philosophers holding to this view recognize, as sentient beings, the activities of mental life, especially those that are so readily available to conscious awareness, for example, the intentional attitudes of believing, knowing, or desiring, they dispute the validity of these and other descriptors of cognition as descriptors of the activity of the brain during acts of cognition. They argue that the state of functional descriptors and explanations of cognition is primitive and, like the primitive structures of other sciences in their earliest stages of development, undoubtedly incorrect. Such structures, as a consequence, should not be driving (constraining) forces in the construction of neurobiological theories of cognition. Rather, as the argument continues, once there is a completed science of neurobiology, a full understanding and explanation of cognition will be naturally and readily derived consequences. Within this view it is of course possible, although unlikely – argue the eliminative materialists given the history of science – that (some of) the constructs of modern cognitive science, the present descriptions and terms of explanation, will find correspondence with the descriptors of neurobiology. This is all to say that the science of cognition in its present guise will be (to some extent) reduced to the science of neurobiology, rather than replaced by some other cognitive description. Of course, if the eliminative materialists are correct and the descriptive categories of mind are incorrect, then one aspect of the problem is eliminated, namely the translation (reduction) of these cognitive mentalistic constructs into the descriptive terms of brain science. But even if this view is true, there still remains the problem of describing the levels of organization of the brain and determining how they result in, for example, the comprehension of a specific sentence or connected discourse, however they are represented in cognitive theory. The position of the eliminative materialists would seem only to eliminate one set of descriptors that presently inform a considerable part of the effort to understand human cognition, while leaving a physical solution as open (our polite word for uninformative) as it is at present.

These views are, of course, modern philosophical reflections on the mind–body problem, and not part of the working assumptions of modern neuroscience, although we suspect that the basic premises of eliminative materialism are not infrequently received with considerable sympathy by neurobiologists as well as by a substantial number of cognitive scientists. Like those who claim that the science of cognition is in principle an irreducible, autonomous science (e.g., Fodor, 1975), the eliminative materialists offer an extreme view of the mind–body problem – one that does not easily fit with our intuitions. We offer no further comment on either of these extreme views. Rather, we note only that we prefer the stance of most scientists in both fields, or what we believe to be the majority view, namely, that whether there are complex cognitive functions, ranging from intentional attitudes to perception, to understanding language, and to problem solving, that are explicable in neurobiology is simply an open empirical question. And on this view rests this special issue of *Cognition.*

For completeness we should add that there is the strong belief among many that there is a third, algorithmic (i.e., computational) level of analysis in addition to the level of brain and the level of cognition (Marr & Poggio, 1979). This level is presumed to be logically distinct from either the activities of the mind or the hardware that instantiates (i.e., implements) activities and computations, but still constrained by both the possible activities and the hardware of the species. This view of three logically independent levels of analysis does not, however, find universal acceptance. Changeux and De-haene (this issue) and Edelman (1987a), among others, argue against a separate level of computation, which they view as a program that requires instruction, if not by a homunculus, then by the environment *or* a detailed genetic code, which in their view are equally improbable. It remains, how-ever, to be empirically determined whether there is really a logically indepen-dent computational level and, if so, whether it will find a neurobiological explanation, although we will assume for the present discussion that a compu-tational level exists.

Brain and mind, the objects of study of neurobiology and cognitive science respectively, also represent in the history of science interesting and attractive metaphors to explain the evolution of the behavior of complex systems, most notably that of humankind. For example, natural selection acts most obvi-ously on behavioral capacities. Consequently, these capacities, and the mind they presumably reflect, are the clearest measure of the accomplishments of human evolution, and their study, when comparative in nature, can enlighten the origins of the characteristics that define humanity – an endeavor of im-mense inherent interest even if the methodology by its very nature leaves the mechanisms of evolution unspecified. By contrast, the phylogenetic path taken by the human brain over its 2.5 million years of evolution (or thereab-outs), and its computational characteristics, are most likely slavish to the behavioral consequences of its physical and computational changes. On the other hand, of course, the metaphor of brain takes its strength, its appeal, in the fact that the brain has an undeniable physical presence that permits more directly the study of the evolutionary mechanisms underlying this most com-plex of biological structures. Indeed, with sufficient knowledge of the relation between neurophysiology and cognition the (partial) reconstruction of our cognitive evolution may be possible from the reconstruction of neural struc-tures from fossil records.

The problem for a neurobiology of cognition, however, lies not in whether each metaphor, brain and mind, represents a valid, if not always mutually interesting, approach to the study of cognition, the behavioral acts and mental events of complex biological organisms, most notably human beings. Instead, the main issue, as we have noted – empirically answerable and hence the focus of this special issue – is the extent to which it will be possible to explain observations made under the guise of one metaphor in terms of observations derived from use of the other metaphor. Of course, adequate theoretical descriptions will enable us to move beyond explanations, for example, to formulate predictions about degree and type of change in one plane from observations of change in the other – an advancement that should have enormous practical consequences.

Structure of mind

For all of us, there is the mind, that seemingly lofty structure that is perceptive, thoughtful, and even reflective, the most mysterious of all its functions. However, as most scientists believe, these and other workings of the mind reflect a set of inherited dispositions to behave according to principles and rules, slowly being discovered, that were established over the long course of our species' evolution (phylogeny) and also the individual's personal history of interactions with the environment (ontogeny). The latter determines the actualization of individualized cognitive structures, just as is true of course for physical structures. In the metaphor of mind, there is a functional architecture that represents the organization of cognitive structures and that determines their manner of interaction with the environment and with each other. It is this functional architecture that presumably provides a theory of the workings of mind, that is, of cognition. It is a neurobiological description of the functional architecture that is sought when we speak of the physical instantiation of cognitive theory.

The functional architecture that represents mind and the processes of cognition can be analyzed at many levels. This is perhaps made most explicit in our descriptions of the processes – the representations, their transformations, and the use of knowledge structures – that are involved in the production and understanding of spoken language. On most views of spoken language understanding, representations of the physical signal are available at auditory, phonetic, lexical, syntactic, and semantic levels. The knowledge structures that are presumed to underlie the transformations include the processes of speech perception and production, the phonological and syntactic rules, the meanings of individual lexical units as well as rules and constraints on their generalization and combination, the pragmatics of language use, and finally world knowledge. But, as is well known, we do not as yet have a comprehensive and coherent theoretical description of the content, organization, or manner in which these levels of representation and knowledge structures operate so as to permit the rapid and effortless execution and interpretation of speech acts. Nevertheless, sufficient knowledge and theory exist to begin a detailed search for neurobiological understanding of language and its manner of function. Similar analyses can be given for other aspects of cognition – the perception of form, for example, which is actually an interesting and relatively rare example, inasmuch as both functional and physical descriptions and explanations are advancing and are even beginning to find correspondence (see, for example, Hubel & Wiesel, 1977; Marr, 1982).

Structure of brain

Brain by the very fact of its being a physical structure has seemed to many inadequate to capture the properties of mind, especially its intentionality and its awareness of itself. But this seeming inadequacy, as we have tried to argue, is not to be taken as an *a priori* truth, but rather an issue to be empirically determined. Like mind, brain reflects phylogenetic and ontogenetic experience. The phylogenetic history delimits the overall physical architecture, the types of elements constituting this architecture, and the rules and principles governing their interaction, all arising from a narrow range of possibilities that involve highly regulated combinations and chronologies of gene expression; for example, Jane's brain and all normal human brains are large, have temporal lobes, Heschl's gyri, callosal connections, Meynert stellates, asymmetrical synapses, testosterone receptors, and cell adhesion molecules. The ontogenetic history, through environmental (epigenetic) interactions capable of modifying the expression of the more modifiable of these genes, determines the particular brain architecture that emerges from within the genetically determined range of possibilities and thus, to continue our example, Jane's brain weighs 1500 g, has asymmetric temporal lobes, two Heschl's gyri on the right, a thick corpus callosum, and increased sensitivity to testosterone possibly as a result of abnormal early exposure to the sex steroid, and a tendency to tomboyish behaviors (Money & Ehrhardt, 1972); thus, this variability has functional correlates. In other instances of epigenetic influences, the receptive fields in the sensory cortex for the hand surface of adult monkeys varies among adult individuals (Merzenich et al., 1987), a developmentally determined decrease in the magnitude of anatomical asymmetry of some language areas correlates with disorders of reading acquisition (Galaburda et al., 1985), and a proportion of humans do not show aphasic symptoms after lesions in the left frontal lobe (Mohr et al., 1978). But, in all cases the variation of normal individuals finds expression within the constancy of the species.

An understanding of the architecture of brain requires delineation and understanding of its many levels of functioning. First, there is the gross anatomical level of hemispheres and lobes, frontal and occipital poles, dorsal and ventral and medial and lateral surfaces, cortical and subcortical grey masses, gyri and sulci which during the phrenological period were thought to correlate with cognitive and emotional traits and which today are found to be moderately useful for predicting functional deficits after injury and some gross developmental abnormalities. At the next level, in terms of decreasing structural complexity, there are widely distributed neuronal systems or more locally restricted networks or maps. These assemblies are composed of specific numbers and types of neurons and interconnections, with each assembly presumably having separate and distinct functional properties. For example, there is the neuronal assembly that contains huge numbers of parvocellular neurons in the lateral geniculate nucleus and "blob" and thin-stripe neurons in the visual cortices and participates in (motionless) color perception (Livingstone & Hubel, 1988). Conversely, there may be a much smaller neuronal assembly such as that responsible for the vestibulo-ocular response, for instance, which contains only a few thousand input neurons, motor neurons, interneurons, cerebellar neurons, and sensory feedback neurons (Lisberger, 1988). Next we find the level of the individual neuron with specific functional properties, for example, the orientation (Zeki, 1983) or color-sensitive (Hubel & Livingstone, 1983; Zeki, 1983) neuron, useful for determining "receptive field" maps of *neural representation* of the external space, or the Mauthner neuron, which appears to play a role in impulse propagation (Yasargil, Adert, & Sandri, 1986).

At subcellular levels of description, the first is that of synapses. Examples of brain functioning at this level are illustrated by the presynaptic impingement of the mantle neurons onto the tail neuron, which modifies the latter's influence on the motor neuron to the gill of *Aplysia* during that invertebrate animal's habituation or sensitization (Kandel, 1976). The level of membrane is next in order with the activity of the postsynaptic N-methyl-d-aspartate (NMDA) receptor for excitatory amino acids in the mammalian hippocampal neuron, thought to mediate plasticity associated with long-term (declarative, but not procedural) memory (Morris, Anderson, Lynch, & Baudry, 1986; also see Cotman & Lynch, this volume), as well as with the actions of chemoreceptors, adhesion molecules, and ionic channels. Here local cell–cell interactions are determined, for example, by the closing of a calcium channel and decreasing release of neurotransmitter that is associated with habituation to a sensory stimulus in the behaving *Aplysia* and by the transformation of the cell adhesion molecule seen at the point when the cells forming a feather adopt the desired architecture (Gallin, Chuong, Finkel, & Edelman, 1986). The process of an emerging structure – resulting from the interaction between genetic and epigenetic effects – continues at each of these levels throughout life, albeit less at maturity and senescence (e.g., McKinley, Jenkins, Smith, & Merzenich, 1987; Wall & Eggers, 1971).

As we have claimed and attempted briefly to show, analysis of the architecture of the brain at multiple levels is necessary if the functional architecture and the complexities of human cognition evident in even its most basic forms, including perception, learning, categorization, and memory, are to be understood in terms of neurobiological principles. Moreover, the structural development of the brain, specifically, the change in morphology during ontogenesis (Edelman, 1987b; Hubel & Wiesel, 1970) that might accommodate a new memory, or percept, or category (Changeux & Dehaene, this issue), has been demonstrated at many levels. For example, it has been shown in the number of cells comprising a neuronal assembly (Cowan, 1973; Graziadei & Monti Graziadei, 1979a, 1979b; Hamburger & Oppenheim, 1982; Oppenheim, 1981; Williams & Rakic, 1988), in the detailed structure of individual neurons (their dendritic and axonal structure) (Altman & Tyrer, 1977; Bastiani, du Lac, & Goodman, 1985; Kramer, Goldman, & Stent, 1985; Purpura, 1974; Ramón y Cajal, 1929), and in the detailed pattern of connections (inputs, outputs, overlaps; local circuits and long-ranging projections) (Easter, 1983; Ebesson, 1984; Hubel & Wiesel, 1977; Innocenti & Clarke, 1983; Ivy, Akers, & Killackey, 1979; Jones, 1981; Wise & Jones, 1976). This variation has, in addition, been shown in the arrangement of neurons in specific laminar and columnar arrays (cytoarchitectonics), with each cell type present in particular positions and at appropriate densities (Rakic, 1988; Woolsey et al., 1981), in the type of chemical transmission available to cells in a group and to cells at different times (Anderson & Cohen, 1977; Bixby & Spitzer, 1982; Goodman & Spitzer, 1981), in the electrical properties of single and distributed neurons (Goodman & Spitzer, 1981; Kano, 1975; Miyake, 1978; Mountcastle, 1978), in the chemical and electrical properties of synapses and membranes, which determine their dynamic responses (Carew, Hawkins, Abrams, & Kandel, 1984; Changeux & Danchin, 1976; Kandel, 1976; Llinás, Steinberg, & Walton, 1976; Lynch, Dunwiddie, & Gribkoff, 1977; Scholz & Byrne, 1987; Goodman & Spitzer, 1981), in the metabolic and transport properties of neurons (Bayon et al., 1979; Giacobini, 1975; Shaw & Meinertzhagen, 1986; Sokoloff, 1981; Swaab & Boer, 1983; Van Orden, Bloom, Barnett, & Giarman, 1966), including the effects of hormones originating in distant endocrine sites (McEwen, De Kloet, & Rostene, 1986; Nottebohm, 1981), and, finally, in the interactions between neurons and other elements such as glia (Fedoroff, 1978; Hatten, Liem, & Mason, 1984).

Mind–brain correspondences

The first problem to be solved in the quest for a neurobiology of cognition is how levels of description of mind correspond to levels of description of brain. On one extreme, some behaviors are associated with change in an ionic channel or a protein constituent (Alkon, 1984; Scholz & Byrne, 1987; also see Cotman & Lynch, this issue); others may require change in the response properties of a whole neuron (Braak & Braak, 1976; Chan-Palay, Palay, & Billings-Gagliardi, 1974; Winfield, 1982; Yasargil et al., 1986); and, still others, on the other extreme, are associated only with demonstrable changes in a large neuronal network (Fox, Burton, & Raichle, 1987; Ingvar, 1983; Larsen, Skinhoj, & Lassen, 1978; Llinás, 1981). But the problem is even more complex. We know that a particular knowledge structure may be neurally represented in more than a single locus, with some representations in distinct architectonic areas (Fox et al., 1987; Ingvar, 1983; Larsen et al., 1978; Posner, Petersen, Fox, & Raichle, 1988; also see Damasio, this issue). Obviously these multiple representations for a single knowledge structure, as well as for the many structures that are needed to represent the things and events of the world, must be concatenated in terms of time and space if neurological explanations are to capture the complexity and coherence that are characteristic of the world we know. An idea of the enormity of this problem is readily forthcoming when we contemplate the possible neurological requirements for the production or comprehension of even a single sentence, to draw once more on our favorite example, that of language. Thus, we need to know what are the physical counterparts of cognitive representations and their temporal organizations as we move from auditory to phonetic to lexical to syntactic and to semantic structures, and how internalized information in the form of rules and knowledge of varying forms are physically instantiated (See Miller & Juczyk, this issue) so as to yield the multi-leveled, yet unified description that is apparently necessary for any instance of language understanding or production. There is some thinking (see Damasio, this issue), but little empirical evidence, informing the problem of binding, that is, the reconstitution of an entity from parts that appear to be spatially segregated in the nervous system, and the problem of bonding, that is, the unification of sequential experience into whole events.

Empirical challenges and approaches

With our improving capacity to describe behavior and brain at several levels at once, and to measure accurately changes in functional (cognitive) and physical (brain) states, it is becoming increasingly probable that we shall be able to detect how the structures and mechanisms of brain and the processes of cognition map onto one another, if indeed they do. If this is ultimately to occur, however, a fastidiously chronological approach is crucial in both descriptive planes. As is amply demonstrated in the brain, changes occurring at one anatomical level and locus usually propagate to other levels and to other anatomically or humorally related loci, which can potentially obscure the level and locus at which physical change is relevant (causally related) to the originally observed behavior. This potentially confounding phenomenon, moreover, occurs with both relatively long and quite short time spans and in both immature and mature nervous systems. For example, at relatively longer spans of time, monocular enucleation (and to an extent even less severe environmental deprivation) in developing monkeys leads to cellular, architectonic, and connectional changes in the visual thalamus and visual cortex (see Rakic, 1988; Sretavan & Shatz, 1986a, 1986b); similarly, injury to the developing visual system of the hamster leads to plastic reorganization that further complicates the original visual loss (Schneider, 1981). At lower levels injury might be associated with the release of trophic molecules (Needels et al., 1986), which themselves can alter the behavioral capacities of the brain by their actions on these levels (Aloe, Cozzari, Calissano, & Levi-Montalcini, 1981). Even in the mature state damage to the (possibly) behaviorally relevant architecture of a neuronal circuit will propagate rapidly to the lowest levels of gene regulation and expression, and the physical events that follow may merely reflect attempts at repairing the damage, whereas the physical state that actually explains the behavior may not be as easily observed. In other words, before one can say that a particular protein or messenger is responsible for a particular behavioral state, it is important to determine whether these substances might not be involved in epiphenomena such as maintenance and upkeep of the machinery or even reaction to the behavior. This is a particularly sticky point in contemporary research on neurodegenerative disorders such as Alzheimer's disease, in which it is difficult to tell whether accumulated substances in the brain parenchyma cause the disease and its behavioral accompaniments, or simply reflect a point in a cascade of secondary changes. In some well-documented experimental research involving lesion-induced abnormal behaviors, the observed behaviors appear indeed to be the result of anatomical reactions to the injury more so than a direct consequence of the injury itself (Schneider, 1981).

At quite short periods of time, we need to be able to describe how interactions with environmental forces operate so as to change synaptic resistances, electrical activity, metabolic characteristics, and network organization, as well as their subsequent effects on levels at a far remove. Numerous data (Bartlett et al., 1987; Byrne, 1987; Fischler et al., 1983; Hillyard & Kutas, 1983; Ingvar, 1983; John et al., 1986; Lang et al., 1987; Mazziotta, Phelps, & Carson 1984; Rugg, Kok, Barrett & Fischler, 1986; Posner et al., 1988) are available on local changes in metabolic activity, electrical activation, and blood flow related to language, visual perception, and memory functions, which provide an idea about the structures involved in the processes (actively or passively; excited or inhibited), within the time scales tapped by the procedures, but not about the nature of the processes themselves or their relationship to the observed behaviors. In other words, the "physiological" codes, which these measures appear to represent, do not approximate the explanatory value that would be afforded by a truly computational code, that is, the brain's algorithm for the observed behavior. And similarly, if the current metaphor of mind is correct, the various representations that are presumed to be formed for brief periods of time in response to environmental signals, whether they be simple visual forms or the complex acoustic signals of connected discourse, require that we be able to independently measure them and the processes of transformation across real time if we are to discover how the presumed stages of processing in the mental plane find instantiation in the physical domain of brain. And longer experiences that result in relatively permanent modifications of functional structures, such as must occur after we have acquired (or fixed) the rules or codes that determine how various objects and events in the environment are to be categorized and sentences are to be defined, must likewise be carefully measured across time. There would seem to be no other course if we are to understand the locus of these modifications and how such relatively permanent modifications exert their influence in both an upward and downward fashion and how they are mapped onto physical descriptions.

The incorporation of developmental phenomena, including descriptions of the initial state(s) (Mehler & Fox, 1985) and their development into stable states (cf. Changeux & Dehaene, this issue, and Edelman, 1987a), into material and functional theories of cognition is but a further example of what we have labeled a chronological approach to the study of mind and brain. It offers a precious opportunity for observing and comparing changes in states of brain and mind. Moreover, it permits examination of the functional or physical plane at, or close to, its beginning, when there has not been sufficient time for the unfolding of every physical and behavioral disposition and their subsequent modifications. Systems of interest are thus caught at relatively simple states of being, which surely must enhance the chances of successful mappings between the cognitive and neurobiological planes of description.

Experiments of nature, whether originating in corrupted genetic blueprints (presenting anomalous initial states), or in deviant environmental interactions during sensitive periods of development or maintenance, or in mature states that have sustained damage, can lead to variability or frank abnormality characterized by extraordinary functional and physical architectures. The study of these architectures can enlighten the understanding of the relationship between mind and brain. For instance, preliminary research has suggested a relation between processing styles in language activities and variants of cerebral lateralization that are distinguishable from one another by virtue of their distinct patterns of neuronal and connectional organization (Bever et al., in press; Galaburda, Aboitiz, Rosen, & Sherman, 1986;

Galaburda, Corsiglia, Rosen, & Sherman, 1987a; Galaburda, Rosen, & Sherman, 1987b). Similarly, individuals with some developmental language disorders differ in the patterns of cerebral laterality and asymmetry, and may exhibit alterations in local and widespread cortical architecture and connections (Galaburda & Kemper, 1979; Galaburda et al., 1987a, 1987b). Analysis of the plasticity and regenerative capacities of physical structures after experimentally induced injury can refine this understanding through carefully timed manipulations and observations in both physical and functional structures. As with developmental studies, experimentally induced loss of physical structures can be examined for the emergence of new functional properties or the alteration of old properties. Furthermore, the degree of change at one level of the physical plane can be evaluated with respect to the degree of change at other physical levels and at multiple levels within the functional plane. Such observations can help to answer questions regarding, for example, the extent of change in the physical state, in terms of source and propagation, that is required before changes in functional capacities will be detected, and whether continuous changes in one level of alterations result in continuous or discontinuous effects in other physical levels and in functional capacities.

The study of biological systems that are simple by virtue of their ontogenetic state may be complemented by studies of animals that are simple by virtue of their phylogenetic history (see Cotman & Lynch, this issue). These (usually invertebrate) animals exhibit extremely simple neuronal arrangements and behavioral repertoires, perhaps only distantly telling of the human brain and mind. Nevertheless, some fundamental aspects of the human brain and mind appear to be highly conserved in evolution and thus found in these relatively easily studied organisms. A particularly striking example of this is the work by Kandel and his associates (Kandel, 1976; also see Cotman & Lynch, this issue). Thus, the retraction of a gill and similar simple motor responses in association with either conditioned or unconditioned stimuli have been shown to relate to specific changes in the ionic channels of the presynaptic neuron, and longer lasting effects have been linked to new protein synthesis. Even these simple paired associate effects, however, do not occur (as some might suggest) in an unbiased "connectionist" arrangement (see below) of input, output, and hidden units, but rather presuppose an already complex innate structure, an initial state, upon which certain stimuli and not others are capable of producing certain responses and not others. Similar statements can be made about research done on cell cultures and tissue slices, which reflect attempts to simplify the biology of complex vertebrate nervous systems.

Beyond empirical knowledge

We note as a final comment on strategies for realizing a neurobiology of cognition that there is need for formalisms that go beyond empirical research. What we have offered in our discussion to this point is in effect a metatheoretical discourse on the neurobiology of cognition. We have related some rather uncontroversial general principles, or so we believe, describing brain and mind that would be necessary in one form or another in any neurobiological or functional account of cognition. Thus, for example, we see no potential counter to the idea that operation of both brain and mind are multi-leveled and that the initial steps in constructing a neurobiological theory of some facet or facets of cognition will be to delineate these levels within each descriptive plane, determine the mappings across planes, and show how change in the levels in one plane of description determines and maps onto change in levels of the other. Recent examples of the use of principles of this nature are found in Kosslyn (1988) and Posner et al. (1988) in their analyses, respectively, of mental imagery and the codes (representations) that are involved in reading. Nor do we foresee objections to the idea that this analysis into levels within each descriptive plane must by necessity have a chronological character. The acts of cognition are not momentary, nor do they consist of single, discrete entities. Quite to the contrary, even relatively simple acts of perception and most certainly acts of problem solving, language comprehension, foresight, and remembering, are best described as being constituted of sets of continuously unfolding events that are coherent because of their chronological order, which by necessity must be functionally and neurally represented. To ignore this chronicity can only result in theoretical descriptions that have no correspondence with environments or organisms.

But even with problems of this nature solved, and this is certainly far from the case at present, and perhaps not for some considerable time despite increasing recognition of the issue (Changeux & Dehaene, this issue; Damasio, this issue; Edelman, 1987a), a comprehensive neurobiology of cognition requires more. First, biological descriptions of cognition cannot, given the current state of technology, rest solely on descriptions of genomic activity, synaptic strengths and connections, neural groupings or networks, and the anatomical interactions and interconnections across levels. This is not to claim that such descriptions are not necessary. Rather our contention is that such descriptions must, in view of present (and quite possibly future) methodologies, remain incomplete, given that they involve 10^{11} neurons and as many as 10^{15} connections. What descriptions there are at present must be augmented by abstract generalizations and formalisms that go well beyond our empirical knowledge. Thus, just as we require an innate predisposition early in life for deriving rules and meanings from the otherwise chaotic and seemingly disorganized spoken language around us during language acquisition, a theoretical "predisposition" of a formal nature is indispensable for the efficient acquisition of knowledge about the mind and its relationship to brain. Only in this manner, or so we believe, will neurobiologists overcome the obviously inherent limitation on our abilities to determine empirically the architectural and organizational details that are necessary for providing a neurobiological description of the complexities and coherence of cognition that we seek. Alternatives must be sought, and they have been, in the form of mathematical descriptions of neural functioning and neural networks. Of course, this is not a new development. Since the writings of McCulloch and Pitts (1943), formal descriptions of neural mechanisms and organized structures, based to varying degrees on known principles of neurophysiology and neurobiology, have been proffered in the attempt to explain behavior, including often quite complex acts of human cognition. At no time, however, has this endeavor been more prevalent than at present (e.g., Anderson & Hinton, 1981, Anderson & Rosenfeld, 1988; McClelland & Rumelhart, 1986), and equally impressive are the increasing sophistication of the formalisms that are used and the growing adherence to neurological realism.

Nevertheless, there is also a large body of criticism of this theoretical effort (e.g., Pinker & Mehler, 1987). A major concern of some cognitivists is whether formalisms based solely on associatively organized neural networks, without a formal representation of rules, will accommodate what appears to them to be rule-governed domains of cognition. And indeed the accomplishments of these formal models, while impressive in some domains, for example the acquisition and dissolution of associative links among lexical items (Kawamoto, 1985; Rossen, 1988), have done little to dispel the skepticism of those who hold that one of the benchmarks of cognition, especially in such domains as that of human language, is its rule-governed nature. We offer another complaint, namely, the very nearly universal lack of concern for inherited dispositions. It is our contention that it is the initial state(s) of a species – the very early, and, later, maturationally driven, biologically determined dispositions – that provide the origins of many specific cognitive achievements. Indeed, it is possible to argue that without such dispositions, without constraints on cognitive development, the very bases of our mental live, a rich conceptual network and a language, would in principle not be possible (e.g., Chomsky, 1965, 1980a, 1980b; Fodor, 1980). Evidence showing rather remarkable cognitive abilities in very young human infants has done much to strengthen our view that there are strong and pervasive innate dispositions that must find expression in neural models of cognition (e.g., Mehler & Fox,

1985, provide a number of reviews of the cognitive capacities across a wide range of activities). For how else are we to accommodate the findings that infants well within the first half year of life are able to perceive objects as unified entities (Kellman & Spelke, 1983), to form categorical representations for the sounds of speech and a seemingly indefinite number of groupings based on geometrical shapes and various artifacts (see Eimas, Miller, & Jusczyk, 1987; and Quinn & Eimas, 1986, for recent reviews), as well as to imitate motions and facial expressions (Meltzoff & Moore, 1977; and Field, Cohen, Greenberg, & Woodson, 1982)? In our view there is no other way; nor is there any alternative for accommodating the species-specific coherence that all successful organisms find in their environments, despite the indefinite number of alternatives that are available to all. In all fairness, we should note that the problem of innate dispositions has been a concern of neuronal group selection theory (e.g., Changeux & Dehaene, this issue, and Edelman, 1987a) and there is even evidence that the computational formalisms of the connectionists are beginning to change, and growing attention is now being paid to attempts to build "innate" properties into models (Hinton, 1988); these, so-called, innate properties will of course only make sense if they are constrained by knowledge of the behaviors (cognitive science) and of the brain (neuroscience).

The contributions

Having presented a general overview of what we believe is necessary for neurobiologically based theories of cognition and a brief review of recent accomplishments that makes us reasonably confident that successes will be forthcoming, we note in closing the plan of this issue.

There are six contributions, selected in part to provide a view of the range of activities that we believe constitute the growing endeavor to provide a neurobiology of cognition. Our selections range from what might be considered approaches in the style of the "grand scheme", that is, an attempt to provide the means of encompassing and explaining the full range of human cognition, to an examination of the functional structures for echolocation in the bat and their possible means of neuronal instantiation, and finally to the cellular and molecular structures of memory and learning.

The first contribution is by Antonio Damasio. He describes a global view of brain functioning. His treatise is a true example of a "grand scheme" – an overarching view showing how brain operates as an organized and organizing entity in contacting the world, in placing the organism in the world, and in directing cognition and the actions that result from cognition. Damasio presents the brain as a complex system with multiple levels and assemblies that represent aspects – features – of the world and the manner in which those aspects are bound together spatially to form entities and how entities are bound temporally to form coherent events. He introduces us to the interesting concept of convergence zones that perform the operation of binding. Working from these basic ideas, he attempts to describe a coherent view of brain: one that can ultimately accommodate human cognition from its simplest functions to its most complex accomplishments in the realm of perception and memory, and even provide an account of consciousness. This approach puts us in mind of Hebb's *Organization of behavior*.

The second contribution is by Jean-Pierre Changeux and Stanislas Dehaene. Their discussion provides us with a sophisticated and we believe realistic framework for the construction of abstract, formal models, the purpose of which is to capture and explain human cognition at both its simplest and most complex levels of functioning. In their overview they describe how their position is by necessity developmental (and chronological) in nature, both in a phylogenetic and ontogenetic sense, and tied deeply (not nominally) to the facts of neuroscience. Changeux and Dehaene also describe the principles and mechanisms for the acquisition and memory of knowledge at cellular and subcellular levels, briefly here and in greater detail in their other publications. They bring to their readers a picture of how synaptic organizations occur and assemblies of ever-changing neuronal arrangements form and reform and are "selected" by environment events for a role in cognition. Their Darwinistic approach is rare among theoretical neuroscientists, but in our view correct – there is little reason to believe that the growth of neuronal structures and the acquisition of knowledge follows principles other than those that have applied to the organism as an evolving entity or to other systems within the organism – the immune system, for example. Their contributions can be viewed as providing a means for the acquisition and retention of knowledge as well as a framework for constructing another form of "grand scheme", one that like Damasio's is potentially capable of accommodating even the most complex forms of cognition, for example, the recognition and execution of organized sequences of activity.

Next is a discussion of speech perception by Joanne Miller and Peter Jusczyk. Here, we contact that unique functional structure in humans – language. The authors are concerned solely with perception at the level of phonetics, which in being in closest contact with the acoustic representations of speech offers us the greatest hope of beginning the enterprise of building a neurobiological description of language that goes beyond descriptions of linguistic functions in anatomical terms. Although, as Miller and Jusczyk note, we have a good understanding of the physical signal and of a large number of perceptual phenomena as well as considerable knowledge of mammalian auditory systems, neurophysiological models of speech perception that can accommodate the basic, but complex, functions of segmentation and perceptual invariance remain as yet a matter for the future. What we have at present consists of a number of reasonably well-grounded speculations of a neurophysiological nature that are beginning to accommodate a number of interesting perceptual phenomena. The reasons for this state of affairs, as described by Miller and Jusczyk, include ethical limitations on investigations into the human auditory system as well as the fact that we are dealing with a highly complex system that may well be species specific and uniquely dedicated to the perception of speech. If the latter is true, our neurobiological theorizing must proceed to a large extent in the absence of directly comparable animal models, even from those primates that number among our closest relations. Nevertheless, this does not mean that principles of animal communication including those of a neurobiological nature may not inform our physical descriptions of how human language is acquired and used at least at the level of speech, as Miller and Jusczyk extensively argue.

In the fourth contribution, Held provides a discussion of how the modern view of the nervous system can provide a basis for conscious perceptions – one that is less mysterious, less magical than the classical view that assumes a very special transformation in a specific anatomical locus is the means by which we become aware of the world about us. He uses his findings on infant visual development to illustrate his view of perception and how we are to understand the necessary and sufficient neuronal mechanisms, as well as the processing characteristics that underlie perception. More specifically, he shows how the (functional) processes of grating, vernier and stereo acuity, when examined at or near the time of their initial state, enable neurobiologically based explanations that include processes of development. What is particularly interesting for those who have followed Held's work is that his approach and findings provide not only a means for considering the difficult problem of how perception arises, but also insights into development itself and a rationale for remedial procedures to help children who have been afflicted with ocular and visual perceptual disorders early in life.

The fifth contribution is a detailed description of the most recent research of James Simmons and his colleagues on the manner in which echolocating bats represent the distance and physical characteristics of targets in three-dimensional space. Simmons gives us a remarkably detailed picture of how one form of biologically significant information is perceived and what information in what form must ultimately be represented in the neural structures. He also provides us with some ideas as to how this complex representation is instantiated in neuronal structures of the bat. This work provides a clear example that a detailed neurobiology of an extraordinary processing systems appears to be possible. This is true undoubtedly because of the fine-grained description of what the bat represents that is now available, and quite possibly also because Simmons is concerned with what certainly appears to be a modular system (cf. Fodor, 1983) that serves a unique function in the bat. Moreover, a neurophysiological theory of echolocation should, we believe, provide principles of functioning that are applicable to other systems that process information of biological significance, for example, the mechanisms for speech perception.

In the final contribution, Cotman and Lynch offer a comprehensive discussion of recent developments concerning the acquisition and remembrance of information at systemic, cellular, and subcellular levels of neuronal organization. Thus, the authors review recent work, a substantial portion of which is their own, reinforcing the distinction, in neuroanatomical terms, between declarative or factual memory and procedural or rule memory. They also underline synaptic turnover and other processes that evidence the neuronal plasticity that is under environmental influence. Their examples illustrate that some of the basic mechanisms of classical conditioning, sensitization, habituation, short-term and long-term memory are beginning to be understood in terms of changes in synaptic properties at molecular levels. Their work, and that of their many colleagues, has been one of the major accomplishments of the neurosciences over the past decade or two. They show that we are approaching a solution to Lashley's search for the engram, and we are doing so at multiple levels of description, from the biochemical to the gross anatomical. The latter, as Cotman and Lynch interestingly inform us, has benefited considerably from studies of neurologically impaired humans. This reinforces our view that progress toward a neurobiology of cognition must by the nearly overwhelming complexity of the task take many forms ranging from the study of very simple organisms to complex organisms who have suffered neurological injuries of varying types.

A final comment on our selection of contributors is perhaps in order if only to begin to explain what must seem to some a rather eccentric view of a neurobiology of cognition. Our selections resulted from our own interests and opinions (biases, perhaps) as to what constitutes progress in the neurobiology of cognition and what is exciting, as well as an attempt to bring together a wide range of the approaches to a neurobiology of cognition. We were eager to show examples of work at very global levels as well as examples at quite molecular levels of analysis. Of course, our selections also reflect constraints imposed by space – handbooks can take a more comprehensive approach to their domains than can a single issue of a journal. In addition, the willingness of researchers to contribute to this endeavor, especially some who are less optimistic about the ultimate success of a neurobiology of cognition, was a source of limitation. But the latter is another story, one more in keeping perhaps with a special issue on the ever-shifting battle lines in the philosophy of mind and brain.

References

Alkon, D.L. (1984). Changes of membrane currents during learning. *Journal of Experimental Biology, 112,* 95–112.

Aloe, L., Cozzari, C., Calissano, P., & Levi-Montalcini, R. (1981). Somatic and behavioral postnatal effects of fetal injections of nerve growth factor antibodies in the rat. *Nature, 291,* 413–415.

Altman, J.S., & Tyrer, N.M. (1977). The locust wing hinge stretch receptors. II. Variation, alternative pathways, and "mistakes" in the central arborizations. *Journal of Comparative Neurology, 172,* 431–439.

Anderson, J.A., & Hinton, G.E. (1981). Models of information processing in the brain. In G.E. Hinton & J.A. Anderson (Eds.), *Parallel models of associative memory.* Hillsdale, NJ: Erlbaum.

Anderson, J.A., & Rosenfeld (Eds.) (1988). *Neurocomputing: Foundations of research.* Cambridge, MA: MIT Press.

Anderson, M.J., & Cohen, M.W. (1977). Nerve-induced and spontaneous redistribution of acetylcholine receptors on cultured muscle cells. *Journal of Physiology, 268,* 757–773.

Bartlett, E.J., Brown, J.W., Wolf, A.P., & Brodie, J.D. (1987). Correlations between glucose metabolic rates in brain regions of healthy male adults at rest and during language stimulation. *Brain and Language, 32,* 1–18.

Bastiani, M.J., du Lac, S., & Goodman, C.S. (1985). The first neuronal growth cones in insect embryos: Model systems for studying the development of neuronal specificity. In A.I. Selverston (Ed.), *Model neural networks and behavior.* New York: Plenum Press.

Bayon, A., Shoemaker, W.J., Bloom, F.E., Mauss, A., & Guillemin, R. (1979). Perinatal development of the endorphin- and enkephalin-containing systems in the rat brain. *Brain Research, 179,* 93–101.

Bever, T.G., Carrithers, C., Cowart, W., & Townsend, D.J. (1989). Language processing and familial handedness. In A.M. Galaburda (Ed.), *From reading to neurons.* Cambridge, MA: Bradford Books/MIT Press (in press).

Bixby, J.L., & Spitzer, N.C. (1982). The appearance and development of chemosensitivity in Rohen-Beard neurons of the *Xenopus* spinal cord. *Journal of Physiology, 330,* 513–536.

Braak, H., & Braak, E. (1976). The pyramidal cells of Betz within the cingulate and precentral gigantopyramidal field in the human brain. A Golgi and pigmentarchitectonic study. *Cell Tissue Research, 172,* 103–119.

Byrne, J.H. (1987). Cellular analysis of associative learning. *Physiological Reviews, 67,* 329–439.

Carew, T.J., Hawkins, R.D., Abrams, T.W., & Kandel, E.R. (1984). A test of Hebb's postulate at identified synapses which mediate classical conditioning in Aplysia. *Journal of Neuroscience, 4, 1217–1224.*

Changeux, J.-P., & Danchin, A. (1976). Selective stabilization of developing synapses as a mechanism for the specification of neuronal networks. *Nature, 264,* 705–711.

Chan-Palay, V., Palay, S.L., & Billings-Gagliardi, S.M. (1974). Meynert cells in the primate visual cortex. *Journal of Neurocytology, 3,* 631–658.

Chomsky, N. (1965). *Aspects of the theory of syntax.* Cambridge, MA: MIT Press.

Chomsky, N. (1980a). On cognitive structures and their development: A reply to Piaget. In M. Piattelli-Palmarini (Ed.), *Language and learning: The debate between Jean Piaget and Noam Chomsky.* Cambridge, MA: Harvard University Press.

Chomsky, N. (1980b). *Rules and representations.* New York: Columbia University Press.

Churchland, P. (1986). *Neurophilosophy.* Cambridge, MA: MIT Press.

Cowan, W.M. (1973). Neuronal death as a regulative mechanism in the control of cell number in the nervous system. In M. Rockstein (Ed.), *Development and aging in the nervous system.* New York: Academic Press.

Easter, S.S., Jr. (1983). Postnatal neurogenesis and changing connections. *Trends in Neuroscience, 6,* 53–56.

Ebesson, S.O.E. (1984). Evolution and ontogeny of neural circuits. *Behavioral and Brain Sciences, 7,* 321–366.

Edelman, G.M. (1987a). *Neural Darwinism.* New York: Basic Books.

Edelman, G.M. (1987b). Epigenetic rules for expression of cell adhesion molecules during morphogenesis. *CIBA Foundation Symposium, 12,* 192–216.

Eimas, P.D., Miller, J.L., & Jusczyk, P.W. (1987). On infant speech perception and the acquisition of language. In S. Harnad (Ed.), *Categorical perception.* New York: Cambridge University Press.

Fedoroff, S. (1978). The development of glial cells in primary cultures. In E. Schoffeniels (Ed.), *Dynamic properties of glial cells.* Oxford: Pergamon Press.

Field, T.M., Cohen, D., Greenberg, R., & Woodson, R. (1982). Discrimination and imitation of facial expressions by neonates. *Science, 218,* 179–181.

Fischler, I., Bloom, P.A., Childers, D.G., Roucos, S.E., & Perry, N.W., Jr. (1983). Brain potentials related to stages of sentence verification. *Psychophysiology, 20,* 400–409.

Fodor, J.A. (1975). *The language of thought.* New York: Crowell. (Paper edition, 1979. Cambridge, MA: Harvard University Press).

Fodor, J.A. (1980). On the impossibility of acquiring "more powerful" structures. In M. Piattelli-Palmarini (Ed.), *Language and learning: The debate between Jean Piaget and Noam Chomsky.* Cambridge, MA: Harvard University Press.

Fodor, J.A. (1983). *The modularity of mind.* Cambridge, MA: MIT Press.

Fox, P.T., Burton, H., & Raichle, M.E. (1987). Mapping human somatosensory cortex with positron emission tomography. *Journal of Neurosurgery, 67,* 34–43.

Galaburda, A.M., Aboitiz, F., Rosen, G.D., & Sherman, G.F. (1986). Histological asymmetry in the primary visual cortex of the rat: Implications for mechanisms of cerebral asymmetry. *Cortex, 22,* 151–160.

Galaburda, A.M., Corsiglia, J., Rosen, G.D., & Sherman, G.F. (1987a). Planum temporale asymmetry: Reappraisal since Geschwind and Levitsky. *Neuropsychologia, 25,* 853–868.

Galaburda, A.M., & Kemper, T.L. (1979). Cytoarchitectonic abnormalities in developmental dyslexia: A case study. *Annals of Neurology, 6,* 94–100.

Galaburda, A.M., Rosen, G.D., & Sherman, G.F. (1987b). Connectional anomaly in association with cerebral microgyria in the rat. *Society for Neuroscience Abstracts, 13,* 1601.

Galaburda, A.M., Sherman, G.F., Rosen, G.D., Aboitiz, F., & Geschwind, N. (1985). Developmental dyslexia: Four consecutive cases with cortical anomalies. *Annals of Neurology, 18,* 222–233.

Gallin, W.J., Chuong, C.M., Finkel, L.H., & Edelman, G.M. (1986). Antibodies to L-CAM perturb inductive interactions and alter feather pattern and structure. *Proceedings of the National Academy of Sciences USA, 83,* 8235–8329.

Giacobini, E. (1975). Neuronal control of neurotransmitters biosynthesis during development. *Journal of Neuroscience Research, 1,* 315–331.

Goodman, C.S., & Spitzer, N.C. (1981). The mature electrical properties of identified neurones in grasshopper embryos. *Journal of Physiology, 313,* 369–384.

Graziadei, P.P.C., & Monti Graziadei, G.A. (1979a). Neurogenesis and neuron regeneration in the olfactory system of mammals. I. Morphological aspects of differentiation and structural organization of the olfactory sensor neurons. *Journal of Neurocytology, 8,* 1–18.

Graziadei, P.P.C., & Monti Graziadei, G.A. (1979b). Neurogenesis and neuron regeneration in the olfactory system of mammals. II. Degeneration and reconstitution of the olfactory sensory neurons after axotomy. *Journal of Neurocytology, 8,* 197–213.

Hamburger, V., & Oppenheim, R.W. (1982). Naturally occurring neuronal death in vertebrates. *Neuroscience Commentaries*, *1*, 39–55.

Hatten, M.E., Liem, R.K., & Mason, C.A. (1984). Two forms of cerebellar glial cells interact differently with neurons in vitro. *Journal of Cellular Biology*, *98*, 193–204.

Hillyard, S.A., & Kutas, M. (1983). Electrophysiology of cognitive processing. *Annual Review of Psychology*, *34*, 33–61.

Hinton, G. (1988). *How the brain works*. Paper presented at the *Nature* Conference, Cambridge, Massachusetts, September 28, 1988.

Hubel, D.H., & Livingstone, M.S. (1983). The 11th J.A.F. Stevenson memorial lecture. Blobs and color vision. *Canadian Journal of Physiology and Pharmacology*, *61*, 1433–1441.

Hubel, D.H., & Wiesel, T.N. (1970). The period of susceptibility to the physiological effects of unilateral eye closure in kittens. *Journal of Physiology*, *206*, 419–436.

Hubel, D.H., & Wiesel, T.N. (1977). Functional architecture of macaque monkey visual cortex. *Proceedings of the Royal Society of London Biological Sciences*, *198*, 1–59.

Ingvar, D.H. (1983). Functional landscapes of the brain pertaining to mentation. *Human Neurobiology*, *2*, 1–3.

Innocenti, G.M., & Clarke, S. (1983). Multiple sets of visual cortical neurons projecting transitorily through the corpus callosum. *Neuroscience Letters*, *41*, 27–32.

Ivy, G.O., Akers, R.M., & Killackey, H.P. (1979). Differential distribution of callosal projection neurons in the neonatal and adult rat. *Brain Research*, *173*, 532–537.

John, E.R., Tang, Y., Brill, A.B., Young, R., and Ono, K. (1986). Double-labeled metabolic maps of memory. *Science*, *233*, 1167–1175.

Jones, E.G. (1981). Anatomy of cerebral cortex: Columnar input–output organization. In F.O. Schmitt, F.G. Worden, G. Adelman, & S.G. Dennis (Eds.), *The organization of the cerebral cortex*. Cambridge, MA: MIT Press.

Kandel, E.R. (1976). *Cellular basis of behavior*. San Francisco: Freeman Press.

Kano, M. (1975). Development of excitability in embryonic chick skeletal muscle cells. *Journal of Cellular Physiology*, *86*, 503–510.

Kawamoto, A.H. (1985). Dynamic processes in the (re)solution of lexical ambiguity. Unpublished Doctoral Dissertation, Brown University.

Kellman, P.J., & Spelke, E.S. (1983). Perception of partly occluded objects in infancy. *Cognitive Psychology*, *15*, 483–524.

Kosslyn, S.M. (1988). Aspects of a cognitive mental imagery. *Science*, *240*, 1621–1626.

Kramer, A.P., Goldman, J.R., & Stent, G.S. (1985). Developmental arborization of sensory neurons in the leech *Haementeria ghilianii*. I. Origin of natural variation in the branching pattern. *Journal of Neurosciences*, *5*, 768–775.

Lang, M., Lang, W., Uhl, F., & Kornhuber, A. (1987). Slow negative potential shifts in a verbal concept formation task. *Electroencephalography and Clinical Neurophysiology* (Suppl.), *40*, 335–340.

Larsen, B., Skinhoj, E., & Lassen, N.A. (1978). Variations in regional cortical blood flow in the right and left hemispheres during automatic speech. *Brain*, *101*, 193–209.

Lisberger, S.G. (1988). The neural basis for learning of simple motor skills. *Science*, *242*, 728–735.

Livingstone, M., & Hubel, D. (1988). Segregation of form, color, movement, and depth: anatomy, physiology, and perception. *Science*, *240*, 740–749.

Llinás, R.R. (1981). Electrophysiology of the cerebellar networks. In V.B. Brooks (Ed.), *Handbook of physiology. Vol. 2: The Nervous system. Part II*. Bethesda, MD: American Physiological Society.

Llinás, R., Steinberg, I.Z., & Walton, K. (1976). Presynaptic calcium currents and their relation to synaptic transmission: Voltage clamp study in squid giant synapse and theoretical model for the calcium gate. *Proceedings of the National Academy of Sciences of the United States of America*, *73*, 2918–2922.

Lynch, G.S., Dunwiddie, R., & Gribkoff, V. (1977). Heterosynaptic depression: A post-synaptic correlate of long-term potentiation. *Nature*, *266*, 737–739.

Marr, D. (1982). *Vision*. San Francisco: W.H. Freeman.

Marr, D., & Poggio, T. (1979). A computational theory of human stereo vision. *Proceedings of the Royal Society of London Biological Sciences, 204*, 301–328.

Mazziotta, J.C., Phelps, M.E., & Carson, R.E. (1984). Tomographic mapping of human cerebral metabolism: Subcortical responses to auditory and visual stimulation. *Neurology, 34*, 825–828.

McClelland, J.L., & Rumelhart, D.E. (1986). *Parallel distributed processing: Explorations in the microstructure of cognition. Vol. 2: Applications*. Cambridge, MA: MIT Press.

McCulloch, W.S., & Pitts, W. (1943). A logical calculus of the ideas immanent in nervous activity. *Bulletin of Mathematical Biophysics, 5*, 115–133.

McEwen, B.S., De Kloet, E.R., & Rostene, W. (1986). Adrenal steroid receptors and actions in the nervous system. *Physiology Review, 66*, 1121–1188.

McKinley, P.A., Jenkins, W.M., Smith, J.L., & Merzenich, M.M. (1987). Age-dependent capacity for somatosensory cortex reorganization in chronic spinal cats. *Brain Research, 428*, 136–139.

Mehler, J., & Fox, R. (1985). *Neonate cognition: Beyond the blooming, buzzing confusion*. Hillsdale, NJ: Erlbaum.

Meltzoff, A.N., & Moore, M.K. (1977). Imitation of facial and manual gestures by human neonates. *Science, 198*, 74–78.

Merzenich, M.M., Nelson, R.J., Kaas, J.H., Stryker, M.P., Jenkins, W.M., Zook, J.M., Cynader, M.S., & Schoppmann, A. (1987). Variability in hand surface representations in areas 3b and 1 in adult owl and squirrel monkeys. *Journal of Comparative Neurology, 282*, 281–296.

Miyake, M. (1978). The development of action potential mechanism in a mouse neuronal cell line in vitro. *Brain Research, 143*, 349–354.

Mohr, J.P., Pessin, M.J., Finkelstein, J., Funkenstein, H.H., Duncan, G.W., & Davis, K.R. (1978). Broca's aphasia: Pathologic and clinical. *Neurology, 4*, 311–324.

Money, J., & Ehrhardt, A.A. (1972). Gender dimorphic behavior and fetal sex hormones, In E.B. Astwood (Ed.), *Recent progress in hormone research* (Vol. 28). Academic Press, New York.

Morris, R.G., Anderson, E., Lynch, G.S., & Baudry, M. (1986). Selective impairment of learning and blockade of long-term potentiation by an *N*-methyl-*D*-aspartate receptor antagonist, AP5. *Nature, 319*, 774–776.

Mountcastle, V.B. (1978). An organizing principle for cerebral function: The unit module and the distributed system. In G.M. Edelman & V.B. Mountcastle (Eds.), *The mindful brain: Cortical organization and the group-selective theory of higher brain function*. Cambridge, MA: MIT Press.

Needels, D.L., Nieto-Sampedro, M., & Cotman, C.W. (1986). Induction of a neurite-promoting factor in rat brain following injury or deafferentiation. *Neuroscience, 18*, 517–526.

Nottebohm, F. (1981). A brain for all seasons: Cyclical anatomical changes in song control nuclei of the canary brain. *Science, 214*, 1368–1370.

Oppenheim, R.W. (1981). Cell death of motoneurons in the chick embryo spinal cord. V. Evidence on the role of cell death and neuromuscular function in the formation of specific peripheral connections. *Journal of Neuroscience, 1*, 141–151.

Pinker, S., & Mehler, J. (Eds.) (1987). Special issue: Connectionism and symbol systems. *Cognition, 28*, 1–247.

Posner, M.I., Petersen, S.E., Fox, P.T., & Raichle, M.E. (1988). Localization of cognitive operations in the human brain. *Science, 240*, 1627–1631.

Purpura, D.P. (1974). Dendritic spine "dysgenesis" and mental retardation. *Science, 186*, 1126–1128.

Quinn, P.C., & Eimas, P.D. (1986). On categorization in early infancy. *Merrill-Palmer Quarterly, 12*, 331–361.

Rakic, P. (1988). Specification of cerebral cortical areas. *Science, 241*, 170–176.

Ramón y Cajal, S. (1929). *Étude sur la neurogenèse de quelques vertébrés*. Translated by L. Guth (1960) as *Studies on vertebrate neurogenesis*. Springfield, IL: Charles C. Thomas.

Rossen, M.L. (1988). A neural model of deep dyslexia. *Program of the Ninth Annual Conference of the Cognitive Science Society*, 983–989.

Rugg, M., Kok, A., Barrett, G., & Fischler, I. (1986). ERPs associated with language and hemispheric specialization. A review. *Electroencephalography and Clinical Neurophysiology, 38*, 273–300.

Schmitt, F.O. (1978). Introduction. In G.M. Edelman & V.B. Mountcastle (Eds.), *The mindful brain*. Cambridge, MA: MIT Press.

Schneider, G.E. (1981). Early lesions and abnormal neuronal connections. *Trends in Neurosciences, 4*, 187–192.

Scholz, K.P., & Byrne, J.H. (1987). Long-term sensitization in *Aplysia*: Biophysical correlates in tail sensory neurons. *Science, 235*, 685–687.

Shaw, S.R., & Meinertzhagen, I.A. (1986). Evolutionary progression at synaptic connections made by identified homologous neurones. *Proceedings of the National Academy of Sciences (USA), 83*, 7961–7965.

Sokoloff, L. (1981). The relationship between function and energy metabolism: Its use in the localization of functional activity in the nervous system. *Neurosciences Research Program Bulletin, 19*, 159–210.

Sretavan, D.W., & Shatz, C.J. (1986a). Prenatal development of retinal ganglion cell axons: Segregation into eye-specific slayers within the cat's lateral geniculate nucleus. *Journal of Neuroscience, 6*, 234–251.

Sretavan, D.W., & Shatz, C.J. (1986b). Prenatal development of cat retinogeniculate axon arbors in the absence of binocular interaction. *Journal of Neuroscience, 6*, 990–1003.

Swaab, D.F., & Boer, G.J. (1983). Neuropeptides and brain development. Current perils and future potential. *Journal of Developmental Physiology, 5*, 67–75.

Van Orden, L.S., Bloom, F.E., Barnett, R.J., & Giarman, N.J. (1966). Histochemical and functional relationships of catecholamines in adrenergic nerve endings. I. Participation of granular vesicles. *Journal of Pharmacology and Experimental Therapeutics, 154*, 185–199.

Wall, P.D., & Eggers, M.D. (1971). Formation of new connexions in adult rat brains after partial deafferentation. *Nature, 232*, 542–544.

Williams, R.W., & Rakic, P. (1988). Elimination of neurons from the rhesus monkey's lateral geniculate nucleus during development. *Journal of Comparative Neurology, 272*, 424–436.

Winfield, D.A. (1982). The effect of visual deprivation upon the Meynert cell in the striate cortex of the rat. *Brain Research, 281*, 53–57.

Wise, S.P., & Jones, E.G. (1976). The organization and postnatal development of the commissural projection of the rat somatic sensory cortex. *Journal of Comparative Neurology, 168*, 313–343.

Woolsey, T.A., Durham, D., Harris, R.M., Sinions, D.J., & Valentino, K.L. (1981). Somatosensory development. In R.N. Aslin, J.R. Roberts, & M.P. Petersen (Eds.), *Development of perception* (Vol. 1). New York: Academic Press.

Yasargil, G.M., Adert, K., & Sandri, C. (1986). Further morphological (freeze-fracture) evidence for an impulse generating function of Mauthner axon collaterals in the tench (*Tinca tinca* L.) spinal cord. *Neuroscience Letters, 71*, 43–47.

Zeki, S.M. (1983). The distribution of wavelength and orientation selective cells in different areas of monkey visual cortex. *Proceedings of the Royal Society of London (Biological Sciences), 217*, 449–470.

2

Time-locked multiregional retroactivation: A systems-level proposal for the neural substrates of recall and recognition*

ANTONIO R. DAMASIO

University of Iowa College of Medicine

Abstract

Damasio, A.R., 1989. Time-locked multiregional retroactivation: A systems-level proposal for the neural substrates of recall and recognition. Cognition, 33: 25–62.

This article outlines a theoretical framework for the understanding of the neural basis of memory and consciousness, at systems level. It proposes an architecture constituted by: (1) neuron ensembles located in multiple and separate regions of primary and first-order sensory association cortices ("early cortices") and motor cortices; they contain representations of feature fragments inscribed as patterns of activity originally engaged by perceptuomotor interactions; (2) neuron ensembles located downstream from the former throughout single modality cortices (local convergence zones); they inscribe amodal records of the combinatorial arrangement of feature fragments that occurred synchronously during the experience of entities or events in sector (1); (3) neuron ensembles located downstream from the former throughout higher-order association cortices (non-local convergence zones), which inscribe amodal records of the synchronous combinatorial arrangements of local convergence zones during the experience of entities and events in sector (1); (4) feed-forward and feedback projections interlocking reciprocally the neuron ensembles in (1) with those in (2) according to a many-to-one (feed-forward) and one-to-many (feedback) principle. I propose that (a) recall of entities and events occurs when the neuron ensembles in (1) are activated in time-locked fashion; (b) the synchronous activations are directed from convergence zones in (2) and (3); and (c) the process of reactivation is triggered from firing in convergence zones

*This work was supported by NINCDS grant PO1 NS19632. I thank my associates Hanna Damasio, Gary Van Hoesen, and Daniel Tranel for helping me shape many of the ideas summarized here, over the past decade. I also thank other colleagues who read previous versions of this manuscript over the past few years and made numerous helpful suggestions: Patricia Churchland, Victoria Fromkin, Jack Fromkin, Edward Klima, Francis Crick, Terry Sejnowski, Jaques Paillard, Marge Livingstone, David Hubel, Freda Newcombe, Ursula Bellugi, Arthur Benton, Peter Eimas and Albert Galaburda. Requests for reprints should be sent to Antonio R. Damasio, Professor and Head, Department of Neurology, University of Iowa Hospitals and Clinics, Iowa City, IA 52242, U.S.A.

and mediated by feedback projections. This proposal rejects a single anatomical site for the integration of memory and motor processes and a single store for the meaning of entities of events. Meaning is reached by time-locked multiregional retroactivation of widespread fragment records. Only the latter records can become contents of consciousness.

Introduction

This proposal describes a neural architecture capable of supporting the experiences that are conjured up in recall and are used for recognition, at the level of systems that integrate macroscopic functional regions. It arose out of dissatisfaction with available accounts of the neural basis of higher behaviors, especially those implicit in center localizationism, behaviorism, functional equipotentiality, and disconnection syndrome theory.

The title captures the two principal notions in the proposal. First, perceptual experience depends on neural activity in multiple regions activated simultaneously, rather than in a single region where experiential integration would occur. Second, during free recall or recall generated by perception in a recognition task, the multiple region activity necessary for experience occurs near the sensory portals and motor output sites of the system rather than at the end of an integrative processing cascade removed from inputs and outputs. Hence the term retroactivation to indicate that recall of experiences depends on reactivation close to input and output sites rather than away from them.

The two critical structures in the proposed architecture are the fragment record of feature-based sensory or motor activity, and the convergence zone, an amodal record of the combinatorial arrangements that bound the fragment records as they occurred in experience. There are convergence zones of different orders; for example, those that bind features into entities, and those that bind entities into events or sets of events, but all register combinations of components in terms of coincidence or sequence, in space and time. Convergence zones are an attempt to provide an answer to the binding problem, which I see as a central issue in cognitive processing, at all taxonomic levels and scales of operation.

The adult organization described here operates on the basis of neurobiological and reality constraints. During interactions between the perceiver's brain and its surround, those constraints lead to a process of feature, entity, and event grouping based on physical structure similarity, spatial placement, temporal sequence, and temporal coincidence. The records of those perceptuomotor interactions, both at fragment level and at combinatorial level, are inscribed in superimposed and overlapped fashion; yet, because of the different conditions according to which they are grouped, they become committed to separate neural regions. In cognitive terms I will refer to these processes as domain formation (a creation of relatively separable areas of knowledge for faces, man-made objects, music, numbers, words, social events, disease states, and so on), and recording of contextual complexity (a recording of the temporal and spatial interaction of entities within sets of concurrent events). In neural terms I will refer to these grouping processes as regionalization.

The same type of neuron ensembles, operating on the same principles, constitutes the substrate for different cognitive operations, depending on the location of the ensemble within the system and the connections that feed into the ensemble and that feed back out of it. Location and communication lines determine the topic of the neuron ensemble. The connectivity of functional regions defines the systems-level code for cognitive processes.

The neuroanatomical substrates for this organization are:

(1) primary and early association cortices, both sensory and motor, which constitute the substrate for feature-based records;

(2) association cortices of different orders, both sensory and motor, some limbic structures (entorhinal cortex, hippocampus, amygdala, cingulate cortices), and the neostriatum/cerebellum, which constitute the substrate for convergence zones;

(3) feed-forward and feedback connectivity interrelating (1) and (2), at multiple hierarchical levels, with reciprocal patterns;

(4) non-specific thalamic nuclei, hypothalamus, basal forebrain, and brainstem nuclei.

The cognitive/neural architecture outlined above can perform: (1) perceptuomotor interactions with the brain's surround; (2) learning of those interactions at the representational level defined above; (3) internal activation of experience-replicative representations in a recall (perception-independent) mode; (4) problem solving, decision making, planning, and creativity; and (5) communication with the evironment. All those functions are predicated on a key operation: the attempted reconstitution of learned perceptuomotor interactions in the form of internal recall and motor performance. Attempted perceptuomotor reconstitution is achieved by time-locked retroactivation of fragmentary records, in mutiple cortical regions as a result of feedback activity from convergence zones. The success of this operation depends on attention, which is defined as a critical level of activity in each of the activated regions, below which consciousness cannot occur.

According to this proposal, there is no single site for the integration of sensory and motor processes. The experience of spatial integration is brought about by time-locked multiple occurrences. I thus propose a recursive, iterative design to substitute for the traditional unidirectional processing cascades.

Although the notion of representation covers all the inscriptions related to an entity or event, that is, both fragment and binding code records, the proposal posits that only the multiregional retroactivations of the fragment components become a content of consciousness. The perceptuomotor reconstitutions that form the substrate of consciousness thus occur in an anatomically restricted sector of the cerebrum, albeit in a distributed, multiple-site manner.

In this proposal, and unlike traditional neurological models, there is no localizable single store for the meaning of a given entity whithin a cortical region. Rather, meaning is reached by widespread multiregional activation of fragmentary records pertinent to a stimulus, wherever such records may be stored within a large array of sensory and motor structures, according to a combinatorial arrangement specific to the entity. A display of the meaning of an entity does not exist in permanent fashion. It is recreated for each new instantiation. The same stimulus does not produce the same evocations at every instantiation, though many of the same or similar sets of records will be evoked in relation to the same or comparable stimuli. The records that pertain to a given entity are distributed in the telencephalon both in the sense that they are inscribed over sizable synaptic populations and in the sense that they are to be found in multiple loci of cerebral cortex and subcortical nuclei.

The proposal permits the reinterpretation of the main types of higher cognitive disorder – the agnosias, the amnesias, and the aphasias – and prompts testable hypotheses for further investigation of those disorders. It also provides a basis for neural hypotheses regarding psychiatric conditions such as sociopathy, phobias and schizophrenia. Several predictions based on this proposal are now being tested in humans, with or without focal brain lesions, using advanced imaging methods and cognitive probes. Some anatomical and physiological aspects of the proposal can be investigated in experimental animals. The concept of convergence zone can be explored with computational techniques.

The need for temporo-spatial integration and its traditional solution

Current knowledge from neuroanatomy and neurophysiology of the primate nervous system indicates unequivocally that any entity or event that we normally perceive through multiple sensory modalities must engage geographically separate sensory modality structures of the central nervous system. Since virtually every conceivable perception of an entity or event also calls for a motor interaction on the part of the perceiver and must include the concomitant perception of the perceiver's somatic state, it is obvious that perception of external reality and the attempt to record it are a multiple-site neurophysiological affair. This notion is reinforced by the discovery, over the past decade, of a multiplicity of subsidiary functional regions that show some relative dedication not just to a global sensory modality or motor performance but also to featural and dimensional aspects of stimuli (see Damasio, 1985a; Van Essen & Maunsell, 1983; Livingstone & Hubel, 1988, for a pertinent review). The evidence from psychological studies in humans is equally compelling in suggesting featural fragmentation of perceptual processes (see Barlow, 1981; Julesz, 1971; Posner, 1980; Triesman & Gelade, 1980). Early geographic parcellation of stimulus properties has thus grown rather than receded, and the condition faced by sensory and motor representations of the brain's surround is a fragmentation of the inscription of the physical structures that constitute reality, at virtually every scale. The physical structure of an entity (external, such as an object, or internal, such as a specific somatic state) must be recorded in terms of separate constituent ingredients, each of which is a result of secondary mappings at a lower physical scale. And the fragmentation that obtains for concrete entities is even more marked for abstract entities and events, considering that abstract entities correspond to criterion-governed conjunctions of dimensions and features present in concrete entities, and that events are an interplay of entities.

The experience of reality, however, both in ongoing perception as well as in recall, is not parcellated at all. The normal experience we have of entities and events is coherent and "in-register", both spatially and temporally. Features are bound in entities, and entities are bound in events. How the brain achieves such a remarkable integration starting with the fragments that it has to work with is a critical question. I call it the *binding problem* (I use the term binding in a broader sense than it has been used by Treisman and others, to denote the requisite integration of components at all levels and scales, not only in perception but also in recall). The brain must have devices capable of promoting the integration of fragmentary components of neural activity, in some sort of ensemble pattern that matches the structures of entities, events, and relationships thereof. The solution, implicitly or overtly, has been, for decades, that the components provided by different sensory portals are projected together in so-called multimodal cortices in which, presumably, a representation of integrated reality is achieved. According to this intuitively reasonable view, perception operates on the basis of a unidirectional cascade of processors, which provides, step by step, a refinement of the extraction of signals, first in unimodal streams and later in a sort of multimedia and multitrack apparatus where integration occurs. The general direction of the cascade is caudo-rostral, in cortical terms, and the integrative cortices are presumed to be in the anterior temporal and anterior frontal regions. Penfield's findings in epileptics undergoing electrical stimulation of temporal cortex seemed to support this traditional view (Penfield & Jasper, 1954), as did influential models of the neural substrates of cognition in the post-war period, such as Geschwind's (1965) and Luria's (1966). The major discoveries of neurophysiology and neuroanatomy over the past two decades have also seemed compatible with it. On the face of it, anatomical projections do radiate from primary sensory cortices and do create multiple-stage sequences toward structures in the hippocampus and prefrontal cortices (Jones & Powell, 1970; Nauta, 1971; Pandya & Kuypers, 1969; Van Hoesen, 1982). Moreover, without a doubt, single-cell neurophysiology does suggest that, the farther away neurons are from the primary sensory cortices, the more they have progressively larger receptive fields and less unimodal responsivity (see Desimone & Ungerleider, 1988, for a review and restatement of the traditional view). Until recently, the exception to this dominant view of anterior cerebral structures as the culmination of the processing cascade was to be found in Crick's (1984) hypothesis for a neural mechanism underlying attention.

The purpose of this text is to question the validity of the conventional solution. I doubt that there is a unidirectional cascade. I also question the information-processing metaphor implicit in the solution, that is, the notion that finer representations emerge by progressive extraction of features, and that they flow caudo-rostrally. Specifically, we believe that by using this view of brain organization and function the experimental neuropsychological findings in patients with agnosia and amnesia become unmanageably paradoxical. I also suggest that there is a lack of neuroanatomical support for some requirements of the traditional view, and that there are neuroanatomical findings to support an alternative model. Finally, I believe that available neurophysiological data can be interpreted to support the alternative theory I propose.

Paradoxes and contradictions for the traditional solution

Objections from human studies with the lesion method

If temporal and frontal integrative cortices were to be the substrate for the integration of neural activity on the basis of which perceptual experience and its attempted recall unfold, the following should be found:

(a) That the bilateral destruction of those cortices should preclude the perception of reality as a coherent multimodal experience and reduce experience to disjointed, modality-specific tracks of sensory or motor processing to the extent permitted by the single modality association cortices; (b) That the bilateral destruction of the integrative cortices should reduce the quality of even such modality-specific processing, that is, reduce the richness and detail of perception and recall commensurate with the quality obtainable by the level of non-integrative stations left intact; (c) That the bilateral damage to the rostral integrative cortices should disable memory for any form of past integrated experience and interfere with all levels and types of memory, including memory for specific entities and events, even those that constitute the perceiver's autobiography, memory for non-unique entities and events, and memory for relationships among features, entities, and events.

The results of bilateral destruction of the anterior temporal lobes, either in the medial sector alone or the entire anterior temporal region, as well as bilateral destruction of prefrontal cortices, either in separate sectors or in combination, deny all but a fraction of one of these predictions.

Evidence from anterior temporal cortex damage

It is *not* true that coherent, multimodal, perceptual experience is disturbed by bilateral lesions of the temporal integrative units, and it is *not* true that those lesions cause the perceptual quality of experience to diminish. On the contrary, all available evidence indicates that at both consciously reportable and non-conscious covert levels, the quality of perceptual experience of subjects who have sustained major selective damage to anterior temporal cortices is comparable to controls (see Corkin, 1984; Damasio et al., 1985a,b, 1987). Such subjects can report on what they see, hear, and touch, in ways that observers cannot distinguish from what they themselves see, hear, and touch. A variety of covert knowledge paradigms (e.g., forced recognition and passive skin conductance) indicates that they can also discriminate stimuli, probably on the basis of non-conscious activation of detailed knowledge about the items under scrutiny (Bauer, 1984; Tranel & Damasio, 1985, 1987, 1988). More importantly, the knowledge that such subjects can evoke consciously, at a non-autobiographical level, indicates that ample memory stores of "integrated experience" remain intact after damage to the alleged integrative units. These facts support the contentions: (1) that a considerable amount of integration must take place early on in the system well before higher-order cortices are reached; (2) that integrated information can be recorded there without the agency of rostral integrative units; and (3) that it can be re-evoked there too, without the intervention of rostral integrative structures.

The only accurate prediction regarding the role of alleged integrative units applies to anterior temporal cortices and concerns the loss of the ability to recall unique combinations of representations that were conjoined in experience within a specific time lapse and space unit. That ability is indeed lost, along with the possibility of creating records for new and unique experiences. This is exemplified by the neuropsychological profile of the patient Boswell, whose cerebral damage entirely destroyed, bilaterally, both hippocampal systems (including the entorhinal cortex, the hippocampal formation, and the amygdala), the cortices in anterolateral and anteroinferior temporal lobes (including areas 38, 20, 21, anterior sector of 22, and part of 37), the entire basal forebrain region bilaterally (including the septal nuclei, the nucleus accumbens and the substantia innominata, which contains a large sector of the nucleus basalis of Meynert), and the most posterior part of the orbitofrontal cortices. Boswell's perception in all modalities but the olfactory is flawless and the descriptions he produces of complex visual or auditory entities and events are indistinguishable from those of his examiners. All aspects of his motor performance are perfect. His use of grammar, his phonemic and phonetic processing, and his prosody are intact. His memory for most entities is preserved, and at generic/categorical levels his defect only becomes evident when subordinate specificity is required for the recognition of uniqueness or for the disambiguation of extremely similar exemplars. For instance, he recognizes virtually any man-made object such as a vehicle, tool, utensil, article of furniture or clothing, but cannot decide whether he has previously encountered the specific exemplar, or whether or not it is his. Although he can recognize the face of a friend as a human face, or his house as a house, and provide detailed descriptions of the features that compose them, he is unable to conjure up any event of which the unique face or house was a part, and which belong to his autobiography. In short, his essential perceptuomotor interaction with the environment remains normal provided uniqueness of recognition, recall, or action are not required. Recognition, recall, and imagery operate as they should for large sectors of knowledge at the generic/categorical level.

Evidence from anterior frontal lobe damage

Damage to bilateral prefrontal cortices, especially those in the orbitofrontal sector, is compatible with normal perceptual processes and even with normal memory for entities and events, except when they pertain to complex domains such as social knowledge (Damasio & Tranel, 1988; Eslinger & Damasio, 1985). Bilateral lesions in superior mesial and in dorsolateral cortices cause defects in drive for action, attention, and problem solving, that may secondarily influence perceptual tasks. However, even extensive ablation of virtually the entire prefrontal cortices is compatible with normal perception. The study of Brickner's patient A, of Hebb's and Ackerly and Benton's patients (see Damasio, 1985b for a review), and of our subject EVR (see Eslinger & Damasio, 1985) provides powerful evidence in this regard. Frontal lobe structures, with their multiple loci for the anchoring of processing cascades (Goldman-Rakic, 1988), are even less likely candidates to be the single, global site of integration than their temporal counterparts.

Evidence from damage in single-modality cortices

Perhaps the most paradoxical aspect of these data, when interpreted in light of the traditional view, is that damage in certain sectors of sensory association cortices does affect the quality of some aspects of perception within the sensory modality of those cortices. For instance, damage in early visual association cortices can disrupt perception of color, texture, stereopsis, and spatial placement of the physical components of a stimulus. The range of loss depends on which precise region of visual cortex is most affected (Damasio, 1985a).

The perceptual defect is accompanied by an impairment of recall and recognition. For instance, achromatopsia (loss of color perception) also precludes imaging color in recall (Damasio, 1985; Farah, 1989 and unpublished observations), that is, no other cortices, and certainly no other higher-order, integrative cortices, are capable of supporting the recall of the perceptually impaired feature. The coupling of perceptual and recall impairments is strong evidence that the same cortices support perception and recall. This finding, based on lesion method studies, is in line with evidence from normal human experiments (Kosslyn, 1980). It also suggests an economical approach to brain mapping of knowledge that might obviate the problem of combinatorial explosion faced by the traditional view. In my proposal, the brain would not re-inscribe features downstream from where it perceives them. Furthermore, damage within some sectors of modal association cortices can disturb recall and recognition of stimuli presented through that modality, even when basic perceptual processing is not compromised. The domain of stimuli, and the taxonomic level of the disturbance, depend on the specification of the lesion in terms of site, size, and uni- or bilaterality (Damasio & Tranel, 1989; see also work on category-related recognition defects reviewed in Damasio, 1989; and McCarthy & Warrington, 1988). Lesions within visual association cortices may impair the recognition of the unique identity of faces, while allowing for the recognition of facial expressions, non-unique objects, and visuo-verbal material. Or lesions may compromise object recognition and leave face recognition untouched (Feinberg, Rothi, & Heilman, 1986; Newcombe & Ratcliff, 1974), or compromise reading but not object or face recognition (Damasio & Damasio, 1983; Geschwind & Fusillo, 1966). The key point is that damage in a caudal and modal association cortex *can disrupt recall and recognition at even the most subordinate taxonomic level*. It can preclude the kind of integrated experience usually attributed to the rostral cortices, that is, an evocation made up of multiple featural components, based on different modalities, constituting entities and events. This can happen without disrupting perception within the affected modality and without compromising recall or recognition in other modalities. Damage in modal cortices also disrupts learning of new entities and events presented through the modality (Damasio et al., 1989a).

These findings indicate that a substantial amount of perceptual integration takes place within single-modality cortices, and that knowledge recalled at categoric levels (also known as semantic, or generic)[1] is largely dependent on records and interactions among posterior sensory cortices and the interconnected motor cortices.

It also indicates that recall and recognition of knowledge at the level of unique entities or events (also known as episodic)[1] requires *both* anterior *and* posterior sensory cortices, an indication that a more complex network is needed for intricate subordinate-level mappings and that anterior integrative structures alone are not sufficient to record and reconstruct knowledge at such levels.

The implications are:

(a) that the posterior sensory cortices are sites where fragment records are inscribed and reactivated, according to appropriate combinatorial arrangements (by fragments I mean "parts of entities", at a multiplicity of scales, most notably at the feature level, for example color, movement, texture, and shape); such cortices are also capable of binding features into entities and thus re-enact the perceptual experience of entities and their operations ("local" or "entity" binding). But posterior cortices cannot map non-local contextual complexity at event level, which is to say they cannot map the spatial and temporal relationships assumed by entities within the multiple concurrent events that usually characterize complex interactions with the environment.

(b) the inscription of contextual complexity, that is, the complexity of the

---

[1]The terms semantic and episodic were proposed by Tulving (1972). Our term generic is largely equivalent to semantic and categorical. Elsewhere in the text I refer generic or categorical knowledge as "supraordinate" or "basic object level" knowledge, and to episodic knowledge as "subordinate level" knowledge. The latter terms are drawn from Rosch's nomenclature for taxonomic levels (Rosch et al., 1976).

combinatorial arrangement exhibited by many concurrent events (non-local or event binding), requires anterior cortices, although its re-enactment also depends on posterior cortices.

The posterior cortices contain all the fragments with which experiences can potentially be reconstituted, given the appropriate combinatorial arrangement (binding). But as far as combinatorial arrangements are concerned, the posterior cortices contain primarily the records for "local" entity or simple event binding. They do not contain records for "non-local" concurrent event binding and are thus unable to reconstitute experiences based on the contextually complex, multi-event situations that characterize one's autobiography.

The anterior cortices do contain such non-local, concurrent event binding records. The critical point is that since posterior cortices contain *both* fragment and local binding records, they are essential for *all* experience-replicative operations. Anterior cortices are only required to assist experiences that depend on high-level contextual complexity.

I would predict, based on the above hypotheses, that simultaneous damage in strategic regions of *several* single-modality cortices, for example visual, auditory, somatosensory, in spite of intactness of the so-called rostral integrative cortices, would preclude recognition and recall of a sweeping range of stimuli defined by features and dimensions from those modalities, *both* at generic and episodic levels. The central premise behind my proposal, then, is that extensive damage in "early" sensory cortices is the only way of producing the effect normally posited for destruction of the anterior units, namely the suspension of multimodal recognition and recall, from which would follow the abolition of experiences.

A testable hypothesis drawn from this premise is that damage in intermediate cortices (cortices in parts of areas 37, 36, 35, and 39 that constitute virtual "choke points" for the feed-forward–feedback projections that interlock earlier and higher-order cortices) should have a comparable disrupting effect. There is preliminary evidence that this is so from findings on patients with lesions in these areas (Damasio et al., unpublished; Horenstein, Chamberlin, & Conomy, 1967), and a study is currently under way to analyze additional evidence.

Neuroanatomical and neurophysiological evidence

Leaving aside the fact that no bilateral lesion in a presumed "anterior integrative cortex" is capable of precluding coherent perception of any entity or event, or categorical recall, one might turn around and pose a purely neuroanatomical question: which area or set of areas could possibly function as a fully encompassing and single convergence region, based on what is currently known about neural connectivity? The simple answer is: none. The entorhinal cortex and the adjacent hippocampal system (hippocampal formation and amygdala) do receive connections from all sensory cortices, and come closest to the mark. Prefrontal cortices, inasmuch as one can envisage their connectivity from neuroanatomical studies in non-human primates, do not fit the bill either. They have no single point of anatomical convergence equivalent to the entorhinal cortex, only separate convergence points with different and narrower admixtures of innervation. The hypothesis suggested by these facts is that the integration of sensory and motor activity necessary for coherent perception and recall must occur in multiple sites and at multiple levels. A single convergence site is nowhere to be found.

In fact, developments in neuroanatomy and neurophysiology have emphasized the notion of segregation while beginning to reveal different possibilities for integration. For instance, Hubel and Livingstone (1987) and Livingstone and Hubel (1984) have demonstrated that separate cellular channels within area 17 are differently dedicated to the processing of color, form and motion. Beyond area 17 the evidence shows:

(1) Early channel separation and divergence into several functional regions revealed by neurophysiological studies (Allman, Miezin, & McGuinness, 1985; Hubel & Livingstone, 1987; Livingstone & Hubel, 1984; Van Essen & Maunsell, 1983), and characterized in part by studies of connectivity (Gilbert, 1983; Livingstone & Hubel, 1987a; Lund, Hendrickson, Ogren, & Tobin, 1981; Rockland & Pandya, 1979, 1981). This form of organization is describable by the attributes divergent, one-to-many, parallel, and sequential.

(2) The existence of back-projections to the feeding cortical origin, capable of affecting processing in a retroactive manner, and capable of cross-projecting to regions of the same level (Van Essen, 1985; Zeki, 1987, personal communication). This anatomical pattern opens the possibility for various forms of local integration.

(3) Existence of convergence into functional regions downstream (projections from visual, auditory, and somatosensory cortices) can be encountered in combinations from two and three modalities, in progressively more rostral brain regions such as areas 37, 36, 35, 38, 20 and 21 (Jones & Powell, 1970; Seltzer & Pandya, 1976, 1978; Pandya & Yeterian, 1985),[2] a design feature

---

[2]The human areas 37 (mesially), 36, and 35 largely correspond to fields TF and TH in the monkey, and to fields TF and TH of von Economo and Koskinas in the human. They are extremely developed in the human, especially area 37. Area 38 corresponds to TG; areas 20 and 21 to TE. Area 39 (the angular gyrus) also represents a major human development and may correspond to expansion of cortices in both posterior superior temporal sulcus and inferior parietal lobule. Area 40 (the supramarginal gyrus) is largely a new human area.

describable by the attributes convergent, many-to-few, parallel, and sequential. In humans, judging from evidence in non-human primates, trimodal combinations are likely to occur in functional regions within Brodmann's areas 37, 36, 35, 38, 39; bimodal combinations are likely in areas 40, 20 and 21.

(4) Existence of further feedback from the latter cortices, that is, "convergence regions", have the power to back-project divergently to the feeding cortices.

The pattern of forward convergence and retrodivergence is repeated in the rostral cortices of the entorhinal and prefrontal regions. For instance, neuron ensembles in higher-order cortices project into the circumscribed clusters found in layer II and superficial parts of layer III of the entorhinal cortex (Van Hoesen, 1982; Van Hoesen & Pandya, 1975a,b; Van Hoesen, Pandya, & Butters, 1975). I describe this design feature as convergent, and few-to-fewer. Convergence continues into the hippocampal formation proper, by means of perforant pathway projections to the dentate gyrus and of projections from there into CA3 and CA1. Convergence is again followed by divergent feedbacks via several anatomical routes: (1) a direct route, using the subiculum and layer IV of the entorhinal cortex, diverges into the cortices that provide the last station of input into the hippocampus (Kosel, Van Hoesen, & Rosene, 1982; Rosene & Van Hoesen, 1977); as noted above, those cortices project back to the previous feeding station; (2) an indirect route, so far only revealed in rodents but possibly present in primates, which feeds back into virtually all previous stations, divergently and in saltatory fashion, rather than in recapitulatory manner (Swanson & Kohler, 1986); (3) an even less direct and specific route, which uses pathways in the fornix and exerts influence over thalamic, hypothalamic, basal forebrain, and frontal structures, all of which in turn, directly and indirectly, can influence the operation of the cerebral cortices in widespread fashion. The latter route provides the cortex with regionally selective or widespread neurochemical influence (e.g., acetylcholine, norepinephrine, dopamine, and serotonin) based on the activity of neurotransmitter nuclei in basal forebrain and brainstem (Lewis et al., 1986; Mesulam, Mufson, Levey, & Wainer, 1983).

The findings clearly indicate that the hippocampus-bound projection systems point as much forward as backward. Furthermore, the convergence noted anteriorly is always partial, never encompassing the full range of sensory and motor processes that may be involved in complex experiences. Precisely the same argument could be presented for the multiplicity of prefrontal cortices that serve as end-points for projections from parietal and temporal regions. The feed-forward projections remain segregated among parallel streams and are reciprocated by powerful feedbacks to their originating cortices or their vicinity (Goldman-Rakic, 1988).

The fact that the receptive fields of neurons increase dramatically in a caudal–rostral direction has implicitly supported the notion of rostral integration. A look at this issue in the visual system reveals that the size of the receptive field of neurons in area 17 (V_1) is extremely small; it enlarges by as much as one hundred times at the level of V_4, and at the level of the higher-order cortices of areas 20 and 21 virtually encompasses the entire visual scene (Desimone, Schein, Moran, & Ungerleider, 1985). This gradual enlargement of receptive fields, all the way from small and lateralized to large and bilateral, has been viewed as an indication that anteriorly placed neurons not only see more of the world but represent a finer picture of it (Desimone & Ungerleider, 1989, Perrett et al., 1987). However, nothing in those data indicates that the fewer and fewer neurons that are linked to larger and larger receptive fields contain any concrete representation whatsoever of the perceptual detail upstream or that those neurons are committed and the end-point of multiple-channel processing. Those data are certainly compatible with the proposal I present below: (a) that fewer and fewer neurons placed anteriorly in the system are projected on by structures upstream and thus subtend a broader compass of feed-forwarding regions; (b) that they serve as pivots for reciprocating feedback projections rather than as the recipients and accumulators of all the knowledge inscribed at earlier levels; and (c) that in such a capacity they are intermediaries in a continuous process that systematically returns to early cortices.

The unavoidable conclusion is that, while it is possible to conceive of the integration of sensory processes within a few neuronal regions necessary to define a single entity, it is apparent that no single area in the human brain receives projections from all the regions involved in the processing of an event. More importantly, it is inconceivable that any single region of the brain might integrate spatially all the fragments of sensory and motor activity necessary to define a set of unique events. An answer to this puzzle, namely the ability to generate an integrated experience in the absence of any means to bring the experience's components together in a single spatial meeting ground, might be a trick of timing. It would allow the perceiver or recaller to experience spatial integration and continuity in relation to sets of activity that are spatially discontinuous but do occur in the same time window, an illusory intuition.

A different solution

Following on the evidence and reflections outlined above and incorporating additional neuropsychological and neuroanatomical data, I propose the following solution:

(a) The neural activity that embodies physical structure representations entity occurs in *fragmented fashion and in geographically separate cortices* located in modal sensory cortices. The so-called integrative, rostral cortices of the anterior temporal and prefrontal regions cannot possibly contain such fragmentary inscriptions.

(b) The integration of multiple aspects of reality, external as well as internal, in perceptual or recalled experiences, both within each modality and across modalities, depends on the time-locked co-activation of geographically separate sites of neural activity within sensory and motor cortices, rather than on a neural transfer and integration of different representations towards rostral integration sites. The conscious experience of those co-activations depends on their simultaneous, but temporary, enhancement (here called co-attention), against the background activity on which other activations are being played back.

(c) The representations of physical structure components of entities are recorded in precisely the same neural ensembles in which corresponding activity occurred during perception, but the combinatorial arrangements (binding codes) which describe their pertinent linkages in entities and events (their spatial and temporal coincidences) are stored in separate neural ensembles called *convergence zones*. The former and the latter neuron ensembles are interlocked by reciprocal projections.

(d) The concerted reactivation of physical structure fragments, on which recall of experiences depends, requires the firing of convergence zones and the concomitant firing of the feedback projections arising from them.

(e) Convergence zones bind neural activity patterns corrseponding to topographically organized fragment descriptions of physical structure, which were pertinently associated in previous experience on the basis of similarity, spatial placement, temporal sequence, temporal coincidence, or any combination of the above. Convergence zones are located throughout the telencephalon, at multiple neural levels, in association cortices of different orders, limbic cortices, subcortical limbic nuclei, and non-limbic subcortical nuclei such as the basal ganglia.

(f) The geographic location of convergence zones varies among individuals but is not random. It is constrained by the subject matter of the recorded material (its domain), by degree of contextual complexitiy in events (the number of component entities that interact in an event and the relations they adopt), and by the anatomical design of the system.

(g) The representations inscribed in the above architecture, both those that preserve topographic/topologic relationships, and those that code for temporal coincidences, are committed to populations of neuron ensembles and their synapses, in distributed form.

(h) the co-occurrence of activities at multiple sites, which is necessary for temporary conjunctions, is achieved by iteration across time phases.

Thus I propose not a single direction of processing, along single or multiple channels, but rather a recursive and iterative form of processing. Such processing is parallel and, because of the many time phases involved in multiple steps, it is also sequential. Convergence zones provide integration, and, although the convergence zones that realize the more encompassing integration are more rostrally placed, the activities that all levels of convergence zone end up promoting, and on the basis of which representations are reconstituted and evoked, actually take place in caudal rather than rostral cortices. And because convergence zones return the chain of processing to earlier cortices where the chain can start again towards another convergence zone, there is no need to postulate an ultimate integration area. In other words, this model can accommodate the astonishing segregation of processing streams that the work of Livingstone and Hubel has revealed so dramatically.

The sensory and motor cortices are thus seen as the distributed and yet restricted sector of the brain on which both perception and recall play themselves out, and on which self-consciousness must necessarily be based. Perception and self-consciousness are assigned the same brain spaces at the border between the world within and the world without.

In the following section I present a framework based on these views and discuss its structures, systems, organization, and operation.

Timelocked multiregional retroactivation: framework, structures, systems organization, and operation

Framework

Because of its origin in mutually constraining sets of cognitive and neural data, the theory developed here is both cognitive and neural. The cognitive architecture implicit in the theory assumes representations that can be described as psychological phenomena and interrelated according to combinatorial semantics and syntax. The proposed neural organization, however, is not a mere hardware implementation apparatus for any potential type of cognitive processes, in that its specifications severely restrict the range of representations and algorithms that it can implement; that is, it is not likely to implement representations other than the ones its anatomy and physiology embody and are destined to operate. The key level of neural architecture is that of systems of macroscopic functional regions in cerebral cortex and gray matter nuclei.

The theory describes an adult neural/cognitive organization presumed to be relatively stable and yet modifiable by experience, to produce temporary or long-lasting partial reorganizations. The issues of neural and cognitive development are not addressed, nor does the theory deal with microneural specifications at synaptic and molecular levels. However, it does assume that any inscription of perceptuomotor activity is based on a distributed transformation of physiological parameters, occurring over ensembles of neurons at the level of their synapses, according to some variant of Hebbian principles. The theory operates on the basis of neurobiological and reality constraints.

Neurobiological constraints

These correspond to the structural design of the nervous system prior to interactions with the environment: the basic circuitry of cellular structures and their interconnectivity, which can be changed by epigenetic interactions. The design includes neuroanatomically embodied values of the organism (e.g., goals and drives of the species), external and internal spatial reference maps, and a variety of processing biases that are likely to guide, in part, the mapping of interactions with the environment, that is, the domains of knowledge that the brain prefers to acquire and the choice of neural sites to support such knowledge. The effect of these constraints is to provide a certain degree of innate modularization of "faculties" upon exposure to the reality constraints discussed below.

Reality constraints: the world without and the world within

The description of the characteristics of the universe surrounding the brain, both inside and outside the organism, can be made at the multiple levels that current knowledge of philosophy, psychology, physics, chemistry, and biology permit. From my point of view, however, it is sensible to focus the description on the levels from which we derive psychological meaning: (1) a broad range of objects to which I will refer to as entities and which encompass both natural and man-made kinds; (2) the features and dimensions that compose those entities; and (3) the interplay of entities in unique events or episodes occurring in temporal and spatial units. Thus, the set of reality constraints corresponds to:

(1) The existence of concrete entities external to both brain and organism, and external to the brain but internal to the organism (somatic). External entities are themselves composed of various aggregated features and dimensions in an entity-intrinsic space (the space defined by the physical limits of the entity) and are, in turn, placed within an entity-extrinsic space (the coordinate space where the entity and other entities lie or move). Internal entities consist of: (a) motor interactions of the organism with external entities by means of movements in hands, head, eyes, and whole body; (b) baseline somatic states of internal milieu and of smooth and striated musculature during interaction with external entities; and (c) modification of somatic states triggered by and occurring during interaction with external entities.

(2) The existence of abstract entities are criterion-governed conjunctions of features and dimensions present in the concrete entities outlined above.

(3) The fact that entities necessarily occur in unique interactive combinations called events, and that events often take place concurrently, in complex sets.

Entities are definable by the number of components, the modality range of those components (e.g., single or multiple modality), the mode of assembly, the size of the class formed on the basis of physical structure similarity, their operation and function, their frequency of occurrence, and their value to the perceiver.

As is the case with entities, events can be both external and internal, and both concrete and abstract. The concurrence of many events which characterize regular life episodes generates "contextual complexity", which can be defined by the number of entities and by the relational links they assume as they interplay in such complex sets of events. Naturally, during the unfolding of events, other entities and events are recalled from autobiographical records. The records co-activated in that process add further to the contextual complexity of the experiences that occur within a given time unit. It is thus contextual complexity which sets entities and events apart and which confers greater or lesser uniqueness to those entities and events. In other words, contextual complexity sets the taxonomic level of events and entities along a continuum that ranges from unique (most subordinate) to non-unique (less subordinate and more supraordinate).

Domain formation and recording of contextual complexity

During interactions between the perceiver's brain and its surround, the two sets of constraints lead to some critical operations that can be described as follows from a psychological standpoint:

(1) domain formation, which is a process of feature, entity, and event grouping based on physical structure similarity, spatial placement, temporal sequence, and temporal coincidence;

(2) the creation of records of contextual complexity that register the temporal coincidence of entities and their interrelationships within sets of events.

It is on the basis of this psychological-level description and on the evidence that category-related recognition defects can be associated to damage in specific brain loci that we hypothesize neural substrates for different knowledge domains and levels of knowledge processing. It must be noted that for the purposes of modeling we are here inverting the natural order of things: domains exist *because* of neurobiological and reality constraints, not the other way around.

Functional regionalization

The process of regionalization occurs for both fragments of perceptuomotor activity and convergence zones. I conceive it as a way of recruiting a neuron population for a limited range of cortical inputs (and, by extension, to the domain or level defined by the feed-forwarding neuronal populations). In other words, certain topics (at feature, entity, or event level) are assigned to a circumscribed neuronal population. Within that polulation, however, different synaptic patterns define individual features, or entities, or events. In simple terms one might say that generally similar material stacks up together within the same regions and systems.

As I will discuss further on, the superimposed, overlapped nature of the records poses problems for their appropriate separation during recall. The solution I envisage, and that may appear counterintuitive at first glance, resides with the wealth and complexity of the record at the synaptic level. The greater the number of defining sub-components and distinctive links, the greater the chance of establishing uniqueness at the time of recording and at the time of reactivation.

The key to regionalization is the detection, by populations of neurons, of coincident or sequential spatial and temporal patterns of activity in the input neuron populations. Precisely the same type of neuron ensembles, operating on precisely the same principles, will constitute the substrate for different cognitive operations depending on the location of the ensemble within the system and the connections that feed into the ensemble and that feed back out of it. In other words, location and communication lines determine the topic of the synaptic patterns within a given neuron ensemble (the domain of a convergence zone), without there being a need to posit special neuron types or special physiological codes in order for convergence zones to serve different domains or cognitive operations.

The nature of representations

Human experiences as they occur ephemerally in *perception* are the result of multiple sensory and motor processing of a collection of features and dimensions in external and internal entities. Specifically they are based on the cerebral representation of concrete external entities, internal entities, abstract entities, and events.

Such representations are interrelated by combinatorial arrangements so that their internal activation in recall and the order with which they are attended, permits them to unfold in a "sentential" manner. Such "sentences" embody semantic and syntactic principles.

In my view, the words of any language are also concrete external entities. The combinatorial semantics and syntax of thought and language might be embodied in the relationships that describe the constitution of entities and events (although the universal grammar behind language may be based on additional language-specific principles and rules).

This cognitive/neural architecture implies a high degree of sharing and embedding of representations. Both the representation of abstract entities and of events are derived from the representation of concrete entities and are thus individualized on the basis of combinatorial arrangement rather than remapping of constituents. The representation of concrete entities themselves share subrepresentations of component features so that individuality is again conferred by combinatorial formulas.

Human experiences, as they occur ephemerally in *recall,* are based on records of the multiple-site and multiple-level neural activities previously engaged by perception. Recalled experiences constitute an attempted reconstruction of perceptual experience based on activity in a set of pertinent sensory and motor cortices, controlled by a reactivation mechanism specified below.

The components of representations

Feature-based fragments

I propose that the experienceable (conscious) component of representations results from an attempt at reconstituting feature-based, topographic or topologically organized fragments of sensory and motor activity; that is, only the feature-based components of a representation assembled in a specific pattern can become a content of consciousness. The maximal size of the feature-based fragment is a critical issue. Stimuli such as human faces, verbal lexical entities, and body parts of the self, must be permanently represented by large-scale fragments on the basis of which rapid reconstitution can occur. It is unlikely that such stimuli would depend on a reconstruction from the smallest-scale level of neural activity (equivalent, for the visual system, to Bela Julesz' textons, 1981). But many fragments are small-scale and can be shared by numerous entities and used interchangeably in the reconstitution attempt.

Convergence zones

1. The structure and role of convergence zones

Because feature-based fragments are recorded and reactivated in sensory and motor cortices, the reconstitution of an entity or event so that it resembles the original experience depends on the recording of the combinatorial arrangement that conjoined the fragments in perceptual or recalled experience. The record of each unique combinatorial arrangement is the binding code, and it is based on a device I call the convergence zone.

Convergence zones exist as synaptic patterns within multi-layered neuron ensembles in association cortices, and satisfy the following conditions: (1) they have been convergently projected upon by multiple cortical regions according to a connectional principle that might be described as many-to-one; (2) they can reciprocate feed-forward projections with feedback projection (one-to-many); (3) they have additional, interlocking feed-forward/feedback relations with other cortical and subcortical neuron ensembles. The signals brought to convergence zones by cortico-cortical feed-forward projections, represent temporal coincidences (co-occurrence) or temporal sequences of activation in the feeding cortices (rather than re-representations of inscriptions contained in the feeding cortices). I envision the binding code as a synaptic pattern of activity such that when one of the projections which feed-forward to it is reactivated, firing in the convergence zone leads to simultaneous firing in all or most of the feedback projections which reciprocated the feed-forward from the original set. By means of those reciprocating feedback lines, convergence zones can trigger simultaneous activity in all or part of the originally feeding cortices, in a retroactive and divergent manner, according to certain principles of operation specified below. The proposal does not address the issue of the number or size of convergence zones, although it assumes that the zone's size is defined during development as a result of input–output connection patterns, and the patterns of lateral interaction that help structure the ensemble as a unit.

Convergence zones are *amodal*, in that they receive signals from the same or different modalities but do *not* map sensory or motor activity in a way that preserves feature-based, topographic and topological relations of the external environment as they appear in psychological experience. Convergence zones do not embody a refined representation, in the sense that would be assumed in an information-processing model, although they do route information in the sense of information theory. They know "about" neural activity in the feeding cortices and can promote further cortical activity by feedback/retroactivation. In themselves, however, they are uninformed as to the content of the representations they assist in attempting to reconstruct. The role of convergence zones is to enact formulas for the reconstitution of fragment-based momentary representations of entities or events in sensory and motor cortices—the experiences we remember.[3]

2. Operating principles

Convergence zones signal the related binding of the similarity, spatial placement, temporal sequence, or temporal coincidence of feature-based fragments highlighted in the perceiver's experience. Convergence zones prompt sensory and motor co-activation by means of back-projections into cortices located upstream. In the extreme view (a mere caricature), all that would be required of a convergence zone would be to function as a pivot, that is, to cause retroactivation in sites that it fed back to, after a threshold defined by concurrent inputs had been reached. The general operating principle would be stated as: (a) reactivate itself when fired upon; (b) reactivation promotes firing toward any site to which there are back-projections, recip-

---

[3]The notion of separating storage of fragments of experience, from storage of a catalogue for their reconstitution, was inspired by our study of patient Boswell, along with the notion that a unidirectional caudal–rostral processing cascade was less likely than a multidirectional, recursive organization. The idea of convergence zones came from reflection on patterns of cortico-limbic projections, especially the multiplicity of parallel and converging channels, and the progressive size reduction of the neural convergence sites along a caudal–rostral axis. The pattern of disruption of cortico-limbic and cortico-cortical feed-forward and feedback projections in patients with Alzheimer's disease (see Van Hoesen & Damasio, 1987, for a review) provided the blueprint for the construct.

rocating feed-forward inputs that generated the synaptic pattern that defines the zone. But because of superimposition and overlapping of convergence zones within the same neuron population, and of the ensuing high number of synaptic interactions, the range of back-firing of each convergence zone is modulated rather than rigid. It depends on the momentary number and nature of cortical feed-foward inputs (relative to the total number of possible feedback outputs that the zone can have), and on the momentary inputs from other areas of cortex and from limbic system, thalamus, basal forebrain, and so forth.

As a consequence, convergence zones can produce different ranges of retroactivation in the cortex, depending on the concurrent balances of inputs they receive. Also, convergence zones can blend responses, that is, produce retroactivation of fragments that did not originally belong to the same experiential set, because of underspecification of cortical feed-forward inputs, or higher-order cortical feedbacks, or subcortical feedbacks. When pathological combinations of input are reached, the zone malfunctions, for example, it may generate "fantastic" or "psychotic" responses, or not operate at all.

It is important to note that the lines activated by feedback from convergence zones are not rigid. They should be seen as facilitated paths that may or may not be travelled depending on the ensemble pattern of synaptic interactions within a population.

3. Types of convergence zones

I envisage permanent convergence zones in the cortex and temporary convergent zones in limbic structures and basal ganglia/cerebellum, based on current findings regarding the profile of retrograde amnesia following hippocampal damage. The domain of the convergence zone is determined by its immediate and remote feed-forward inputs which are co-extensive with its back-projection targets.

I propose two types of convergence zones. In Type I, the zone fires back simultaneously and produces concomitant activations. Type I zones inscribe temporal coincidences and aim at replicating them. Type II convergence zones fire back in sequence, producing closely ordered activations in the target cortices. Such zones have inscribed temporal sequences and aim at replicating them. The time scale for firing from Types I and II convergence zones would be different.

Type I convergence zones are located in sensory association cortices of low and high order, and are assisted in learning by the hippocampal system. Type II convergence zones are the hallmark of motor-related cortices, and are assisted in learning by basal ganglia and cerebellum.

In the normal condition, the two types of convergence zone interlock at multiple levels so that learning relative to an entity or event recruits both types of convergence zones. Likewise normal recall and recognition involve operations in both types of convergence zone, even when the triggering stimulus only activates one type of convergence zone at the outset of the process.

4. The development of convergence zones

The placement of convergence zones is partly the result of the genetically expressed neuroanatomical design and partly the result of the sculpting process introduced by learning. Convergence zones develop in association cortices that: (a) receive projections in a convergent manner from a wider array of cortices located upstream; (b) can reciprocate projections to the feeding cortices; (c) can project downstream to other cortices and subcortical structures; and (d) can receive a wide array of projections from several subcortical and motor structures.

It is the genetic pattern of neuroanatomical connections that first constrains the potential domain of convergence zones. For example, a convergence zone in early visual association cortices cannot possibly bind anything but visually related activity at the level of component features, whereas a convergence zone in anterior temporal cortices can be told about activity related to numerous simultaneous events and bind their coincidence. But the ultimate anatomical location and functional destiny of convergence zones is determined by learning, as neuron ensembles become differentially dedicated to certain types of occurrence in feeding cortices.

Convergence zones are created during learning as a result of concurrent activations in neuron ensembles within association cortices of different order, hippocampus, amygdala, basal ganglia, and cerebellum. The concurrent activations come from convergent feed-forward signals generated by neural activity in: (a) sensory and motor cortices (as caused by perception or recall of external or internal entities); (b) feedback projections from other convergence zones in association cortices; (c) direct and indirect feedback projections from convergence zones in limbic cortices and from limbic related nuclei: (d) direct and indirect feedback projections from basal ganglia, non-motor thalamus, and cerebellum; and (e) local microcircuitry interactions.

As noted above, convergence zones have thresholds and levels of response. The activation of a convergence zone depends on its internal constitution, the size, locus, number, and location of sensory and motor representation sites that it subtends. It also depends on the momentary concurrent combination of potential trigger weights, from neural activity related to externally generated representations, internally recalled representations, and back-projection from all the neuronal sites listed previously.

5. Superposition of signals

Convergence zones contain overlapping binding codes for many entities and events. Such rich binding is the source of the widening retroactivation that permits recognition and thought processes, and yet its wealth, if unchecked, would eventually result in co-activations bearing only minimal relationships to previous specific experiences and on inability to reconstitute unique events. Ultimately, fantastic and cognitively catastrophic combinations would occur, as they do in fact occur in a variety of neuropsychological disorders caused by the neuropathological processes at several levels of the system. In the normal brain, the constraints that impose specificity of co-evocations depend on concurrent inputs from the following systems: (a) other convergence zones, at multiple neural levels, whose subtended retroactivation provides neural context and thereby helps constrain co-activation; and (b) non-specific limbic nuclei (basal forebrain and brain stem) activated by antero-temporal limbic units (amygdala, hippocampus).

6. Attention

In a system that produces multiple-site activations incessantly, it is necessary to enhance pertinently linked sites in order to permit binding by salient coincidences. I use the term attention to designate the "spotlighting" process that generates simultaneous and multiple-site salience and thus permits the emergence of evocations. Consciousness occurs when multiple sites of activation are simultaneously enhanced in keeping or not with real past experiences. (Some psychotic and demential states are possibly examples of simultaneous enhancement of activations whose combination does not conform to reality; in non-pathological states the same applies to day-dreams). As defined here, attention depends on numerous factors and mechanisms. First, there is a code for enhancement of activations that is part of the record of the activation pattern it enhances. Type II convergence zones are especially suited to this role. Secondly, the state of the perceiver and the context of the process play important roles in determining the level of activations. The reticular activating system, the reticular complex of the thalamus, and the limbic system mediate such roles under partial control of the cerebral cortex.

The evocations that constitute experienced recall occur in specified sensory and motor cortices, albeit in parcellated fashion. Experienced recall thus occurs where physical structures of external entities or body states were mapped in feature fragment manner, notwithstanding the fact that a complex neural machinery made up of numerous other areas of cortex and subcortical nuclei cooperates to reconstruct the co-activation patterns and enhance them.

7. The placement of convergence zones

Convergence zones have different placements within association cortices and other gray matter regions, and varied activation thresholds. There are numerous levels of convergence zone depending on knowledge domain and contextual complexity (taxonomic level). The functional regionalization of a domain corresponds to the neural inscription of separate sensory and motor activities related to features and dimensions of different exemplars. The inscriptions are naturally superimposed to the extent that the respective features and dimensions overlap, or coincide in time. The inscriptions are naturally contiguous when the respective features or acts they represent occurred in temporal sequence. As superimpositions accrue, categories emerge from the blends and mergings of separate exemplars. It is important to note that for each separate exemplar to be recalled as an individual entity, it is necessary to add contextual complexity to its representation. This is accomplished by connecting its inscription to the inscription of other entities and events so that an entirely unique set can be defined. When additional inscriptions are not linked to create unique or nearly unique sets, the superimposition of exemplars remains categorical or generic, and recall can reconstitute any one previously learned exemplar or else a blend of exemplars. The creation of records of contextual complexity, which code for the temporal entities and events, is thus critical for recall or recognition at unique (episodic) level.

It is important to note that in this perspective the building of categories occurs while inscribing episodes. The system operates so that it always attempts to inscribe as much as possible of the entire context. Even if the system fails to inscribe the whole episode—or if it does inscribe it, but recall cannot fully reconstitute it—the operation preserves enough of the core inscription of an entity (or event) for categorization to develop from this and other related inscriptions. The inscription of categories precedes episode inscription; that is, it is neuroanatomically and neurophysiologically more caudal. This disposition explains the impairment of episodic memory and preservation of generic memory following damage to anterior temporal cortices.

Knowledge of objects, faces, numbers, among many others, created by perceptuomotor interactions, is anatomically and functionally regionalized in a manner different from classic localizationism of function, but that does admit a notable degree of anatomical specialization. This form of specialization does not follow traditional anatomical boundaries such as are known for sensory modalities, or cytoarchitectonic brain areas. Nor does it conform to the functional centers of traditional neurology. The fragment representations that comprehensively describe an entity are dispersed by multiple functional regions which are, in turn, located in different cytoarchitectonic areas. The many convergence zones necessary to bind the fragments relationally are located in yet other neural sites. The region thus formed obeys anatomical criteria dictated by the nature of the entity represented, and by the interaction between perceiver and entity, and is secondarily constrained by the potential offerings of the anatomy. The comprehensive representation of a specific entity or category is distributed not only within a population of neurons but is also distributed in diverse types of neural structure, cortically and subcortically. In this proposal, the term localization can only refer to an imaginary space defined by neural sites likely to contain convergent zones necessary for the retroactivation of a given set of entities or events. The borders of such a space are not only fuzzy but changeable, in the sense that for different instantiations of retroactivation of a given entity the set of necessary convergence zones varies considerably.

Applications of the framework

In the following two sections I discuss briefly the application of this proposal to learning and memory and language.

Learning and memory

1. The relative segregation of memory domains
The fact that different neural regions support memory for different domains is the reason why striking performance dissociations can occur in human amnesia. For instance, after lesions in the hippocampal system, patients retain previously learned perceptuomotor skills (so-called procedural knowledge) or even learn new ones, while memory and learning for new faces or objects is no longer possible (Cohen & Squire, 1980; Damasio et al., 1985a,b, 1987; Eslinger & Damasio, 1986; Milner, Corkin, & Teuber, 1968). This dissociation occurs because the representations of motor entities rely on structures that remain intact in those patients: somatosensory and motor cortices, neo-striatum and cerebellum. As noted above, the functional essence behind the system formed by those structures is the recording and re-encactment of temporal sequences and relies on Type II convergence zones.
Participation of the hippocampal system is not at all necessary for the acquisition and maintenance of procedural memories, provided they are used only at a covert level, and the subject is not required to recollect the factual information related to the acquisition of the skill or to the circumstances in

which the skill has been previously exercised. Conscious recall of the source of knowledge requires patency of at least one hippocampal region.

By contrast, the weight of recording factual knowledge, in spite of its diverse base on sensory and motor activities, relies most importantly on sensory cortices and necessitates hippocampal activity. The functional essence in this system is the recording of neural activity related to physical structure (of features, entities, and events), spatial contiguity (of features and entities), and temporal coincidence (of entities and events). Type I convergence zones in the hippocampal-bound association cortices are required. Perhaps the most dramatic lesion-related dissociation within factual knowledge is the one that compromises memory for complex social events but spares general knowledge of entities and events outside of a social context (Damasio & Tranel, 1988; Eslinger & Damasio, 1985). Other striking dissociations abound, however, for different categories of objects, for verbal and non-verbal knowledge, and for different types of verbal knowledge (Damasio et al., 1989b).

2. Different levels of memory processing

In essence, the distinction between generic and episodic memories is a distinction of processing levels during recall or recognition. We can recall at generic levels, with little contextual complexity attached to an entity, no definition of uniqueness, and no connection to our autobiography. Or we can recall at progressively richer episodic levels, with the evocation of greater contextual complexity and the experience of autobiographic events in which entities play more specific roles. I believe the brain normally attempts to capture the maximal complexity of every event, although the stability of the recording of such complexity varies with the value of the event and with the anticipated need to recall it.

3. The mapping of uniqueness and of entity-centered knowledge

The critical distinction between generic and episodic knowledge, from the standpoint of learning, resides with the ability to record temporal coincidence (co-occurrence) of entities within a wide and complex context. It is a matter of magnitude that distinguishes generic from episodic levels of processing, somewhat artificially, along a continuum.

When a perceiver interacts with a novel entity, learning consists of recording any additional patterns of physical structure, somatic state, or relational binding that transpired during the interaction but were *not previously recorded*. The same applies to learning of new events.

In virtually all instances of learning beyond the early acquisition periods of infancy and childhood, any new pattern of activity related to perception of new entities and events also evokes multiple and previously stored patterns that are thus co-experienced with the novel stimuli. Learning does not entail the recording of all the information contained in a new event. Rather, it calls for the co-evocation of many physical structures and relations previously recorded for related events, the recording of any novel features that had not been recorded before, and the linking of novel records with the pre-existing records so that a new specific set is defined and the code for its potential reconstitution committed to a convergence zone.

There is a large sharing of memory records such that the same neural patterns can be applied to many entities and events by superimposition and overlap whenever and wherever their physical structure or relational bindings are shared. The inscription of a specific entity or event can be made unique only by means of connecting a particular component to others. Such an organization is extremely economical and promotes a large memory capacity. However, it is also prone to ambiguity and an easily disordered operation if one of its many supporting devices malfunctions. Confusional states and some amnesic syndromes caused by subcortical lesions are an expression of such malfunctions. At a milder level, fatigue, sleep deprivation, or distraction can cause the same.

4. Neural substrates for learning and memory at systems level
The critical neural substrate for learning and memory comprises two major subsystems: one that interconnects sensory cortices assigned to mapping physical structure and temporal coincidence with the hippocampus; and a second that interconnects sensory and motor cortices assigned to mapping temporal sequence with the basal ganglia/cerebellum and the dorsolateral frontal cortices. Normal operation of these subsystems is cooperative rather than independent.

The neuroanatomical design of the entorhinal cortex and of the sequence of cellular regions in the hippocampus to which it projects deserves special mention. This subsystem provides a set of auto-interacting convergence zones of great complexity. It is the only brain region in which signals originally triggered by neural activity in all sensory cortices and in centers for autonomic control can actually co-occur over the same neuron ensembles. As such, this is the appropiate substrate for a detector of temporal coincidences, the function that I have previously proposed for this system and that I believe to be lost in amnesia following hippocampal damage (see Damasio et al., 1985a). Such a function is compatible, in essence, with the type of physiological basis for learning proposed by Hebb, a presynaptic/postsynaptic coincidence mechanism. It is also compatible with a variety of recent cellular and molecular evidence regarding the phenomenon of long-term potentiation (LTP) and the role of NMDA-gated calcium channels as detectors of coincidence (see Gustafsson & Wigstrom, 1988, for a review).

Once detection of co-occurrence takes place, the region acts via its powerful feedback system into cortical and subcortical neural stations, to assist in the creation or modification of convergence zones located in the cortices that originally projected into the entorhinal cortex. It is also apparent that such a structure, especially the autocorrelation matrix of CA_3, could store within itself binding codes of the kind I envisage for convergence zones, capable of content-addressed completion. It appears unlikely, however, that the hippocampal complex remains as a storage site for long periods, not only because of what that would mean in terms of capacity limits and risk of malfunction, but also because bilateral damage confined to the entorhinal cortex/hippocampus appears to cause only limited impairments of retrograde memory (Corkin, 1984), and the same appears to be true of bilateral damage to the hippocampus alone (Zola-Morgan, Squire, & Amaral, 1986). The definitive account on this issue is not available yet. In humans, the left and right hippocampi appear to be dedicated to different operations and may also operate differently in terms of their long-term role in retrieval.

5. Consciousness and self-consciousness

As previously noted, consciousness emerges when retroactivations attain a level of activity that confers salience. Coincident salient sites of activity define a set that separates itself from background activity and emerges, in psychological terms, as a conscious content on evocation as opposed to non-salient retroactivations that remain covert.

Conscious contents are all contents about which one can give testimony, in verbal narrative form, but I wish to distinguish them from the subset of conscious content we call self-conscious contents. The difference resides with the notion of self and autobiography. In my view, self-consciousness only emerges when conscious contents relative to an ongoing stimulus are experienced in the context of pertinent autobiographical data. The distinction is not specious. Patient Boswell is conscious of his environment and properly recognizes the stimuli around him but not in relation to his autobiography. Whether the stimulus is something that he ought to have recognized as unique, or something truly new to him, his ability to put it in the perspective of his life experience is restricted. His self-consciousness is thus limited and unlike that of perceivers in whom evocations generated by novel percepts are co-attended simultaneously with autobiographical evocations.

Language

The representations related to language, that is, the representations of lexical entries and grammatical operations, including syntactic rules or principles, phonology, morphology, and semantics which constitute the internalized or mental grammar, are perceived, acquired, and co-activated according to the principles articulated for non-verbal entities. As noted above, the framework does not address the issue of innate versus acquired aspects of language, although from a perspective of biological evolution as well as from the investigation of universal properties of the world's diverse languages it is likely that the substrates for combinatorial semantics and syntactical principles are partly innate.

The lexicon and language-specific aspects of the grammar, as cultural artifacts, are a subset of reality characterized by certain physical structures (the physical phonetic articulatory gestures and resultant acoustic correlates of linguistic units and structures, that is, phones, phonemes, morphemes, words, phrases, sentences, etc.) and logical relationships (grammatical functions) at multiple levels. Those external physical structures and relations constitute a corpus of signals capable of symbolizing, in sentential terms, most non-language aspects of reality at any level. By means of both feature-based physical fragment representations and binding convergence zones, the brain stores the potential for reconstituting any lexical entry or relational arrangement that it has learned, as well as the implicit rules by which novel utterances are produced and comprehended. This would not deny the possibility that highly frequent lexical entries would be recorded at large-scale fragment level, for instance, the level of an entire word stem, a condition that would be highly adaptive.

The brain not only inscribes language constituents but also provides direct and dynamic neural links between verbal representations and the representation of non-language entities or events that are signified by language. In other words, the brain embodies (materializes) in neural hardware the combined biological and cultural bond that culture has assigned between a language representation (a signifier) and a segment of non-verbal reality (a signified), to borrow Saussure's suggestive terminology. It is that neural bond that permits the two-way, uninhibitable translation process that can automatically convert non-verbal co-activation into a verbal narrative (and vice versa), at every level of neural representation and operation.

Testing the framework

There are fundamentally four approaches to test the validity of the hypotheses expressed here. One relies on the lesion method, the approach on which most of these ideas are based. Small focal and stable lesions in humans with neurological disease can be used to probe neuropsychological predictions based on the hypotheses expressed here. Another approach involves the use of positron emission tomography in both normals and patients with focal brain damage, to explore temporal correlations among different cortical regions activated by controlled stimuli. Another approach would involve computational modeling and testing of the concept of convergence zone. Finally, it will be possible in experiments using multiple recording from different cortical sites to test the notion of time-locked activations. For instance, in an experiment where one would record simultaneously from multiple cortical sites encompassing two sensory modalities, the following should be observed:

(1)   After a delay compatible with feedback firing, electrical stimulation of convergence zones would produce synchronous activity in separate cortical sites presumed to contain feature-fragments related to the convergence zone.
      The regions chosen for stimulation would be guided by knowledge of neurons in association cortex that respond constantly to specific stimuli, for example, faces. Likewise, the choice of areas to guide the search for time-locked activity in early cortices would come from knowledge of areas known to be activated by the perception of a specific stimulus, for example, a face.
(2)   The lack of finding of time-locked activity across a vast array of cortical regions theoretically presumed to be necessary for the reconstitution of a perceptual set would constitute evidence against the notion of convergence zones proposed here.

Situating the proposal

I see the following features of the theory as distinctive:

(1)   The notion that there is a major distinction between records of physical structure fragments, and records of combinatorial arrangements among those records.
(2)   The notion that the experience of entities or events in recall always depends on the time-locked retroactivation of fragmentary records contained in multiple sensory and motor regions and thus on momentary attempted reconstitutions of the once perceived components of reality.
(3)   The notion that while evocations only exist momentarily, they are the only directly inspectable aspect of brain activity. Their fleeting existence makes them no less real. Furthermore, although their existence depends

on a complex machinery distributed by multiple brain sites and levels, the proposal specifies that the attempted reconstitutions occur in an anatomically restricted sector of the cerebrum.

(4) The notion that certain aspects of the interaction between perceiver and reality generate domains of knowledge, which become regionalized according to neural constraints rather than conceptual-lexical labels.

(5) The notion that the anatomical placement and connectional definition of a convergence zone, that is, the specification of its inputs and outputs at the point in the system that is located, also defines the knowledge domain the convergence zone embodies.

(6) The role attributed to feedback projections, especially cortico-cortical, in the mechanisms of reconstitution of experiences. Feedback is distinguished from re-entry as used in the automata of Edelman and Reeke (1982). Feedback and feed-forward carry signals about activity in interconnected units but they do not transport a movable representation being entered or re-entered. Feed-forward signals mark the presence of activity upstream in the network, and indicate the whereabouts of records of activity. Feedback reactivates such upstream records. The convergence zones record those relationships and operate to route activity. No representations of reality as we experience it are ever transferred in the system; that is, no concrete contents and no psychological information move about in the system.

(7) The value accorded to representations of internal somatic states in all their aspects and levels. Somatic states are generally relegated to a subsidiary position, a matter of non-specific influence on the general workings of a network concerned with representations of external reality. In this proposal somatic states are memorized in feature-based fragment records (linked by binding convergence zones), just as external stimuli are. The source for this notion was our studies of humans with focal lesions, especially those with conditions such as anosognosia and acquired disorders of conduct (Damasio & Anderson, 1989).

It is perhaps useful to compare this proposal to other recent proposals that deal with cognitive processes and the organization of their putative neural substrates. In order to do this we will choose two reference points: the classical model of cognitive architecture, as presented, for instance, by Fodor and Pylyshyn (1988), and a range of models known under the designations "parallel distributed processing" or "connectionism" (see Rumelhart & McClelland, 1986).

    We believe that the structures and operations described in this theory occupy an intermediate position and are compatible with the proposals in these reference points. The neural organization we propose is at the level of systems formed by macroscopic functional regions. It embodies and can implement some predicates of a classical cognitive architecture. On the other hand, it is conceivable that connectionist nets and alogrithms may realize some of the microscopic levels underlying the organization proposed here. By the same token our theory is also compatible with neuronal group selection theory (Edelman & Finkel, 1984). Although the specification of neuron units in those theories is designed in "brain-style", the overall networks are not yet "brain-like". The principles of structure and operation of the machines so designed are not aimed at the superstructure organization necessary for cognitive processes such as thought, language, or consciousness; that is, to our knowledge they do not yet compel separate units to hook themselves up in a particular way capable of making a system thoughtful and self-conscious. By contrast, this theory seeks to propose precisely some of those higher organization principles. Cognitive architecture proposals refer to psychological phenomena that our framework aims at capturing. Connectionist models refer to microstructure and function situated below the levels at which our description concentrates, but that might conceivably carry on some of the necessary implementations, at least in certain sectors of the neural structure.

References

Allman, J., Miezin, F., & McGuinness, E. (1985). Stimulus specific responses from beyond the classical receptive field: Neurophysiological mechanisms for local–global comparisons in visual neurons. *Annual Review of Neuroscience, 8,* 407–430.

Barlow, H.B. (1981). Critical limiting factors in the design of the eye and visual cortex. (The Ferrier Lecture, 1980). *Proceedings of the Royal Society London, (Biology), 212,* 1–34.

Bauer, R.M. (1984). Autonomic recognition of names and faces in prosopagnosia: A neurophysiological application of the Guilty Knowledge Test. *Neuropsychologia, 22,* 457–469.

Bruce, C.J., Desimone, R., & Gross, C.G. (1981). Visual properties of neurons in a polysensory area in superior temporal sulcus of the macaque. *Journal of Neurophysiology, 46,* 369–384.

Chavis, D.A., & Pandya, D.N. (1976). Further observations on corticofrontal connections in the rhesus monkey. *Brain Research, 117,* 369–386.

Cohen, N.J., & Squire, L.R. (1980). Preserved learning and retention of pattern-analyzing skill in amnesia: Dissociation of knowing how and knowing that. *Science, 210,* 207–210.

Corkin, S. (1984). Lasting consequences of bilateral medial temporal lobectomy: Clinical course and experimental findings in HM. *Seminars in Neurology, 4,* 249–259.

Crick, F. (1984). Function of the thalamic reticular complex: The searchlight hypothesis. *Proceedings of the National Academy of Science USA, 81,* 4586–4590.

Damasio, A.R. (1979). The frontal lobes. In K. Heilman & E. Valenstein (Eds.), *Clinical neuropsychology.* New York: Oxford University Press.

Damasio, A.R. (1985a). Disorders of complex visual processing. In M.M. Mesulam (Ed.), *Principles of behavioral neurology.* Philadelphia: Davis.

Damasio, A.R. (1985b). The frontal lobes. In K. Heilman & E. Valenstein (Eds.), *Clinical neuropsychology* (2nd edition). New York: Oxford University Press.

Damasio, A.R. (1989). Category-related recognition defects as a clue to the neural substrates of knowledge. *Trends in Neurosciences,* in press.

Damasio, A.R., & Anderson, S. (1989). Anosognosia as a domain-specific memory defect. *Journal of Clinical and Experimental Neuropsychology, 11,* 17.

Damasio, A.R., & Damasio, H. (1983). The anatomic basis of pure alexia. *Neurology, 33,* 1573–1583.

Damasio, A., Damasio, H., & Tranel, D. (1989a). Impairments of visual recognition as clues to the processes of memory. In G.M. Edelman, W.E. Gall, & W.M. Cowan (Eds.), *Signal and sense: Local and global order in perceptual maps.* In press.

Damasio, A.R., Damasio, H., & Tranel, D. (1989b). New evidence in amnesic patient Boswell: Implications for the understanding of memory. *Journal of Clinical and Experimental Neuropsychology, 11,* 61.

Damasio, A., Damasio, H., Tranel, D., Welsh, K., & Brandt, J. (1987). Additional neural and cognitive evidence in patient DRB. *Society for Neuroscience, 13,* 1452.

Damasio, A., Damasio, H., & Van Hoesen, G.W. (1982). Prosopagnosia: Anatomic basis and behavioral mechanisms. *Neurology, 32,* 331–341.

Damasio, A., Eslinger, P., Damasio H., Van Hoesen, G.W., & Cornell, S. (1985a). Multimodal amnesic syndrome following bilateral temporal and basal forebrain damage. *Archives of Neurology, 42,* 252–259.

Damasio, A., Graff-Radford, N., Eslinger, P., Damasio, H. & Kassell, N. (1985b). Amnesia following basal forebrain lesions. *Archives of Neurology, 42,* 263–271.

Damasio, A.R., & Tranel, D. (1988). Domain-specific amnesia for social knowledge. *Society for Neuroscience, 14,* 1289.

Desimone, R., Albright, T.D., Gross, C.G., & Bruce, C. (1984). Stimulus-selective responses of inferior temporal neurons in the macaque. *Journal of Neuroscience, 4,* 2051–2062.

Desimone, R., Schein, S.J., Moran, J., & Ungerleider, L.G. (1985). Contour, color and shape analysis beyond the striate cortex. *Vision Research, 25,* 441–452.

Desimone, R., & Ungerleider, L. (1989). Neural mechanisms of visual processing in monkeys. In A. Damasio (Ed.), *Handbook of neuropsychology: Disorders of visual processing* (Vol. II, pp. 267–299). Amsterdam: Elsevier.

Edelman, G.M., & Finkel, L.H. (1984). Neuronal group selection in the cerebral cortex. In G.M. Edelman, W.E. Gall, & W.M. Cowan (Eds.), *Dynamic aspects of neocortical function.* New York: Wiley.

Edelman, G.M., & Reeke, G.N. (1982). Selective networks capable of representative transformations, limited generalizations, and associative memory. *Proceedings of the National Academy of Science USA, 79,* 2091–2095.

Eslinger, P.J., & Damasio, A.R. (1985). Severe disturbance of higher cognition after bilateral frontal lobe ablation. *Neurology, 35,* 1731–1741.

Eslinger, P.J., & Damasio, A.R. (1986). Preserved motor learning in Alzheimer's disease. *Journal of Neuroscience, 6,* 3006–3009.

Farah, M. (1989). The neuropsychology of mental imagery. In A. Damasio (Ed.), *Handbook of neuropsychology: Disorders of visual processing.* (Vol. II, pp. 395–413). Amsterdam: Elsevier.

Feinberg, T., Rothi, L., & Heilman, K. (1986). Multimodal agnosia after unilateral left hemisphere lesion. *Neurology, 36,* 864–867.

Fodor, J.A., & Pylyshyn, Z.W. (1988). Connectionism and cognitive architecture: A critical analysis. *Cognition, 28,* 3–71.

Geschwind, N. (1965). Disconnexion syndromes in animals and man. *Brain, 88,* 237–294.

Geschwind, N., & Fusillo, M. (1966). Color-naming defects in association with alexia. *Archives of Neurology, 15,* 137–146.

Gilbert, C.D. (1983). Microcircuitry of the visual cortex. *Annual Review of Neuroscience, 6,* 217–247.

Goldman-Rakic, P.S. (1984). The frontal lobes: Uncharted provinces of the brain. *Trends in Neurosciences, 7,* 425–429.

Goldman-Rakic, P.S. (1988). Topography of cognition: Parallel distributed networks in primate association cortex. In: *Annual Review of Neuroscience, 2*, 137–156.

Gustafsson, B., & Wigstrom, H. (1988). Physiological mechanisms underlying long-term potentiation. *Trends in Neurosciences, 11*, 156–162.

Horenstein, S., Chamberlin, W., & Conomy, J. (1967). Infarction of the fusiform and calcarine regions: Agitated delirium and hemianopia. *Transactions of the American Neurological Association, 92*, 85–89.

Hubel, D.H., Livingstone, M.S. (1987). Segregation of form, color, and stereopsis in primate area 18. *Journal of Neuroscience, 7*, 3378–3415.

Hubel, D.H., & Wiesel, T.N. (1977). Functional architecture of macaque monkey visual cortex. *Proceedings of the Royal Society London Series B, 198*, 1–59.

Jones, E.G., & Powell, T.P.S. (1970). An anatomical study of converging sensory pathways within the cerebral cortex of the monkey. *Brain, 93*, 793–820.

Julesz, B. (1971). *Foundation of cyclopean perception*. Chicago: University of Chicago Press.

Julesz, B. (1981). Textons, the elements of texture perception and their interaction. *Nature, 290*, 91–97.

Kosel, K.C., Van Hoesen, G.W., & Rosene, D.L. (1982) Nonhippocampal cortical projections from the entorhinal cortex in the rat and rhesus monkey. *Brain Research, 244*, 202–214.

Kosslyn S.M. (1980). *Image and mind*. Cambridge, MA: Harvard University Press.

Lettvin, J.Y., Maturana, H.R., McCulloch, W.S., & Pitts, W.H. (1959). What the frog's eye tells the frog's brain. *Proceedings of the IRE, 47*, 1940–1949.

Lewis, D.A., Campbell, M.J., Foote, S.L., & Morrison, J.H. (1986). The monoaminergic innervation of primate neocortex. *Human Neurobiology, 5*, 181–188.

Livingstone, M.S., & Hubel, D.H. (1984). Anatomy and physiology of a color system in the primate visual cortex. *Journal of Neuroscience, 4*, 309–356.

Livingstone, M.S., & Hubel, D.H. (1987a). Connections between layer 4B of area 17 and thick cytochrome oxidase stripes of area 18 in the squirrel monkey. *Journal of Neuroscience, 7*, 3371–3377.

Livingstone, M.S., & Hubel, D.H. (1987b). Psychological evidence for separate channels for the perception of form, color, movement, and depth. *Journal of Neuroscience, 7*, 3416–3468.

Livingstone, M.S., & Hubel, D.H. (1988). Segregation of form, color, movement, and depth: Anatomy, physiology, and perception. *Science, 240*, 740–749.

Lund, J.S., Hendrickson, A.E., Ogren, M.P., & Tobin, E.A. (1981). Anatomical organization of primate visual cortex area VII. *Journal of Comparative Neurology, 202*, 19–45.

Luria, A.R. (1966). *Higher cortical functions in man*. New York: Basic Books.

McCarthy, R.A., & Warrington, E.K. (1988). Evidence for modality-specific meaning systems in the brain. *Nature, 334*, 428–430.

Mesulam, M.M., Mufson, E.J., Levey, A.I., & Wainer, B.H. (1983). Cholinergic innervation of the cortex by basal forebrain: Cytochemistry and cortical connections of the septal area, diagonal band nuclei, nucleus basalis (substantia innominata) and hypothalamus in the rhesus monkey. *Journal of Comparative Neurology, 214*, 170–197.

Milner, B., Corkin, S., & Teuber, H.L. (1968). Further analyses of the hippocampal amnesic syndrome: 14 year follow-up study of H.M. *Neuropsychologia, 6*, 215–234.

Mishkin, M., Malamut, B., & Bachevalier, J. (1984). Memories and habits: Two neural systems. In G. Lynch, J.L. McGaugh, & N.M. Weinberger (Eds.), *Neurobiology of learning and memory* (pp. 65–77). New York: Guilford Press.

Mountcastle, V.B., Lynch, J.C., & Georgopoulous, A. (1975). Posterior parietal association cortex of the monkey: Command functions for operations within extra-personal space. *Journal of Neurophysiology, 38*, 871–908.

Nauta, W.J.H. (1971). The problem of the frontal lobe: A reinterpretation. *Journal of Psychiatric Research, 8*, 167–187.

Newcombe, F., & Ratcliff G. (1974). Agnosia: A disorder of object recognition. In F. Michel & B. Schott (Eds.), *Les syndromes de disconnexion calleuse chez l'homme.* Lyon: Colloque international de Lyon.

Paillard, J. (1971). Les determinants moteurs de l'organization de l'espace. *Cahiere de Psychologie, 14,* 261–316.

Pandya, D.N., & Kuypers, H.G.J.M. (1969). Cortico-cortical connections in the rhesus monkey. *Brain Research, 13,* 13–36.

Pandya, D.N., & Yeterian, E.H. (1985). Architecture and connections of cortical association areas. In A. Peters & E.G. Jones (Eds.), *Cerebral cortex, (Vol. 4).* New York: Plenum Press.

Penfield, W., & Jasper, W. (1954). *Epilepsy and the functional anatomy of the human brain.* Boston: Little, Brown.

Perrett, D.I., Mistlin, A.J., & Chitty, A.J. (1987), Visual neurons responsive to faces. *Trends in Neurosciences, 10,* 358–364.

Perrett, D.I., Rolls, E.T., & Caan, W. (1982). Visual neurons responsive to faces in the monkey temporal cortex. *Experimental Brain Research, 47,* 329–342.

Posner, M.I. (1980). Orienting of attention. *Quarterly Journal of Experimental Psychology, 32,* 3–25.

Rockland, K.S., & Pandya, D.N. (1979). Laminar origins and terminations of cortical connections of the occipital lobe in the rhesus monkey. *Brain Research, 179,* 3–20.

Rockland, K.S., & Pandya, D.N. (1981). Cortical connections of the occipital lobe in rhesus monkey: Interconnections between areas 17, 18, 19 and the superior temporal gyrus. *Brain Research, 212,* 249–270.

Rosch, E., Mervis, C., Gray, W., Johnson, D., & Boyes-Braem, P. (1976). Basic objects in natural categories. *Cognitive Psychology, 8,* 382–439.

Rosene, D.L., & Van Hoesen, G.W. (1977). Hippocampal efferents reach widespread areas of the cerebral cortex in the monkey. *Science, 198,* 315–317.

Rumelhart, D.E., & McClelland, J.L. (1986). *Parallel distributed processing (Vol. 1).* Cambridge, MA: MIT Press.

Sejnowski, T.J. (1986). Open questions about computation in cerebral cortex. In J.L. McClelland & D.R. Rumelhart (Eds.), *Parallel distributed processing* (pp. 372–389). Cambridge, MA: MIT Press.

Seltzer, B., & Pandya, D.N. (1976). Some cortical projections to the parahippocampal area in the rhesus monkey. *Experimental Neurology, 50,* 146–160.

Seltzer, B., & Pandya, D.N. (1978). Afferent cortical connections and architectonics of the superior temporal sulcus and surrounding cortex in the rhesus monkey. *Brain Research, 149,* 1–24.

Squire, L.R. (1987). *Memory and brain,* New York: Oxford University Press.

Swanson, L.W., & Kohler, C. (1986). Anatomical evidence for direct projections from the entorhinal area to the cortical mantle in the rat. *Journal of Neuroscience, 6,* 3010–3023.

Tranel, D., & Damasio, A. (1985). Knowledge without awareness: An autonomic index of facial recognition by prosopagnosics. *Science, 228,* 1453–1454.

Tranel, D, & Damasio, A. (1987). Autonomic (covert) discrimination of familiar stimuli in patients with visual agnosia. *Neurology, 37,* 129; *Society for Neuroscience, 13,* 1453.

Tranel, D., & Damasio, A. (1988). Nonconscious face recognition in patients with face agnosia. *Behavioral Brain Research, 30,* 235–249.

Treisman, A., & Gelade, G. (1980). A feature-integration theory of attention. *Cognitive Psychology, 12,* 97–136.

Tulving, E. (1972). Episodic and semantic memory. In E. Tulving & W. Donaldson (Eds.), *Organization of memory.* New York: Academic Press.

Ungerleider, L.G., & Mishkin, M. (1982). Two cortical visual systems. In D.J. Ingle, R.J.W. Mansfield, & M.A. Goodale (Eds.), *The analysis of visual behavior.* Cambridge, MA: MIT Press.

Van Essen, D.C. (1985). In A. Peters & E.G. Jones (Eds.), *Functional organization of primate visual cortex.* New York: Plenum Publishing.

Van Essen, D.C., & Maunsell, J.H.R. (1983). Hierarchical organization and functional streams in the visual cortex. *Trends in Neurosciences, 6,* 370–375.

Van Hoesen, G.W., & Damasio, A.R. (1987). Neural correlates of the cognitive impairment in Alzheimer's disease. In F. Plum (Ed.), *Higher functions of the nervous system: The handbook of physiology* (pp. 871–898).

Van Hoesen, G.W., & Pandya, D.N. (1975a). Some connections of the entorhinal (area 28) and perirhinal (area 35) cortices in the rhesus monkey. I. Temporal lobe afferents. *Brain Research, 95,* 1–24.

Van Hoesen, G.W., & Pandya, D.N. (1975b). Some connections of the entorhinal (area 28) and perirhinal (area 35) cortices in the rhesus monkey. III. Entorhinal cortex efferents. *Brain Research, 95,* 39–59.

Van Hoesen, G.W., Pandya, D.N., & Butters, N. (1975). Some connections of the entorhinal (area 28) and perirhinal (area 35) cortices in the rhesus monkey. II. Frontal lobe afferents. *Brain Research, 95,* 25–38.

Van Hosen, G.W. (1982). The primate parahippocampal gyrus: New insights regarding its cortical connections. *Trends in Neurosciences, 5,* 345–350.

Zeki, S.M. (1987). Personal communication.

Zola-Morgan, S., Squire, L.R., & Amaral, D. (1986). Human amnesia and the medical temporal region: Enduring memory impairment following a bilateral lesion limited to the CAI field of the hippocampus. *Journal of Neuroscience, 6,* 2950–2967.

Résumé

Cet article esquisse un cadre théorique pour la compréhension des bases neurales de la mémoire. Il propose l'hypothèse que le rappel et la reconnaissance d'entités et d'événements dépendent de l'activation de nombreux ensembles de neurones dans de multiples régions des cortex sensoriels et moteurs où les représentations des fragments de formes sont représentés par des configurations d'activité impliquées à l'origine par les interactions perceptuo-motrices. Le processus d'activation est dirigé à partir de multiples zones de convergence situées dans les cortex d'association et dans certains noyaux gris sous-corticaux. Ces zones de convergence enregistrent de façon amodale l'arrangement combinatoire des différents fragments de formes tels qu'il se présente dans les aires corticales précoces au cours de l'entité ou de l'événement. Les zones de convergence sont reliées avec les ensembles neuronaux primaires par des projections réciproques qui forment des chemins facilités plutôt que des liens rigides. Le fonctionnement des zones de convergence est modulé de façon dynamique par les entrées concurrentes provenant d'autres aires et noyaux sous-corticaux. Ce modèle réfuse l'existence d'un site anatomique unique pour l'intégration sensori-motrice et d'une mémoire unique gardant le sens d'entités ou d'événements. Le sens résulte de la rétro-activation distribuée et synchrone de fragments. Seuls ces derniers atteignent le seuil du conscient.

3

Neuronal models of cognitive functions

JEAN-PIERRE CHANGEUX
URA CNRS 0210 "Neurobiologie Moléculaire", Département des Biotechnologies, Institut Pasteur, Paris

STANISLAS DEHAENE
INSERM et CNRS, Paris

Abstract

Changeux, J.-P., and Dehaene, S. 1989. Neuronal models of cognitive functions. Cognition, 33:63–109.

Understanding the neural bases of cognition has become a scientifically tractable problem, and neurally plausible models are proposed to establish a causal link between biological structure and cognitive function. To this end, levels of organization have to be defined within the functional architecture of neuronal systems. Transitions from any one of these interacting levels to the next are viewed in an evolutionary perspective. They are assumed to involve: (1) the production of multiple transient variations and (2) the selection of some of them by higher levels via the interaction with the outside world. The time-scale of these "evolutions" is expected to differ from one level to the other. In the course of development and in the adult this internal evolution is epigenetic and does not require alteration of the structure of the genome. A selective stabilization (and elimination) of synaptic connections by spontaneous and/or evoked activity in developing neuronal networks is postulated to contribute to the shaping of the adult connectivity within an envelope of genetically encoded forms. At a higher level, models of mental representations, as states of activity of defined populations of neurons, are discussed in terms of statistical physics, and their storage is viewed as a process of selection among variable and transient pre-representations. Theoretical models illustrate that cognitive functions such as short-term memory and handling of temporal sequences may be constrained by "microscopic" physical parameters. Finally, speculations are offered about plausible neuronal models and selectionist implementations of intentions.

*The second author is currently at the Laboratoire de Sciences Cognitives et Psycholinguistique. Reprint requests should be sent to Jean-Pierre Changeux, Département des Biotechnologies, Institut Pasteur, 28 rue du Docteur Roux, 75274 Paris Cedex 15, France

Introduction

> "To think is to make selections"
> W. James (1909)

In the course of the past decade, the development of the cognitive sciences has resulted in many significant contributions, and, for many, the science of mental life constitutes a "special science" (Fodor, 1975). But still one must ask how the physical world supports mental processes. The radical proposal was made (Johnson-Laird, 1983) that "the physical nature [of the brain] places no constraints on the pattern of thought ... any future themes of the mind [being] completely expressible within computational terms". The computer thus became the last metaphor, which "needs never be supplanted" (Johnson-Laird, 1983).

In parallel, the sciences of the nervous system have made considerable progress. Studies of single nerve cells and of their molecular components unambiguously rooted the elementary processes of neurons in physical chemistry, thereby introducing a wide spectrum of constraints, in particular upon their dynamics. Moreover, comparative anatomical investigations of higher vertebrate (see Goldman-Rakic, 1987; Rakic, 1988) and human (Geschwind & Galaburda, 1987; Luria, 1973) brain connectivity, biochemistry (e.g., Hökfelt et al., 1986) and physiology (e.g., Edelman, Gall, & Cowan, 1984) have yielded novel views about the complexity of adult brain organization and about its morphogenesis (Changeux, 1983a, 1983b; Edelman, 1987; Geschwind & Galaburda, 1987). On such bases, the alternative radical program was proffered that, ultimately, the science of mental life will be reduced to neural sciences and the tenets of psychology will be eliminated (Churchland, 1986).

The aim of this paper is *not* to deal, once more, with this philosophical debate (Churchland, 1986; Fodor, 1975; see also Mehler, Morton, & Jusczyk, 1984; Stent, 1987), but rather to report recent theoretical and experimental work that actually lies at the frontier between cognitive science and neuroscience and that might ultimately bridge these two disciplines. It is hoped that such neurocognitive approaches will serve to create positive contacts between the two disciplines rather than to stress their differences. The real issue becomes the specification of the relationships between a given cognitive function and a given physical organization of the human brain. From an experimental point of view, our working hypothesis (rather than philosophical commitment) is that levels of organization exist within the brain at which a type-to-type physical identity (Fodor, 1975) might be demonstrated with cognitive processes. Yet, it should be stressed that we address this problem from the neurobiological point of view in an attempt to *reconstruct* (rather than reduce) a function from (rather than to) its neural components. This is, of course, not to deny the bridges that some psychologists have already thrown to the neural sciences in areas like language, neonate cognition, memory or neuro-psychology. Our aim is to review recent contributions from the neurosciences to psychological concepts like innateness, learning, internal representations, and intentionality, and to offer relevant models that, in many cases, still remain speculative.

It is beyond the scope of this article to present an exhaustive review of data and models that fall within this approach. The discussion is limited to a few selected issues. First, the notion of level of organization and the relation-ship between structure and function in biological systems is introduced, to-gether with evidence for the existence of multiple levels of functional organi-zation within the human brain. A generalized Darwinian-like theory is pro-posed to describe the relationships between levels of organization and, in particular, the transition from one level to the next higher one. This empirically testable theory assumes that selection at a given level takes place in real time as a result of pressure from the immediately higher level, yielding a two-way dependency. Such Darwinian views are applied to the epigenesis of develop-ing neuronal networks. The last two parts deal with the more conjectural neural bases of mental representations and "mental Darwinism", where the above-mentioned two-way dependency is assumed to take place at a higher level, between representations and the goals they subserve. In both instances, Darwinian views are extended to evolutive systems that are *not* based on variations of their genetic material itself, but of their phenotypic expression in developmental and psychological time-scales.

We have deliberately omitted from the discussion complex cognitive func-tions such as problem solving or language processing, especially those aspects of language interpretation that require access to very large stores of knowl-edge. Our feeling is that, at this stage, the neurobiological basis is too com-plex and the relevant data still too scarce for pertinent modelling in neuronal terms.

I. The notion of level of organization in biological systems

The debate over the relative contributions of cognitive psychology, connec-tionist modelling and neurobiology to the understanding of the higher func-tions of the human brain hinges primarily upon a basic confusion about the levels of organization at which models of cognitive function and their neural implementations have been designed. The specification of such levels should precede any theoretical approach, and might even constitute the substance of a full theory. The cleavage of the world into pertinent units – from atoms, molecules and cells, up to, for example, syntactic structures and social classes – is neither trivial nor unequivocal. In highly evolved organisms, the relevant levels are expected to be multiple and intricate. Before dealing with the cognitive level(s), three basic questions must be answered:

(1) What characterizes a given level of organization within a living organism?
(2) To what extent are the levels dependent on each other?
(3) Does a general mechanism account for the transition from one level to the next?

The definition of a given level relies upon the anatomical organization of its elementary components and upon characteristic properties or functions that are unique to this level. The programme of the life sciences is, of course, to specify functions but, most of all, to relate a given function to an appropriate anatomical organization of its components in a causal and reciprocal manner. A quick look at the history of biology shows that unravelling the actual "physical" implementation of a given function has always been at the origin of considerable progress in the understanding of biological functions (see Clarke & O'Malley, 1968, in the case of neurobiology). As a metaphor to illustrate this point, let us consider the well-known example of the catalytic activity of enzymes. Enzymes are proteins made up of linear chains of amino acids that spontaneously fold into three-dimensional edifices of rather large size – macromolecules. At the turn of the century, such a macromolecular organization of enzymes was not known, but their function as catalysts was already well recognized (see Debru, 1983, for a review). The laws of their action on substrates were described in great detail, and in still valid computational terms, by the Henri and Michaelis–Menten *algorithms*, which, to a first approximation, adequately fit the measured kinetics. The rapid progress of molecular biology, in particular the unravelling of the three-dimensional topology of folded polypeptide chains by X-ray diffraction methods at the atomic level, led to an explanation of the way their active sites function. It showed, for instance, that the fixed orientation in space of a few of the protein amino acid side chains suffices for matching to the shape of the substrate and, through chemical bonding, for activating the transformation of the enzyme–substrate complex, a feature that disappears upon unfolding of the protein. The function of the enzyme (which Jacques Monod (1970) already referred to as "cognitive") is thus directly bound to the macromolecular level of organization and may even be viewed as characteristic of this level. The implementation of the function in terms of chemical bonds, including their nature, strength and topology, would never have been predicted from the algorithmic description of the active site function. Yet, this new understanding did not lead to an abandonment of the Michaelis–Menten algorithm, but rather raised many novel functional questions at a more microscopic level.

Another example is that of the material bases of inheritance. Mendel's observations on the heredity of flower colour in peas, and its description in simple algorithmic terms which constitute the Mendelian laws, may, at a glance, appear sufficient from a functional point of view. Yet, the identification of chromosomes and (subsequently) DNA as the physical basis of heredity opened many new avenues of research without, at any moment, contradicting the Mendelian algorithm.

II. The multiple levels of functional organization within the nervous system

The notion of organization and the relationship between physical structure (architecture) and function can legitimately be extended to the nervous system (Changeux, 1983b; Chomsky, 1979; Jackson, 1932). However, to what extent can the entire nervous system be viewed as one such level, above which would stand both a functional algorithmic level and a formal level of abstract grammatical rules (Marr 1982)? Should we follow the classical view (Fodor & Pylyshyn, 1988), which distinguishes among physical, syntactic and knowledge (semantic) "levels", and further assumes that the "functional organization of the nervous system crosscuts its neurological organization" (Fodor, 1975)? Or even, to be more schematic, may we say that the nervous system is the mechanism, the hardware of the machine, above which would stand autonomously the program with its semantic and syntactic levels? We deliberately reject such a view, for within the nervous system, several distinct levels of organization can be defined. Distinct levels of cognitive function relate to these different levels of physical organization, thus shattering the simple-minded (and actually reductionistic) behaviour/algorithm/hardware metaphor for the relationship between psychology and neural science.

The first level, the architecture of which can be related to functional characteristics of the nervous system, is the *"cellular level"*, because of the unique ability of nerve cells to make topologically defined networks through their axonal and dendritic branches and their synaptic contacts. This physical architecture is described by the topology of the cell arborization and its synaptic connections. Its function includes both the patterns of electrical and chemical signals produced by the cell (Prince & Huguenard, 1988) and the actions of these signals on effector cells, which lead to either overt behaviour or a covert process that might contribute to further operations within the system. At the single-cell level, the ability of the neuron to generate electrical impulses (or modulate its spontaneous firing) as a function of the inputs it receives (and several other functions it displays) can be expressed in a global algorithmic form, and implemented in terms of the molecular properties of its synaptic and cell membrane components. Yet, in this instance already, the algorithmic level cannot be viewed simply as autonomous or distinct from the physical one. It would, of course, be absurd to infer from such cellular and molecular data the nature of the architecture of cognitive functions. Yet, nerve cells are the building blocks of cognitive architectures, and as such they exert severe constraints on the coding of mental representations, on the computations accessible to these representations, and on the modalities of storage and retrieval. After all, the rates of propagation of impulses in nerves and across synapses impose inescapable limits on the speed of higher computations; storage of memory traces has to be considered in terms of changes of molecular properties of nerve cells and synapses; and the production of internal thought processes independently of outside world stimulation relies upon the existence of a spontaneous self-sustained and organized firing of nerve cells (see section VI).

Another level of organization, referred to as the "*circuit level*", is reached with the nervous system of invertebrates (sea-slugs like *Aplysia* or *Hermissenda*, insects like *Drosophila* and worms like *Hirudo*). Circuits are made up of thousands (or even millions) of nerve cells organized in well-defined ganglia, with each (or nearly each) cell possessing a well-defined individual connectivity and function within the organism. Satisfactory attempts have been made to account for simple behaviours strictly on the basis of the anatomy of small circuits and the electrical and chemical activity displayed by the circuit (Alkon, Disterhoft, & Coulter, 1987; Grillner, 1975; Grillner et al., 1987; Kandel et al., 1983; Kleinfeld & Sompolinsky, 1987; Stent et al., 1978). The architecture of the most advanced connectionist models, which aim at imitating humanlike brains, are no more complex than these rather primitive nervous systems, and often remain inferior in complexity even in the most elaborate attempts.

The mutual relations of individual neural circuits define another level of organization. Thus, for example, classical physiology has emphasized the roles of the spinal cord and brainstem in the mediation of reflexes and various other sensorimotor operations. A vast amount of anatomical, physiological and neuropsychological data, moreover, has led to a closer understanding of the participation of various cortical and other brain domains in sensory perception, motor control, language comprehension and production, memory, etc. (Geschwind & Galaburda, 1987; Kolb & Wishaw, 1980; Luria, 1973). The number of these specialized domains appears much larger than initially suspected (Rakic & Singer, 1988): in the primate brain, for instance, there are about a dozen representations of the visual world and half a dozen each of auditory and somatic representations. Many of these are interdigitated, and yet, each fragment displays a distinct characteristic, thus "constructing categories in an unlabeled world" (Zeki, 1988).

The cognitive level lies within reach of this "meta-circuit" level, since the parsing of psychological tasks into elementary operations correlates well with a decomposition of the brain into separate areas (Posner, Petersen, Fox, & Raichle, 1988). However, even these ultimate cognitive functions might themselves be cleaved into distinct faculties. Seventeenth- and eighteenth-century philosophers, Kant in particular, distinguished *"reason"* as the "faculty which contains the principles by which we know things absolutely *a priori"* from *"intendment"* which, from the perceived elements, produces concepts and evaluates them. In a simplified manner, the intendment would make the synthesis of sensible elements into concepts, while pure reason would make computations upon the concepts produced by the intendment. Such distinction of different levels of abstraction bears a relation to recent concepts from experimental psychology (see Kihlstrom, 1987). Accordingly, intendment processes would be mostly modular, automatic and unconscious, although attention may regulate their inputs and their access to memory stores, while in pure reason the processing would essentially (though not exclusively) be conscious, non-modular and require attention. What then are the brain structures, if any, for intendment and reasoning?

In attempting to build bridges across disciplines, it may be useful to relate the intendment/reason distinction with a distinction reached through a different approach in the field of artificial intelligence. Newell (1982) raised questions of levels in computers, of their autonomy and reducibility to lower levels, questions that are indeed familiar to neuroscientists. Thus, he proposed that immediately above the symbol (program) level of standard computers stands a knowledge level, where the agent processes its own knowledge to determine the actions to take. The law governing behaviour is the principle of rationality: actions are selected to attain the agent's goal. "If an agent has the knowledge that one of its actions will lead to one of its goals it will select that action" (4.2, p. 17). According to Newell, the "knowledge level is exactly the level that abstracts away from symbolic processes" (4.3, p. 23), a conclusion not far from Kant's definition of reason. Moreover, and this is a crucial point, the actions may add knowledge to the already existing body of knowledge. As mentioned by Simon (1969) in the case of economic agents, "the adjustment to its outer environment (its substantive rationality) is conditioned by its ability to *discover* an appropriate adaptive behavior (its procedural rationality)". In other words, in selecting actions to achieve a goal, the agent not only relies upon judgments but, in situations of uncertainty, it computes expectations and possible scenarios of complex interactions.

A crucial issue then becomes the specification of the neural architectures that characterize the knowledge level thus defined. Yet, the feasibility of this attempt is under debate. For instance, Pylyshyn (1985) has argued on the basis of Newell's (1982) views, that one should distinguish knowledge-based from mechanism-based explanations. We quote him: "the mechanism is part of the process that itself is not knowledge dependent (it is cognitively impenetrable) hence it does not change according to rational principles based upon decisions, inferences, and the like, but on other sorts of principles, ones that depend on intrinsic properties, which are presumably governed by biological laws" (p. 408). "Ignoring the physics and biology may even be necessary because the categories over which the system's behavior is regular may include such things as the meaning of certain signals and because the entire equivalence class of signals having the same meaning need not have a description that is finitely stable in a physical vocabulary" (p. 405). Our view is that even if the distinction between cognitively penetrable and impenetrable processes may, to some extent and within a limited time-scale, be justified, the separation between the cognitively penetrable and the "biological or biochemical properties" of organisms is not valid. In fact, as will become clear in the following paragraphs, there is hardly any structure in the brain which does not incorporate exterior knowledge during its epigenesis and functioning. We realize that there is more to Pylyshyn's cognitive penetrability than the simple notion of knowledge dependence. For instance, Pylyshyn's mechanistic level, as far as we understand it, comprises the processes that do not vary following a change in conscious beliefs and intentions of an agent. However, the usefulness of this notion is questionable on the grounds that: (1) this particular mechanistic level is not identical to the level of biological laws, since there may be encapsulated psychological processes that cannot be accessed and modified intentionally; (2) its definition depends on the time-scale chosen, since conscious, attention-demanding processes may become automatic and impenetrable in the course of learning (see Baddeley, 1976, 1986); and (3) its definition puts exceptional emphasis on the notions of consciousness and belief, the scientific status of which is now questioned on philosophical as well as neuropsychological grounds.

It is thus part of a concrete scientific programme to describe which (and to what extent) biological structures are penetrable by knowledge at a given level. This programme is necessary if we are to have a biology of goal, knowledge and rational decisions, as well as to know the neural architectures underlying the faculty of reason.

If such a research programme looks plausible, it is far from being achieved (or even undertaken) in neuroscience for many reasons. First of all, in humans, processes as elementary as visual perception, which take place at the intendment level, are deeply impregnated by knowledge from the earliest stages of development (see sections IV and V). Similarly, since storage seems to rely more on semantic than on perceptual cues (Baddeley, 1976, 1986, 1988), it seems almost impossible to analyse the function of long-term memory stores without considering what information they encode. Moreover, from both the phylogenetic and embryological points of view, the faculties for reasoning and for concept formation, among others, cannot be assigned to unique brain domains or areas and, of course, the operations taking place at any level are expected to mobilize important populations of nerve cells with a distributed topology which will *a priori* be difficult to map.

Nevertheless, one may theorize, for example, that the frontal areas of the cortex contribute to the neural architectures of reason (for reviews see Struss & Benson, 1986, and Goldman-Rakic, 1987). Among the many observations supporting this view is the fact that the differential expansion of prefrontal cortical areas from the lowest mammals up to man parallels the development of cognition. Neuropsychological observations of Lhermitte (1983) and Shallice (1982), among others, also relate frontal cortex to high-level cognitive processes. Patients with frontal lobe lesions, for example, display an interesting "utilization" behaviour. They grasp and utilize any object presented to them as if they had become dependent upon sensory stimulation. They also fail in tests such as the "Tower of London", which require planning strategies and control of the execution. Patients no longer employ a general mode of regulation that lets them plan their interactions with the environment, makes them aware of novel situations or errors in the executions of their own strategies, and allows them to generate new hypotheses. Although few studies have investigated the neuronal architecture underlying these functions, brain lesions indicate a dissociation of two levels *within* cognition, which closely approximate the levels of reason and intendment discussed previously.

III. The transition between levels of organization: generalized Variation – Selection (Darwinian) scheme

A given function (including a cognitive one) may be assigned to a given level of organization and, in our view, can in no way be considered to be *autonomous*. Functions obviously obey the laws of the underlying level but also display, importantly, clear-cut dependence on higher levels. Coming back to our favourite metaphor, the function of the enzyme active site is determined by the amino acid sequence of the protein; yet the amino acid sequence is itself the product of a long genetic evolution, which ultimately rested upon survival (stabilization) rules that constrained the structure of the macro-molecule. The macromolecular state, which determines the enzyme catalytic function, is rooted, by its structure, in the underlying levels of physics and chemistry, but also contributes, by its function at a higher level, to the metabolism of the cell and thus to its own existence.

The same interdependence holds for the various levels of neurofunctional organization. If, for instance, the function of the reflex arc can be viewed as strictly determined by a well-defined spinal cord neuronal circuit, its detailed organization is such that higher brain centres may control its actualization within a coordinated motor act. At any level of the nervous system, multiple feedback loops are known to create re-entrant (Edelman & Mountcastle, 1978) mechanisms and to make possible higher-order regulations between the levels.

Our view is that the dual dependence between any two levels must be framed in an evolutionary perspective (see Changeux, 1983b; Delbrück, 1986; Edelman, 1987) and is governed by a generalized variation-selection (Darwi-nian) scheme. Accordingly, a minimum of two distinct components is re-quired: a generator and a test. "The task of the generator is to produce variety, new forms that have not existed previously, whereas the task of the test is to cut out the newly generated forms so that only those that are well fitted to the environment will survive" (Simon, 1969; p. 52). The initial diver-sity may arise from combinatorial mechanisms that produce organizations that are novel (or rare) for the considered level and become transitional forms, bridging it to the next higher level. The rules of stabilization (survival) are governed by the function associated with the novel form, thus creating feedback stabilization loops of function upon structure.

Such a scheme is classical in the case of the evolution of species and is evidenced in the development of the immune response, where diversity arises from genomic reorganization and gene expression, and the test arises from the survival of the fittest (including matching to the antigen). The scheme may also account for the transition from cellular to multicellular organisms and for the general morphogenesis of the brain. Our view, in addition, (Changeux, Courrège, & Danchin, 1973; Changeux & Danchin, 1974, 1976; Changeux, Heidmann, & Patte, 1984; Edelman, 1978, 1985, 1987; Jerne, 1967; Young, 1973; see also Ramon y Cajal, 1909; Taine, 1870; references in Heidmann, Heidmann, & Changeux, 1984), is that the interaction between the nervous system and the outside world during the course of postnatal development through adulthood, during which the acquisition of some of its highest abilities, including language and reasoning, occur (see section V), also follows an analogous Darwinian scheme. Yet, such evolution is expected to take place *within* the brain without any necessary change in the genetic material (at variance with the view of Piaget, 1979, or Wilson, 1975), and inside of short time-scales: days or months in the case of embryonic and early postnatal development and tens of seconds in the case of the processing and reorganization of mental representations. At each level, the generator of variety and the test must be specified, and the time-scale of the evolution must be defined. Moreover, such time-scales are short enough (compared to those spanning the evolution of species) to render the theory experimentally testable.

The justification of such views will constitute the matter of the subsequent sections. In essence the brain will be considered constantly and internally to generate varieties of hypotheses and to test them upon the outside world, instead of having the environment impose (instruct) solutions directly upon the internal structure of the brain (see Changeux, 1983b). The view of the brain as a hardware construct, knowledge-independent, that would be programmed by a computationally autonomous, cognitively penetrable mind has, thus, to be reconsidered for the following reasons:

(1) There exists, within the brain, multiple levels of functional organization associated with distinct neural architectures (see section II).

(2) Several of these neurofunctional levels are cognitively penetrable at some stage of development, and these multiple levels are heavily interconnected via feedback loops, or re-entrant mechanisms, that make possible high-order regulations *between levels* (further examples of such interactions appear below).

(3) The information-processing/input–output scheme has to be abandoned in favour of an internal "generator of variations" continuously anticipating and testing the outside world with reference to its own invariant representation of the world.

IV. The ontogenesis of neural form

A basic principle of cognition is the recognition, storage and internal production of forms in space (patterns) or time (melodies). The Gestalt psychologists have emphasized that this faculty relies on the existence of physiological forms within the organism that display some physical relationship with the psychological ones. Without entering into a debate on the exact nature of this relationship – whether it is isomorphic or not – it is evident that the brain must be viewed as a highly organized system of intertwined architectures whose forms result from pre- and postnatal development. Moreover, as dis-

cussed in the preceding section, several distinct levels of functional organization exist within the brain and develop according to defined biological constraints during both phylo- and ontogenesis. Understanding the formation of
neural forms and their hierarchical organizations, for example those involved
in the architectures of reason, concept formation or pattern recognition, becomes a fundamental step in the understanding of cognition.

1. Preformation and epigenesis. The problem of the origin of animal form
has been at the centre of a long controversy from classical times to the present. According to the extreme *preformationist* view, ontogenesis proceeded
strictly as the enlargement of forms that were thought to be already present
in the egg (Swammerdam) or in the spermatozoon (Van Leeuwenhoek).
Related views are still found in the theory of morphological archetypes advocated by D'Arcy-Thompson (1917), and they have recently been revived by
Thom (1980). Accordingly, such archetypes, mathematically formalized in a
set of abstract rules, would impose global morphological constraints on, or
even direct the ontogenesis of, the adult form. Also, contemporary molecular
biologists frequently refer to a DNA-encoded genetic program according to
which development would proceed in a strictly autonomous manner (see
Stent, 1981, for a criticism of the concept of genetic program). Finally, some
contemporary linguists and psychologists posit the innateness of knowledge
(or at least of a certain body of information) (Chomsky, 1965) or of mental
faculties or structures (Fodor, 1983), although without referring to the actual
neural bases of their development. According to such extreme Cartesian
views, the internal innate structures are rich and diverse, and their interaction
with the environment, although capable of "setting parameters", does not
create new order.

The alternative attitude, illustrated by epigenesis, contrasts with radical
preformationism by postulating a progressive increase of embryonic complexity (rather than simple enlargement by post-generation and after-production).
Such epigenetic conceptualization of the development of animal forms shows
analogies in psychology to the associationist attitude (Helmholtz), or mental
atomism, which assumes, for instance, that perception relies upon the analysis
of external objects into elements and upon their synthesis through association
by continuity in time and repetition. According to such views, in their most
extreme formulation, mental forms would build up strictly from experience,
starting from an initial empty state or *tabula rasa*.

2. The developmental genetics of brain forms. Both the extreme preformationist attitude and the strict epigenetic views are incompatible with current knowledge about development. The contribution of strictly innate,
DNA-encoded mechanisms to the development of animal forms is supported
by a large body of experimental evidence. Yet, the genes involved are not

expressed all at once, whether in the egg or in the early embryo, as postulated by the extreme preformationist view. Rather, they are activated (or blocked) throughout embryogenesis and postnatal development in a sequential and intricate manner and according to well-defined patterns.

The straightforward comparison of the genetic endowment of the organism with the complexity of the adult brain produces, however, two *apparent* paradoxes (Changeux, 1983a, b). The total amount of DNA present in the fertilized egg is limited to a maximum of 2 million average-sized genes which, because a large number of them consist of non-coding sequences, might in fact be in the range of 100,000 genes. There is thus striking parsimony of genetic information available to code for brain complexity. The second paradox is raised by the evolution of the global amount of DNA in mammals, which appears rather stable from primitive species such as rodents up to humans, whereas the functional organization of the brain becomes increasingly complex. There thus exists remarkable non-linearity between the evolution of total DNA content and that of brain anatomy.

The analysis of the early steps of embryonic development by the methods of molecular genetics primarily in *Drosophila* (see Akam, 1987; Doe, Hiromi, Gehring, & Goodman, 1988; Gehring, 1985; Nüsslein-Volhard, Frohnhöffer, & Lehman, 1987) and in the mouse (see Johnson, McConnell, & Van Blerkom, 1984) begins to resolve these paradoxes. For instance, in *Drosophila*, a variety of gene mutations have been identified that affect early embryonic development. The genes involved have been grouped into three main categories. The first controls the Cartesian coordinates of the embryo; the second controls the segmentation of the body; and the third, called homeotic, specifies the identity of the body segments in well-defined territories of the egg and embryo during oogenesis and embryonic development, respectively, both in a hierarchical and parallel manner, and with cross-regulatory interactions. In the course of expression, the symmetry properties of the developing oocyte or embryo change: symmetry breakings (Turing, 1952) take place. In *Drosophila* the expression of the genes that specify the Cartesian coordinates of the embryo occurs in the mother's ovary through the asymmetric diffusion of morphogens from specialized ovary cells into the egg during the latter's maturation. In the mouse (and most likely in humans), the fertilized egg and early embryo (until the 8-cell stage) appear entirely isotropic. All symmetry breakings take place within the embryo after fertilization. Turing (1952) and followers (Meinhardt & Gierer, 1974) have demonstrated mathematically that such symmetry breakings may be created by random fluctuations that generate defined and reproducible patterns within an initially homogeneous system of morphogens reacting together and diffusing throughout the organism. A spatio-temporal network of gene interactions, with convergence, divergence and re-utilization of regulatory signals, thus governs development of the body plan and, as we shall see, governs the plan of the brain.

Several segmentation and homeotic genes are expressed in the nervous system (Awgulewitsch et al., 1986) and are most likely members of a larger but still unidentified population of genes directly concerned with brain morphogenesis, the parsing of the brain into definite centres and areas and even into asymmetric hemispheres. Their combinatorial expression during development thus offers a first answer to the above-mentioned paradox of gene parsimony. Moreover, a quantitative variation in the expression of a few genes at early stages of development may suffice to account for the increase (or decrease) of surface (or volume) of some brain regions such as the cerebral cortex (or the olfactory bulb) in higher mammals (see Changeux, 1983b), thereby providing an explanation for the paradox of non-linear evolution between the complexity of the genome and that of the organization of the nervous system. For instance, since the total number of neurons in the thickness of cerebral cortex appears uniform throughout vertebrate species (Rockwell, Hiorns, & Powell, 1980), its surface area has been the primary target of evolutive changes (Rakic, 1988). One may then speculate that the extremely fast expansion of the frontal lobe surface that, in part, led to the human brain resulted from the prolonged action of some of these genes in the anterior part of the brain (see Changeux, 1983b). The genomic evolution that underlies this process has been extensively discussed in terms of (classical and non-classical) Darwinian mechanisms (Mayr, 1963).

Later in the course of the cellular organization of the nervous system by the mechanism just mentioned, synaptic connections begin to form. In the higher vertebrates, large ensembles of cells are found to project onto other large ensembles of cells, and maps develop. The best-known maps correspond to the projections of sensory organs, but maps also exist that represent projections from one brain region to another. In the course of such transformations symmetry breaking does not, in general, take place, but regular, geometrical deformations frequently occur. They can be mathematically analysed in terms of the theory of transformations (D'Arcy-Thompson, 1917). The actual mechanisms involved in the establishment of ordered connections of neural maps are still largely unknown. In addition to long-range tropism by chemical substances, the conservation of topological relationships between growing axons and a temporal coding by differential outgrowth of nerve fibres have been invoked. Processes of cell surface recognition might also be seminal in these transformations (Edelman, 1985, 1987).

In conclusion, the main forms of brain architecture develop by principles that can be summarized as follows:

(1) The basic operations of symmetry breaking and transformation that occur during the genesis of the geometric outlines and patterns of central nervous system organization are determined by an ensemble of rules. These rules are genetically coded as defined physico-chemical organizations of the brain. The notion of *tabula rasa* does not hold for the developing brain.

(2) The expression of the genes involved in the determination of brain forms follows well-determined spatio-temporal patterns that lead to the progressive establishment of the adult organization. As a consequence, relationships become established between the progressively laid-down forms, with built-in hierarchies, parallelisms and re-entries.

V. Epigenesis of neuronal networks by active selection of synapses

1. Biological premises

If our view of the development of neural forms accounts for species-specific traits of brain organization and function, it does not suffice for a more detailed description of neural anatomy. Indeed, a significant variability of the phenotype of the nervous system is apparent at several levels of its organization. Examination by electron microscopy of identified neurons from genetically identical (isogenic) individuals reveals minor but significant variability. In the small invertebrate *Daphnia magna*, the number of cells is fixed and the main categories of contacts (between optic sensory cells and optic ganglion neurons) are preserved from one isogenic individual to another. Yet, the exact number of synapses and the precise form of the axonal branches varies between pairs of identical twins (Macagno, Lopresti, & Levinthal, 1973). Similar findings have been reported in the case of the Müller cells of a parthenogenetic fish (Levinthal, Macagno, & Levinthal, 1976) and thus they are not restricted to invertebrates. A fluctuation in the details of the connectivity exists. In mammals, the variation also affects the number of neurons. For instance, in the case of the cerebellum of the mouse, the division and migration of Purkinje cells in consanguineous strains are not subject to as rigorous and precise a determinism as the laying down of neurons in invertebrates (Oster-Granite & Gearhart, 1981; Goldowitz & Mullen, 1982). The variability becomes microscopic and may even affect the chemistry (such as the pattern of transmitters and coexisting messengers synthesized (Hökfelt et al., 1986) of entire populations of neurons. In humans, most of the information available on anatomy derives from individuals taken from genetically heterogeneous populations. Nevertheless, the substantial variability noticed in the topology of sites specialized for such language functions as naming, syntax or short-term memory, as identified by electrical stimulation mapping (Ojemann, 1983), cannot be accounted for solely by this heterogeneity. In the extreme case where the left hemisphere has been ablated in infants, the right hemisphere systematically takes over the language functions (Geschwind & Galaburda, 1984; Nass et al., 1985, 1989). More subtle is the topological distinction of sites, the stimulation of which causes different errors in the two languages spoken by bilingual subjects (Ojemann, 1983), a situation which, of course, relies upon reorganization by learning. Finally, in monkeys, transection of peripheral sensory nerves or their functional alteration causes striking reorganization of the topology of the relevant sensory cortical maps (Merzenich, 1987; Edelman, 1987). Thus, an important degree of variation of neural phenotype is manifest at several levels of organization of the nervous system, and this variability seems to increase with the complexity of the brain.

It may be useful to introduce the notion of a *genetic envelope* to delimit invariant characteristics from those that show some phenotypic variance (Changeux, 1983a). Thus, as animals evolve from primitive mammals to humans, the genetic envelope opens to more and more variability. This variability in the organization of the adult brain reflects characteristic features of its developmental history, in particular the way neural networks become interconnected. The growth cones of the dendrite and axon tip navigate by trial and error through the developing neural tissue toward their targets and thus contribute to the variability of the adult neuronal network. Another source of variability resides in recognition of, and adhesion to, the target cells. Little evidence exists for a point-to-point pre-addressing between individual neurons by specific chemical cues (the chemo-affinity hypothesis), except perhaps in small invertebrates (Goodman et al., 1985). On the contrary, the emerging view is that growing nerve endings identify ensembles of target cells further grouped into wider categories by a few intercellular adhesion molecules (N-CAM for instance; Edelman, 1985, 1987). Discrimination between cell categories would emerge from the temporal sequence of the expression of such adhesion molecules on the surface of the cells, from their differential topological distribution in regular patterns within populations of cells, and from their graded combination on the surface of cells. In any case, within a given cell category, a limited randomness and even some overlap between growing nerve fibres and individual target neurons from a given category are expected to occur.

At a critical stage (or sensitive period) of development, the axonal and dendritic trees branch and spread exuberantly. There is redundancy but also maximal diversity in the connections of the network. Yet, as mentioned, this transient fluctuation of the growing connections remains bounded within stringent limits of the genetic envelope. These include, in addition to the overall plan of the nervous system, the rules that command the behaviour of growing tips of nerves (the growth cones) regarding recognition among cell categories and the formation and evolution of synapses. Such limited fuzziness of the network makes a final tuning of the connectivity necessary, but also offers the opportunity for an adaptive shaping.

The classical information-processing scheme of the nervous system is based on the notion that its internal states of activity directly result from interactions with the outside world. In fact, from very early on, there is intense spontaneous electrical and chemical activity within the nervous system of the embryo and of the fetus (Hamburger, 1970). Chick embryos move within the egg as early as 2½ days of incubation. These spontaneous movements are blocked by curare and coincide with electrical activity of the same frequency arising in spinal cord neurons. In the human, these movements start during the eighth week of embryonic development and continue and diversify during the following months. Such spontaneous activity develops in a strictly endogenous manner and results from molecular oscillators consisting of slow and fast ionic channels (Berridge & Rapp, 1979). The cost of this activity in terms of structural genes is very small and bears no relation to its enormous potential for interaction and combination, which results from the activity's eventual contribution to the epigenesis of neuronal synaptic networks.

2. A model for active selection of synapses

The proposed theory (Changeux & Danchin, 1976; Changeux et al., 1973, 1984; also see Edelman, 1987) deals with the stability of the connections. It postulates that the selection of connections by the activity of the developing network (endogenous, or evoked, or both) contributes to the final establishment of the adult organization. Accordingly, the generator of internal diversity would not be based upon genetically determined recombinations, as in the case for the evolution of species or antibody synthesis, but rather stems from multiple neural configurations with connectivities drawn up during the epigenetic formation of a network at the stage(s) of transient redundancy (Figure 1).

According to our theory, during the sensitive period of maximal connectivity, any given excitatory or inhibitory synapse exists in three states: labile, stable and degenerate. Nerve impulses can be transmitted only in the labile and stable states. A given synapse may undergo transitions from labile to stable states (stabilization), from labile to degenerate states (regression), and from stable to labile states (labilization). The ontogenetic evolution of each

Figure 1.   *A diagrammatic representation of the model of epigenesis by selective stabilization. An initial stage of growth precedes the pruning of circuits through
elimination and stabilization of synapses.
(From Changeux, 1983b; reproduced by permission of the publishers, Ar-
theme Fayard, Paris).*

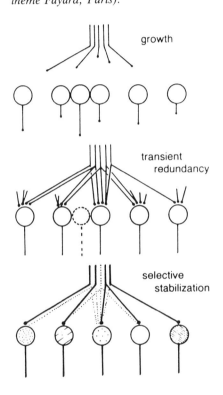

synaptic contact is governed by the combined signals received by the cell on
which it terminates. The activity of the postsynaptic cell within a given time-
window regulates the stability of the synapse in a retrograde manner
(Changeux et al., 1973). As a consequence, a given afferent message will
cause the long-term stabilization of a matching set of synapses from the max-
imally connected neuronal network, while the others will regress.

Detailed models of molecular mechanisms possibly involved in this activity-
dependent synapse selection have been proposed. Some deal with the topology of the postsynaptic clusters of receptors (Changeux, Courrège, Danchin,
& Lasry, 1981), whereas others deal with the selection of multiple afferent
nerve endings (Edelman, 1987; Fraser, 1985; Gouzé, Lasry, & Changeux,

1983). In both instances, the competition takes place for a limited component: in the first case, the receptor for a neurotransmitter; and, in the second, a diffusible growth (or stability) factor produced by the postsynaptic cell and taken up by the nerve ending in a differential manner by active and inactive nerve endings. In both cases, the firing of the postsynaptic cell is assumed to limit the component by repressing its biosynthesis. In addition, rules of release (by the postsynaptic cell) and/or uptake (by the presynaptic nerve endings) based upon the timing relationships between pre- and postsynaptic activity have to be specified in order to yield stable morphogenesis (Kerszberg et al., in preparation).

A straightforward consequence of this theory is that the postulated epigenesis contributes to the specification of the network at a low cost in terms of genetic information, which, in addition, can be shared by different systems of neurons. Such a mechanism offers a plausible way for coding organizational complexity from a small set of genes. By the same token, it also accounts for the paradoxical non-linear increase in complexity of the functional organization of the nervous system compared with that of the genome during the course of mammalian evolution.

3. The theorem of variability

In the course of the proposed epigenesis, diversification of neurons belonging to the same category occurs. Each one acquires its individuality or singularity by the precise pattern of connections it establishes (and neurotransmitters it synthesizes) (see Changeux, 1983a, b, 1986). A major consequence of the theory is that the distribution of these singular qualities may also vary significantly from one individual to the next. Moreover, it can be mathematically demonstrated that the same afferent message may stabilize different connective organizations, which nevertheless results in the same input–output relationship (Changeux et al., 1973). The variability referred to in the theory, therefore may account for the phenotypic variance observed between different isogenic individuals. At the same time, however, if offers a neural implementation for the often-mentioned paradox that there exists a non-unique mapping of a given function to the underlying neural organization.

4. Test of the model

Still, only fragmentary experimental data are available as tests of the theory. Elimination of synapses (and sometimes neurons) during development is well documented at the neuromuscular junction (Redfern, 1970; Van Essen, 1982), at the synapses between climbing fibres and Purkinje cells in the cerebellum (Mariani & Changeux, 1981a, b), and at the autonomic ganglia

(Purves & Lichtman, 1980), whereby in each case individual synapses can be easily counted. The phenomenon had already been noticed by Ramon y Cajal (1909) and interpreted as "a kind of competitive struggle" in Darwinian terms. It looks, in fact, to be rather widespread in the central nervous system (Clarke & Innocenti, 1986; Cowan, Fawcett, O'Leary, & Stanfield, 1984; Huttenlocher, De Courten, Garey, & Vander Loos, 1982; Innocenti & Caminiti, 1980; Price & Blakemore, 1985).

Particularly pertinent to the theory is the effect of nerve activity on these regressive phenomena. As noted, the developing nervous system is already spontaneously active at early stages of embryogenesis. This activity persists into maturity, being eventually modulated by the activity evoked by interaction with the outside world. Chronic blocking of the spontaneous undergoing activity prevents or delays the elimination of connections (Benoit & Changeux, 1975; Callaway, Soha, & Von Essen, 1987; Fraser, 1985; Reiter & Stryker, 1988; Ribchester 1988; Schmidt, 1985; Sretavan et al., 1988). In contrast with the classical empiricist views, activity does not create novel connections but, rather, contributes to the elimination of pre-existing ones. Long-term learning results from disconnection but in a growing network. "To learn is to eliminate" (Changeux, 1983b: p. 246, English translation).

At the larger scale comprising neural maps, activity has also been shown to contribute to the shaping of the adult network. Blocking activity by tetrodotoxin in regenerating fish retinotectal connections interferes with the development of a normal map, both by leading to the maintenance of a diffuse topology of connections and by restricting the receptive fields (Edelman, 1987; Fraser, 1985; Schmidt, 1985). The effect of activity on the segregation of ocular dominance columns in the newborn (but also possibly in the fetus) is well documented (Hubel & Wiesel, 1977; also see references in Reiter & Stryker, 1988; Stryker & Harris, 1986). Lastly, the long-term coordination among maps required, for example, for stereoscopic vision or for the unitary perception of visual and auditory spaces, has also been shown to depend on experience, and models for the synaptic mechanisms involved have been proposed (see Bear, Cooper, & Ebner, 1987).

Finally, the theory also accounts for the sensitive phases of learning and imprinting, which may correspond to the transient stage of maximal innervation (or diversity) in which the synaptic contacts are still in a labile state. This stage is well defined in the case of a single category of synapses. In the case of complex systems, such as the cerebral cortex, multiple categories of circuits become successively established, and, accordingly, many outgrowth and regression steps may take place in a succession of sensitive periods. In this sense the whole period of postnatal development becomes critical, but for different sensory inputs and performances! It is worth recalling that in humans this period is exceptionally long. A prolonged epigenesis of the cerebral cortex would not cost many genes, but for the reasons given above would have a considerable impact on the increased complexity and performance of the adult brain. Possible implications of epigenesis by selective stabilization of synapses in left–right hemispheric differentiation (Nass, Koch, Janowski, & Stiles-Davis, 1985, 1989) for all aspects of language learning have already been extensively discussed (see Changeux, 1983b; Gazzaniga, 1987). The developmental loss of the perceptual ability to distinguish certain phonemes in different languages, such as the initial sounds of *ra* and *la* in Japanese, in contrast to Western languages (Eimas, 1975; Miyawaki et al., 1975), the variability in topological distribution of brain areas in different individuals (Ojemann, 1983), and the remarkable segregation of the cerebral territories utilized in the processing of Japanese Kanji and Kana writings (Sasanuma, 1975) may all be interpreted in such terms. But, convincing demonstrations remain to be established on the basis of neurofunctional data.

In summary:

(1) The brain–computer metaphor does not apply to the development of the brain. The brain does not develop via the part-by-part assembly of prewired circuits.

(2) On the contrary, its morphogenesis is progressive, with forms becoming intricated within forms, including possibly, at each step, sensitive phases of limited transient variability and exuberance followed by drastic elimination of connections.

(3) The proposal is made that a selection of synapses takes place at these sensitive steps and is governed by the state of activity of the developing nervous system.

(4) According to this view, the effect of experience is intertwined with innate processes from development through the adult stage. The formation of brain architectures is not independent of cognitive processes but, rather, is deeply impregnated by them, starting from the early stages of postnatal development.

VI. Mental objects and mental Darwinism

1. *"Representations" and Hebbian assemblies*

J.Z. Young (1964) introduced his insightful book, *Models of the brain*, by defining the brain as the "computer of a homeostat" (p. 14). Being a homeostat the organism can exist in several states, and its adaptation is achieved by selection among possible actions provided by some antecedent process.

Young further speculated that such selection is appropriate in that the homeostat continues its self-maintenance. For it to do so, the organism must adequately represent the situation as a set of physical events (signals) that transmit information. Thus, "The organism is (or contains) a representation of its environment" (p. 20).

The word "representation" has several different meanings. In the cognitive and computer sciences, it refers equally to the structure of internalized information as to its content. Thus, theorists who postulate a "language of thought" (Fodor, 1975) take mental representations to have a combinatorial syntax and semantic content. These representations are often contrasted with the operations performed with them, which are described in algorithmic terms. On the other hand, in neuroscience, the word representation mainly refers to the projections of sensory organs onto defined areas of the brain, or to the mappings of given domains of the brain upon others (Mountcastle, 1978). In his book, *The organization of behavior*, Hebb (1949) introduced the first bridge between the neural and the mental by postulating that "an assembly of association-area cells which can act briefly as a closed system after stimulation has ceased ... constitutes the simplest instance of representative process (image or idea)" (p. 60). For Hebb, the assembly is described by the firing of an anatomically defined population of cells, and "an individual cell or transmission unit may enter in more than one assembly, at different times" (p. 196). Hebb thus posits the assembly as a "three-dimensional lattice", or as a net of neurons, with *coordinated* activity.

Alternative views to Hebb's concept of assembly have been advocated by various authors. For instance, Barlow (1972) has assumed that the coding units of concepts or representations can be identified with the activity of single neurons named "grandmother" or "pontifical" cells. Consistent with such a notion, single cells have been recorded that respond to particular objects, faces or even words (references in Heit, Smith, & Halgren, 1988; Perrett, Mistlin, & Chitty, 1987). In between, there are neuronal groups (Edelman & Mountcastle, 1978) or clusters of cells (Dehaene, Changeux, & Nadal, 1987; Feldman, 1986). Depending on the level at which the coding takes place, pontifical cells or clusters of such cells may be viewed either as autonomous (individual) units or as building blocks for higher order assemblies (Hopfield, 1982).

From both an experimental and theoretical point of view, the actual size of the population of neurons involved in the coding of mental representations remains a debated issue. A wide range of plausible sizes has been suggested, from a single nerve cell to the whole brain. Nevertheless, extensive single-unit recording of populations of cells in awake animals (references in Georgopoulos, Schwartz, & Kettner, 1986; Llinás, 1987; Motter, Steinmetz,

Duffy, & Mountcastle, 1987; Steinmetz, Motter, Duffy, & Mountcastle, 1987) as well as large-scale high-resolution imaging (Posner et al., 1988; Roland & Friberg, 1985) give credence to the notion that these mental objects correspond to privileged activity states of widely distributed domains of the brain and have an identifiable, if not yet specified, physical basis.

Nevertheless, Von der Malsburg (1981, 1987) and Von der Malsburg and Bienenstock (1986) have criticized the cell-assembly concept as formalized by Little (1974) and Hopfield (1982), for two main reasons: (1) in a given brain area, a coding assembly is expected to correspond to only a fraction of a larger ensemble of active units; and (2) states which have the same global distribution of features might be confused with each other. Von der Malsburg and Bienenstock thus propose that the discrimination between coding and non-coding units relies on the temporal correlation between active units rather than on the fact that they are active or not. Such correlations become established between action potentials within a time-scale of a few milliseconds, during the overall time-scale of a representation (tenths of second), and are mediated by fast changes of synaptic strength. On this basis, Von der Malsburg and Bienenstock have developed a formalism whereby topologically organized synaptic patterns can be stored and retrieved, and whereby invariant pattern recognition finds a natural solution. The critical aspect of this formalism is to specify the notion of a firing correlation. Two final remarks have to be made about this view. First, the formalism is fully consistent with Hebb's original proposal of synchronization of activity between active cells, and thus only conflicts with the recent reformulations of the cell assembly concept in terms of statistical physics. Second, under physiological conditions, *both* the actual firing of individual nerve cells and the correlation of firing between cells are likely to contribute to the coding of mental representations.

2. Mental Darwinism

According to Hebb (1949), the growth of the cell assembly is determined by the repeated simultaneous excitation of cells consecutive to sensory stimulation in such a manner that each cell assists each other in firing. The time coincidence of firing between two cells increases the efficiency of the synapse linking the cells. In other words, the genesis of mental representations would occur through an instructive or "Lamarckian" mechanism (cf. Rolls, 1987). As noted, the thesis we wish to defend in the following is the opposite; namely, that the production and storage of mental representations, including their chaining into meaningful propositions and the development of reasoning, can also be interpreted, by analogy, in variation–selection (Darwinian) terms within psychological time-scales (Changeux, 1983b; Changeux et al., 1973, 1984; Dehaene et al., 1987; Edelman & Mountcastle, 1978; Edelman & Finkel, 1984; Finkel & Edelman, 1987; Heidmann et al., 1984).

A basic requirement for such "mental Darwinism" is the existence of a generator of variety (diversity), which would internally produce the so-called Darwinian variations. At psychological time-scales, and at the two levels of intendment and reason, such variations may be viewed as resulting from spontaneous activity of nerve cells. Hebb and many of his followers did not make explicit a possible differential contribution of spontaneous and evoked activity in coding mental representations. But, the occurrence of spontaneous firing by cellular oscillators (see Berridge & Rapp, 1979) and/or oscillatory circuits (see Grillner et al., 1987; Stent et al., 1978) makes possible a strictly internal production of representations.

In a selectionist framework (Changeux, 1983b; Heidmann et al., 1984; Toulouse, Dehaene, & Changeux, 1986), one may thus schematically distinguish: (1) percepts in which the correlation of firing among the component neurons is directly determined by the interaction with the outside world and ceases when the stimulation has stopped; (2) images, concepts and intentions that are actualized objects of memory resulting from the activation of a stabilized trace; and (3) *pre-representations* (analogous to the Darwinian variations), which may be spontaneously developed, multiple, labile, and transient, and which may be selected or eliminated.

Pre-representations would be produced by the neural forms described in the preceding section with both their genetically encoded components (resulting from the evolution of the genome in geological time-scales) and their epigenetic ones (resulting from the consequences of embryonic and postnatal development). Pre-representations would correspond to privileged spontaneous activity states of these wired-in forms, occurring in shorter time-scales (0.1 seconds) and in a transient, dynamic and fleeting manner. At any given time, these pre-representations would be composed of sets of neurons from much larger populations of cells. As a consequence, the correlated firing of diverse combinations of neurons or groups of neurons (or even already stored assemblies) and a wide variety of active neural graphs would be produced successively and transiently. Such pre-representations may arise at the level of intendment and take part in the elaboration and storage of percepts at concepts. They may also arise at the level of reason and contribute to the genesis of higher-order programs and intentions representing the synthesis of concepts (see section VII). The genesis of pre-representations by such a mechanism would thus offer one neural component for the so-called productivity of cognitive processes (Fodor & Pylyshyn, 1988).

At a given stage of the evolution of the organism, some of these spontaneously generated pre-representations may not match any defined feature of the environment (or any item from long-term memory stores) and may thus be transiently meaningless. But, some of them will ultimately be selected in novel situations, thus becoming "meaning full". The achievement of such adequacy (fitness) with the environment (or with a given cognitive state) would then become the basic criterion for selection. The matching between a percept and a pre-representation has been referred to as resonance (Changeux, 1983b; Toulouse et al., 1986) and its unmatching as dissonance. Matching is likely to take place with global, invariant representations of the outside world resulting from the transformation of a set of sensory vectorial components into an invariant functional state (Llinás, 1987; Teuber, 1972).

Finally, mental representations are *not* static states of the brain, but are produced and chained within a system in constant dynamic interaction with the outside world and within itself. They are part of a system in constant evolution within psychological time-scales.

3. The Hebb synapse and elementary mechanism of resonance

To account for the growth of the assembly at the first stage of perception, Hebb (1949) postulates that "when an axon of cell A is near enough to excite cell B and repeatedly, or persistently, takes part in firing it, some growth process or metabolic change takes place in one or both cells such that A's efficiency as one of the cells firing B is increased" (p. 62). This proposal has been much debated from both theoretical and experimental points of view, and many cellular implementations of the Hebb synapse have been suggested since Hebb's original proposal (for instance, see Stent, 1973; Kelso, Ganong, & Brown, 1986; and for a recent review, see Bear et al., 1987).

Heidmann and Changeux (1982) (see also Changeux & Heidmann, 1987; Finkel & Edelman, 1987) have proposed a molecular mechanism whereby synaptic efficacy is governed by the conformational states of the postsynaptic receptor for a given neurotransmitter. The percentage of receptor molecules in activable and inactivable conformations would be a measure of efficacy, and could be modulated by converging electrical and/or chemical postsynaptic signals within a given time-window (Figure 2). This model can account for a variety of modes of regulation of synapse efficacy, as found for instance in *Aplysia* (Abrams & Kandel, 1988; Changeux et al., 1987a; Hawkins & Kandel, 1984) where presynaptic changes appear postsynaptic to a true Hebbian process, or in the cerebellum (Ito, Sakurai, & Tongroach, 1982), and may include so-called non-Hebbian cases.

Most important to our present purpose, such allosteric mechanisms for the Hebb rule and for other rules for synaptic enhancement may serve as basic

Figure 2.   *A model of the regulation of synapse efficacy at the postsynaptic level based on the allosteric properties of the acetylcholine receptor (from Dehaene et al., 1987). The conformation of receptor molecules can be affected by intra- or extracellular chemical potential of the postsynaptic cell.*

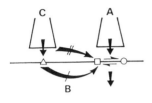

devices to implement the resonance process defined above. It must be stressed that these mechanisms and rules do not imply any revival of "associationist" ideas (Fodor & Pylyshyn, 1988). Spontaneous firing may also regulate the efficacy of afferent synapses by the same rules. Conditions may be defined to occur for synaptic modifications only during a state of resonance between the activity of afferent synapses and the spontaneous firing of the target neuron (Dehaene et al., 1987). Thus, there is no intrinsic empiricist feature in the way these molecular regulatory devices operate.

4. Modelling mental objects by statistical physics

The test of a biological theory may sometimes be carried out succesfully on qualitative grounds without the help of a mathematical formalism. In most instances, however, the predictions appear difficult to derive intuitively, and the elaboration of a formal model in a coherent and simplified form becomes necessary. This is particularly true for assemblies of neurons, and an abundant literature has recently been published on this matter.

McCulloch and Pitts (1943) first described neurons as simple, all-or-none threshold devices. The further introduction of an analogue of temperature (Little, 1974; see Burnod & Korn, 1989) and of variable but symmetrical synapses (Hopfield, 1982) made possible the application of the ready-made formalism of statistical physics to neuronal networks. Hopfield (1982) showed how a content-addressable memory could be constructed, whereby information is stored as stable attractors of the dynamics via synaptic modifications. Several unrealistic features of the model were later revised, such as symmetrical interactions between neurons (Sompolinsky & Kanter, 1986; Derrida, Gardner, & Zippelius, 1987) or catastrophic deterioration of the memory with overloading (Mézard, Nadal, & Toulouse, 1986; Nadal et al., 1986a).

An important aspect of the attempt to formalize neural networks concerns the actual origin of the firing activity and of the interactions between neurons. In the instructive framework, which is the most commonly adopted (Amit, Gutfreund, & Sompolinsky, 1985a, b; Hopfield, 1982), the interaction with the outside world imposes the internal state of activity of the network. In the initial state, the interactions are vanishingly small, and the energy landscape flat. Among several drawbacks, this hypothesis does not take into account the existence of an already heavily connected network and the occurrence of spontaneous activity within the network (see above). In terms of the spin glass formalism (Toulouse et al., 1986), a selectionist model, in contrast, posits an initially rich energy landscape with pre-existing interactions between neurons and an abundance of hierarchically organized attractors. The interaction with the outside world would not enrich the landscape, but rather would select pre-existing energy minima or pre-representations and enlarge them at the expense of other valleys. As a consequence, the whole energy landscape would evolve, the already stored information influencing the pre-representations available for the next learning event. The system possesses internal rigidity so that not every external stimulus would be equally stored. The crucial issue remains to find a learning rule coherent with such a Darwinian picture. A relatively simple initial model was proposed in Toulouse et al. (1986). It begins with a random distribution of synaptic efficacies, and stores patterns using the same rule as the original Hopfield model. Although this does not allow one to make use of the hierarchical structure of pre-existing attractors, such networks do possess an internal rigidity. Moreover, additional biological constraints, such as excitatory synapses not becoming inhibitory and vice versa, are easily implemented, taking this model a step further toward the selective model. Still, one of the major limitations of this model is that it deals with "spin glass" under static conditions, while selection of mental states in the brain always takes place under constant dynamic conditions (see section VII).
     In summary:

(1) Experimental and theoretical evidence from cellular neurophysiology and statistical physics make plausible the hypothesis that mental representations can be defined as states of activity of brain cells.
(2) Models for the Darwinian selection of mental states can be proposed on the basis of:
     (a) the spontaneous productions of transient, dynamic and coherent but fleeting activity states referred to as pre-representations, which would be analogues of the Darwinian variations;
     (b) the selection and stabilization of some of these pre-representations by matching percepts arising from external and somatic internal stimuli

(e.g., see Damasio, this issue), stimuli with already selected internal states.

VII. Neural architecture and the application of theoretical models to cognitive science

Models inspired from statistical physics deal mostly with networks of fully interconnected neurons, whereby neither the singularity of each individual neuron nor higher-order architectural principles of the networks are specified. To better approach a more realistic neurobiology, some modellists have studied simple systems such as *Limax* (Hopfield & Tank, 1986) or *Tritonia* (Kanter & Sompolinsky, 1987) despite the fact that the cognitive abilities of these creatures are rather rudimentary. Our approach is the opposite. While anatomists, physiologists and neuropsychologists decipher the real functional organization of brain connectivity in mammals (see Goldman-Rakic, 1987; Rakic, 1988) and in humans (Geschwind & Galaburda, 1987), it may be possible starting from simple networks to reconstruct cognitive functions by introducing architectural and functional constraints within, and between, neuronal networks and, in a second step, to look for their presence in real brains. In the following section, we try to establish a parallel between the behaviour of networks and well-known cognitive functions, knowing, *a priori*, that such attempts are a simplistic but necessary preliminary to more complex and plausible reconstruction.

1. Short-term memory of a neuronal network

The simplest feature displayed by formal neuronal networks is the storage of memories within a limited-capacity network. As described above, the Hopfield model can be specified and completed in order to retain only the most recent information it received. A direct relation exists between the steady-state, memory capacity of this network and its connectivity. For instance, a network in which each neuron is connected to 500 other neurons has a memory capacity of seven items (Nadal et al., 1986a, b). Both numbers are within a plausible range. Extension of such evaluations to short-term memory in humans is attractive but still highly hypothetical. Yet, at least for the most perceptually driven memory stores, the application of the Hopfield instructive scheme seems legitimate. A long-standing debate in the field has been the origin of forgetting (see Baddeley, 1976, for discussion). Erasure of the short-term memory traces might result from a spontaneous decay or, alternatively, from an interference of recent memories over older ones. Spontaneous decay may simply result from the relaxation kinetics of the molecular transitions of proteins engaged in synaptic transmission. The modelling of formal neuronal networks according to the Hopfield scheme, as exemplified by the palimpsest model (Nadal et al., 1986a, b), illustrates, however, the physical plausibility of an interference mechanism. It further accounts for characteristic features of short-term memory stores such as the "primacy effect", according to which the first item stored is more easily recalled than the subsequent ones (Nadal et al., 1986a, b).

An important feature of this model is that it points to the dependence of global functional features (a fixed memory span) upon elementary synaptic parameters such as the average number of synapses per neuron (see Figure 3). As emphasized by Simon (1969), "the most striking limits to subjects' capacities to employ efficient strategies arise from the very small capacity of

Figure 3. *Model of memory palimpsest. The percentage of memorized patterns drops catastrophically as more and more patterns are added into the Hopfield (1982) model (triangles). A minor modification yields a stationary regime (squares) where only recently learned patterns can be retrieved (palimpsest model: from Nadal et al., 1986a; reproduced by permission of the publishers, Editions de Physique, Les Ulis, France).*

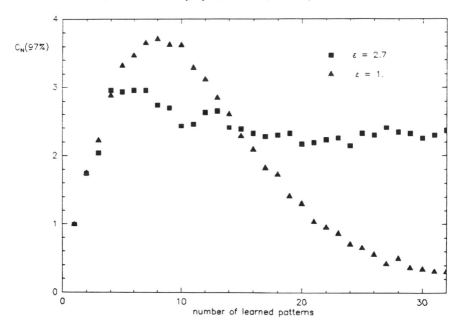

the short-term memory structure" (p. 76). These models, at variance with the classical functionalist point of view, thus illustrate how elementary parameters of the brain may place fundamental constraints on the pattern of thought.

2. Organization of long-term memory

The long-term memory stores in humans possess an apparent unlimited capacity, are strongly hierarchical, and are organized along a semantic, rather than perceptual, space (Baddeley, 1976, 1986, 1988; Massaro, 1975). Storage into long-term memory appears as a rare and slow event compared to the short-term storage of information, and may be viewed as a semantically driven, Darwinist selection from representations present in the short-term store.

Several models for storing a hierarchical tree of memories in a neural network have been proposed (Feigelman & Toffe, 1987; Gutfreund, 1988; Parga & Virasoro, 1985). One of them (Gutfreund, 1988) relies on an architecture based upon multiple distinct networks, one for each level of the tree. The retrieval of a particular memory is achieved at the lowest network, and is assisted by the retrieval of its ancestors, and mimics access to long-term stores in humans (see Baddeley, 1986b, 1988). The models inspired from statistical physics thus offer an elementary physical implementation of semantic relationships in long-term memory, which partially covers the notion of "meaning" (Amit, 1988). In this respect it is worth noting that blood-flow studies involving retrieval of specific memories, such as numbers, nine-word jingles or sequence of visual fields reveal something in the activation of topographically distinct though interconnected cortical areas (Roland & Friberg, 1985). Neuropsychological investigations show that even words belonging to different semantic categories may be represented at different loci in the brain (e.g., McCarthy & Warrington, 1988).

Finally, the so-called unlimited capacity of the long-term store is more apparent than real. First of all, reasonable evaluations of its capacity converge at a value of 10^9 bits (see Mitchinson, 1987), which is a small number compared to the 10^{11} neurons of the human brain and its 10^{15} synapses. Second, the transfer from short- to long-term memory looks rather limited considering the large number of representations transiently circulating in the short-term store. Third, only truly new items, distinct from those already present in long-term memory, are stored at any given time. The transfer from short- to long-term stores may thus be viewed as a selection for novelty occurring via the validation of pre-existing hierarchies and the stabilization of small branches, thereby saving considerable space.

3. Plausible molecular mechanism for long-term storage

Mental objects have been defined as transient physical states of neuronal networks with durations in the time-scale of fractions of seconds. Such activity-dependent changes of neuronal and synaptic properties may be extended to longer time-scales by covalent modifications of neuronal and synaptic proteins and, ultimately, by the regulation of protein synthesis.

Yet, at variance with currently accepted views (Goelet, Castellucci, Schacher, & Kandel, 1986; Montarolo et al., 1986), Changeux and Heidmann (1987) have argued that long-term regulations cannot be equated to regulation of protein synthesis, but rather to the perpetuation of an activity-dependent trace beyond protein turnover. The simplest and most plausible general mechanism is that of a self-sustained metabolic steady-state that includes a *positive* feedback loop (or negative ones in *even* numbers (Delbrück, 1949; Thomas, 1981). Such self-reinforcing circuits may be built at the level of neuronal receptors (Changeux & Heidmann, 1987; Crick, 1984; Lisman, 1985), gene receptors (Britten & Davidson, 1969; Monod & Jacob, 1961), and even at the level of the synapse on the basis of a sequence of chemical reactions. In this last instance (Changeux et al., 1987a) a positive feedback loop may be created by the activity-dependent regulation of the production (by the postsynaptic cell) of a growth factor required for the stability of the afferent nerve ending. There is no theoretical time limit to the maintenance of a trace in a system of that sort up to the life span of the organism.

Plausible molecular mechanisms for the extension to long-term changes of synapse efficacies may thus be envisioned at the level of the synapse in which the short-term modification took place. On the other hand, the occurrence of neuropsychological disconnections in the transfer from short- to long-term stores in human patients supports the notion that in the human brain these two compartments might be topographically distinct though highly interconnected.

4. Recognition, production and storage of time sequences

The attempts to model neuronal networks that have been mentioned concern either stable states or relaxation to stable states. However, as emphasized, the nervous system does not process information under static conditions. At the cellular or simple circuits level, it produces coherent patterns of linear or cyclic sequences of activity (Getting, 1981; Grillner, 1975; Grillner et al., 1987; Stent et al., 1978). At higher levels, including the knowledge level, the nervous system possesses the striking faculty to recognize, produce and store time sequences (Lashley, 1951). One basic function of the frontal cortex mentioned in section II is the control of the temporal evolution of overt behaviour and internal chains of mental representations. An important issue is thus: what are the minimal requirements of neural architecture and function for a network to process temporal sequences?

Complex networks that recognize and produce sequences of higher order have recently been proposed that rely on two sets of synaptic connections: one set which stabilizes the network in its current memory state, while a second set, the action of which is delayed in time, causes the network to make transitions between memories (Kleinfeld, 1986; Sompolinsky & Kanter, 1986; Peretto & Niez, 1986; Amit, 1988). Others (Tank & Hopfield, 1987) are based on delay filters, one for each known sequence. In all these instances, the time delay is built-in as an intrinsic physical parameter of individual neurons, such as postsynaptic potential or axon length.

The network model we have proposed (Dehaene et al., 1987) displays capacities for recognition and production of temporal sequences and for their acquisition by selection. It was inspired by the learning of songs in birds such as *Melospiza* by selective attrition of syllables (Konishi, 1985; Marler & Peters, 1982), whereby identified neurons, called song-specific neurons, detect sequences of syllables. It also makes use of the known properties of allosteric receptors (Changeux, 1981; Changeux & Heidmann, 1987; Heidmann & Changeux, 1982), which may potentially serve as regulators of synapse efficacy at the postsynaptic level (including Hebbian mechanisms: see section V).

The model is based on four assumptions about neural architecture (Figure 4): (1) synaptic triads are composed of three neurons A, B, and C. These are connected so that the efficacy of a synapse of A on B is influenced by the activity of a third modulator neuron C, under conditions that make the postsynaptic neuron B behave as a sequence detector for neurons A and C; (2) a Hebbian learning rule increases the maximal efficacy of the A–B synapse toward an absolute maximum if, after its activation, postsynaptic neuron B fires; (3) the network is formed of juxtaposed clusters of synergic neurons densely interconnected by excitatory synapses, thus able to maintain self-sustained stable activity; and (4) the network is subdivided into three superimposed layers: a sensory layer on which percepts are merely imposed, and an internal production network subdivided into two layers for input clusters and internal clusters, respectively.

The network displays several original properties:

(a) Passive recognition and production of temporal patterns. The few architectural designs of the network, the presence of synaptic triads and the existence of clusters with a linear or hierarchical organization, suffice for the recognition of time sequences. As a consequence of the self-excitatory con-

Figure 4. *Model of formal neuron networks capable of recognition, production and storage of temporal sequences (from Dehaene et al., 1987) (for explanation see text).*

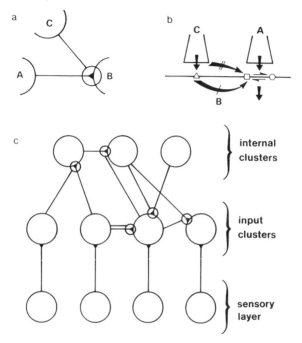

nections within clusters, the activity of previous states remains within the cluster. Individual triads acting as elementary sequence detectors, and the linear and hierarchical arrays of clusters thus behave as detectors of complex sequences that may include repetitions.

Furthermore, the same network produces time sequences. A set of triads between clusters transmits activity with a delay. A memory of previous activity is kept through the persistence, or *remanence*, of former activity within the clusters. Remanent activity may thus influence the pathways that the system takes. The temporal span of this remanence will thus determine the complexity of the sequence produced. It is an elementary neural implementation of context dependence which is basic to cognitive psychology and linguistics. Amit (1988) provides a similar demonstration, although in a different framework, that the same stimulus can elicit different network responses depending on the remanent internal state.

(b) Genesis of internal organization by learning. Introduction of the Hebbian learning rule and the subdivision of the network in two distinct layers, one for the input and the other strictly for internal representations, makes possible the differentiation of hierarchically organized sequence detectors from randomly connected clusters. Conditions can be found in which the imposition of a melody to the input clusters leads progressively to elimination of the initial redundancy and to stabilization of hierarchies of sequence detectors. Conversely, sequences of arbitrary complexity may be produced in the network by stabilization of ongoing spontaneous activity during interaction (resonance) with an externally applied melody.

The model thus illustrates how neurons coding for a temporal relationship between activity clusters may differentiate through experience according to a Darwinian mechanism. It also suggests that abstract relations (rules) may be extracted and stored in hierarchically organized neurons or, conversely, imposed to lower-level neurons coding for a variety of more concrete features.

From an experimental point of view the model points to the role of synaptic triads and to the differentiation through experience of neuronal hierarchies. It has global predictions about variability and its reduction in the course of learning, which are strikingly consonant with observations made on children in the course of phonology acquisition (see Ferguson, 1985).

5. Intentions and inventions

Intentionality and meaning appear so basic to cognition that those who do not address these issues are often viewed as missing the whole field! An elementary step toward the physical implementation of meaning has already been made. On the other hand, the problem of intentionality, even in a very limited sense, has not been considered. Any attempt to unravel its neural bases appears unrealistic *a priori* (Searle, 1983). Our aim is not to propose a neural theory of intentionality. Rather, we limit ourselves to a few remarks and arguments illustrating how such a theory might be constructed, with respect to goals and plans.

(a) Intentions and the frontal cortex

The brief discussion on the contribution of the frontal lobe to the architecture of reason (section II) led to the suggestion that this region of the brain contributes to the elaboration of plans, and controls the temporal unfolding of patterned mental operations or behavioural actions according to a goal. Frontal lesions do interfere with planning behaviour and result in a typical unintentional utilization behaviour (Lhermitte, 1983) that one may associate with the lower intendment level. The prefrontal cortex must thus have a *prospective* function in anticipating and planning and a *retrospective* one in maintaining it in a provisional memory until the goal is reached (Fuster, 1980).

Single-unit recordings in the prefrontal cortex during the delay period of a delayed alternation task disclose cells that remain active for seconds before the response and code for the anticipated direction of the motor response (Bruce, 1988; Niki, 1974). Neural activity therefore can be related to the achievement of a goal. From this it is reasonable to conclude that there exists a neural basis for intentions in humans, as there exists a neural basis for goals in monkeys. Intentions may concern both motor acts and thought processes (Searle, 1983). Accordingly, an intention will be viewed as a particular category of mental object characterized by (1) its occurrence at a high level of organization, such as the level of reason in the frontal cortex, and (2) a long-lasting, *predictive*, activity. Self-excitatory clusters of neurons would offer one implementation for the maintenance of intentions, but the involvement of cellular oscillators or, more likely, of reverbatory closed circuits involving positive feedback loops appears equally plausible (see Changeux, 1983b). The intervention of attentional processes (see Posner & Presti, 1987) would contribute to the fixation of such self-sustained states of activity, which would be determined either externally through percepts or internally through the evocation of memory objects.

(b) Intentionality and context dependence
Intentions are viewed as occurring on top of the hierarchy of brain networks and may create a context for underlying motor actions on the environment and the chaining of mental objects by imposing a frame of semantic constraints on these processes. The model proposed for the recognition, storage and retrieval of time sequences (Dehaene et al., 1987) bases context dependence on the joint contribution of the remanence of activity in self-excitatory clusters and of the recognition (or production) of time sequences by synaptic triads. It might serve as a general framework for the elaboration of more complex models for the context created by intentions, for the development of reasonings and in a more general manner for what Fodor and Pylyshyn (1988) refer to as structure-sensitive operations.

(c) The selectionist (Darwinian) test for intentions and inventions
A basic function of the frontal cortex is to capture errors in the unfolding of a motor program. Similarly, intentions might be subjected to internal tests. The validation of a proposition, for example, would then result from a context-dependent compatibility of a chain of mental objects within a given

semantic frame with already-stored mental objects. Such tests for compatibility or adequateness might be viewed, from a neural point of view, as analogues of the matching by resonance (or un-matching by dissonance) of percepts with pre-representations.

The contribution of attention to the processing of sensory information is currently being investigated in great detail by joint psychological and neurological approaches (Posner & Presti, 1987; Posner et al., 1988). It appears plausible that similar, if not identical, attentional systems are involved in maintaining coherent patterns designed to reach a goal (Posner, 1980; Posner & Presti, 1987). "Attention for action" (Posner et al., 1988) is a generic name for the attentional processes involved in the selection of actions, intentions or goals. As in the case of the selection of meaning, but at a different level and on a different time-scale, the selection of actions and intentions may take place via a Darwinian mechanism among internally evoked and context-dependent pre-representations. Of course, such selection will concern higher-order representations including complex chains of objects from the long-term memory stores. Combinatorial processes may produce novel intentions or inventions at this level. The selection will then be carried out by testing their realism from the cognitive as well as affective point of view. The connections existing between the limbic system and the prefrontal cortex offer a material basis for relationships between the emotional and cognitive spheres (Goldman-Rakič, 1987; Nauta, 1971, 1973).

In summary, on the basis of rather simple architectural designs, physical models of neural networks can be proposed that account for some characteristic features of short-term and long-term memory and for the recognition, production and storage of time sequences. Such models make plausible a neural theory of intentions.

VIII. Conclusions

Despite the rather speculative character of some sections of this presentation, we conclude that it is timely to approach cognition in a synthetic manner with the aim to relate a given cognitive function to its corresponding neural organization and activity state. Such a neurocognitive trend (see also Arbib, 1985; Luria, 1973; Struss & Benson, 1986) contrasts with the classical functionalist approach to cognition (Fodor, 1975; Johnson-Laird, 1983), although it is more compatible with a revised, more recent version (Fodor & Pylyshyn, 1988). This approach has several important consequences.

It contends that data from cognitive psychology often overlook many highly intricate levels of functional organization that have to be distinguished within the human brain. Reconstructing architecture on the basis of external observations alone is a complex matter, if not an ill-defined task, with no unique solution. Neuropsychology and neuro-imagery (Posner et al., 1988) usefully complement the psychological approach by offering ways to dissect such global functions into elementary operations that are localized in the brain, and help to show that the cleavage of brain functions into the classical neurological, algorithmic and semantic levels is no longer appropriate and may even be misleading. Ultimately, both theoretical models and experiments must be devised in such a manner that they specify the particular level of neural organization to which a given function is causally related.

It further argues that the classical artificial intelligence approach, which tries to identify the programs run by the hardware of the human brain, loses much of its attractive power. This may be overcome if one conceives brain-style computers based on the actual architectural principles of the human brain and possessing some of its authentic competences rather than simply mimicking some of its surface performances (for references, see Sejnowski, Koch, & Churchland, 1988). Models of highly evolved functions, for example the acquisition of past tense in English (Rumelhart & McClelland, 1987) or the ability to read a text aloud (Sejnowsky & Rosenberg, 1986) among others (Lehkey & Sejnowski, 1988; Zipser & Andersen, 1988) have been implemented in simplistic connectionist machines. But, despite an "appearance of neural plausibility" (Fodor & Pylyshyn, 1988), the architectures involved are far too simple and even naive compared to those that the human brain actually uses for such multimodal performances with deep cultural impregnation (Pinker & Prince, 1988). As stated by Fodor and Pylyshyn (1988), these systems cannot "exhibit intelligent behavior without storing, retrieving or otherwise operating on structured symbolic expressions" (p. 5). A basic requirement of a plausible neurocognitive approach is thus to unravel the physics of meaning or, in other words, the neural bases of mental representations. The attempt to find the implementation of the semantic content of symbolic expressions in neural terms cannot be viewed as secondary to a psychological theory of meaning (Fodor & Pylyshyn, 1988). Theories of the neural implementation of mental representations may raise useful issues such as the capacity of short-term memory, the hierarchical organization of long-term memory, the recognition and storage of time sequences, and context dependence, as illustrated in a still rather primitive form in this paper. An important issue will be the search for the neural representation of rules (in particular, syntax) and their application to restricted classes of mental representations. In this respect, the model of learning temporal sequences by selection (Dehaene et al., 1987) illustrates how neurons coding for relations between mental objects may differentiate as a consequence of experience.

The model recently served as a starting point for an investigation of the role of prefrontal cortex in delayed-response tasks (Dehaene & Changeux, 1989), which are elementary rule-governed behaviours. Such implementations will one day be described in terms of real neural connections and will thus point to critical experimental predictions. Such abstract neurological theories based upon the most advanced progress of brain anatomy and physiology may ultimately unravel novel algorithms and architectures out of the still largely unexplored universe of human brain connectivity. Our view is that there is much more to expect from such an approach than from strict psychological and/or mathematical theorizing.

Another conclusion that we wish to draw from this discussion is that the brain should be viewed as an evolutive system rather than as a static input–output processing machine. The brain is part of an organism belonging to a species that has evolved (and is still evolving) in geological time-scales according to Darwinian mechanisms at the level of the genome. But the complexity of the brain is such that it may itself be considered as a system evolving *within* the organism with, at least, two distinct time-scales: that of embryonic and postnatal development for the process of organizing neuronal somas and connectivity networks, and that of psychological times for the storage, retrieval and chaining of mental objects and for their assembly into higher-order motor programs, behavioural strategies and schemas. The extension of *selectionist* mechanisms to all these levels breaks down the rigidity (sphexishness; Dennett, 1984) of the strictly nativist or Cartesian schemes (Fodor, 1983) by introducing, at each level, a degree of freedom linked with the production of variations. But as long as these variations are constrained by the genetic envelope, it escapes the pitfalls of Lamarckian associationism. The generator of internal diversity produces, at each of these levels, intrinsic richness, and thereby offers possibilities for creating structures within a given level but also between levels, yielding again one plausible component for the productivity requirements of Fodor and Pylyshyn (1988). Moreover, the number of such choices need not be large to cause an important diversity as long as variability exists at all hierarchically organized levels. The criteria for selection of the pre-representations must be defined at each level. At the lower levels, an obvious criterion is the adequateness or fitness to the environment. At a higher one, the internal thought (Gedanken) experiments might refer to the outcome of former experiences stored in the long-term memory and in the genetic endowment of the species which, *in fine*, ensure its survival (see Dennett, 1984, 1987).

Brain would thus be an evolutive system constantly anticipating the evolution of its physical, social and cultural environment by producing expectations and even intentions that create a lasting frame of reference for a selected set of long-term memories. Brain would not only be a semantic engine (Dennett, 1984) but an intentional engine. At no level would such a machine be neutral about the nature of cognitive processes. Rather, it would be "knowledge-impregnated" from the organization of its genome up to the production of its more labile intentions.

References

Abrams, T., & Kandel, E. (1988). Is contiguity detection in classical conditioning a system or a cellular property? Learning in *Aplysia* suggests a possible molecular site. *Trends in Neuroscience, 11*, 128–135.

Akam, M. (1987). The molecular basis for metameric pattern genes of *Drosophila. Development, 101*, 1–22.

Alkon, D., Disterhoft, J., & Coulter, D. (1987). Conditioning-specific modifications of postsynaptic membrane currents in mollusc and mammal: In J.P. Changeux & M. Konishi (Eds.), *The neural and molecular bases of learning*. New York: Wiley.

Amit, D.J. (1988). Neural networks counting chimes. *Proceedings of the National Academy of Science USA, 85*, 2141–2145.

Amit, D.J., Gutfreund, H., & Sompolinsky, H. (1985a). Spin glass models of neural networks. *Physical Review, A32*, 1007–1018.

Amit, D.J., Gutfreund, H., & Sompolinsky, H. (1985b). Storing infinite numbers of patterns in a spin-glass model of neural networks. *Physical Review Letters, 55*, 1530–1533.

Arbib, M. (1985). *In search of the person*. Amherst, MA: University of Massachusetts Press.

Awgulewitsch, A., Utset, M.F., Hart, C.P., McGinnis, W., & Ruddle, F. (1986). Spatial restriction in expression of a mouse homeobox locus within the central nervous system. *Nature, 320*, 328–335.

Baddeley, A.D. (1976). *The psychology of memory*. New York: Harper & Row.

Baddeley, A.D. (1986). *Working memory*. Oxford: Clarendon Press.

Baddeley, A.D. (1988). Cognitive psychology and human memory. *Trends in Neuroscience, 11*, 176–181.

Barlow, H.B. (1972). Single units and sensations: a neuron doctrine for perceptual physiology? *Perception, 1*, 371–394.

Bear, M.F., Cooper, L.N., & Ebner, F.F. (1987). A physiological basis for a theory of synapse modification. *Science, 237*, 42–48.

Benoit, P., & Changeux, J.P. (1975). Consequences of tenotomy on the evolution of multi-innervation in developing rat soleus muscle. *Brain Research, 99*, 354–358.

Berridge, M., & Rapp, P. (1979). A comparative survey of the function, mechanism and control of cellular oscillations. *Journal of Experimental Biology, 81*, 217–280.

Britten, R.J., & Davidson, E.H. (1969). Gene regulation for higher cells: a theory. *Science, 165*, 349–357.

Bruce, C. (1988). What does single unit analysis in the prefrontal areas tell us about cortical processing? In P. Rakic & W. Singer (Eds.), *Neurobiology of neocortex*, Dahlem Konferenzen. Chichester: Wiley.

Burnod, Y., & Korn, H. (1989). Consequence of stochastic release of neurotransmitters for network computation in the central nervous system. *Proceedings of the National Academy of Science USA, 86*, 352–356.

Callaway, E., Soha, J., & Von Essen, D. (1987). Competition favoring inactive over active motor neurons during synapse elimination. *Nature, 328*, 422–426.

Cavalli-Sforza, L., & Fedelman, M. (1981). *Cultural transmission and evolution: A quantitative approach*. Princeton, NJ: Princeton University Press.

Changeux, J.P. (1981). The acetylcholine receptor: An "allosteric" membrane protein. *Harvey Lectures, 75*, 85–254.

Changeux, J.P. (1983a). Concluding remarks on the "singularity" of nerve cells and its ontogenesis. *Progress in Brain Research, 58*, 465–478.

Changeux, J.P. (1983b). *L'homme neuronal*, Paris: Fayard. English translation by L. Garey (1985). *Neuronal Man*. New York: Pantheon Books.

Changeux, J.P. (1984). Le regard du collectionneur. *Catalogue de la donation Othon Kaufmann et François Schlageter au Departement des peintures, Musée du Louvre*. Paris: Edition de la Réunion des Musées Nationaux.

Changeux, J.P. (1986). Coexistence of neuronal messengers and molecular selection. *Progress in Brain Research, 68*, 373–403.

Changeux, J.P., Courrège, P., & Danchin, A. (1973). A theory of the epigenesis of neural networks by selective stabilization of synapses. *Proceedings of the National Academy of Science USA, 70*, 2974–2978.

Changeux, J.P., Courrège, P., Danchin, A., & Lasry, J.M. (1981). Un mécanisme biochimique pour l'épigénèse de la jonction neuromusculaire. *C.R. Acad. Sci. Paris, 292*, 449–453.

Changeux, J.P., & Danchin, A. (1974). Apprendre par stabilisation sélective de synapses en cours de développement. In E. Morin & M. Piattelli (Eds.), *L'unité de l'homme*. Paris: Le Seuil.

Changeux, J.P., & Danchin, A. (1976). Selective stabilization of developing synapses as a mechanism for the specification of neuronal networks. *Nature, 264*, 705–712.

Changeux, J.P., Devillers-Thiéry, A., Giraudat, J., Dennis, M., Heidmann, T., Revah, F., Mulle, C., Heidmann, O., Klarsfeld, A., Fontaine, B., Laufer, R., Nghiêm, H.O., Kordeli, E., & Cartaud, J. (1987b). The acetylcholine receptor: Functional organization and evolution during synapse formation. In O. Hayaishi (Ed.), *Strategy and prospects in neuroscience*. Utrecht: VNU Science Press.

Changeux, J.P., & Heidmann, T. (1987). Allosteric receptors and molecular models of learning. In G. Edelman, W.E. Gall, & W.M. Cowan (Eds.), *Synaptic function*. New York: Wiley.

Changeux, J.P., Heidmann, T., & Patte, P. (1984). Learning by selection. In P. Marler & H. Terrace (Eds.), *The biology of learning*. Berlin: Springer-Verlag.

Changeux, J.P., Klarsfeld, A., & Heidmann, T. (1987a). The acetylcholine receptor and molecular models for short and long term learning. In J.P. Changeux & M. Konishi (Eds.), *The cellular and molecular bases of learning*. Chichester: Wiley.

Chomsky, N. (1965). *Aspects of the theory of syntax*. Cambridge, MA: MIT Press.

Chomsky, N. (1979). Le débat entre Jean Piaget et Noam Chomsky. In M. Piattelli-Palmarini (Ed.), *Théories du langage – théories de l'apprentissage*. Paris: Le Seuil.

Churchland, P. (1986). *Neurophilosophy*. Cambridge, MA: MIT Press.

Clarke, E., & O'Malley, C. (1968). *The human brain and spinal cord. A historical study illustrated by writings from antiquity to the twentieth century*. Berkeley, CA: University of California Press.

Clarke, S., & Innocenti, G. (1986). Organization of immature intrahemispheric connection. *Journal of Comparative Neurology, 251*, 1–22.

Cowan, M.W., Fawcett, J.W., O'Leary, D., & Stanfield, B.B. (1984). Regressive phenomena in the development of the vertebrate nervous system. *Science, 225*, 1258–1265.

Crick, F. (1984). Memory and molecular turnover. *Nature, 312*, 101.

D'Arcy-Thompson, W. (1917). *On growth and form*. Cambridge: Cambridge University Press.

Debru, C. (1983). *L'esprit des protéines*. Paris: Hermann.

Dehaene, S., & Changeux, J.P. (1989). A single model of prefrontal cortex function in delayed-response tasks. *Journal of Cognitive Neuroscience* (in press).

Dehaene, S., Changeux, J.P., & Nadal, J.P. (1987). Neural networks that learn temporal sequences by selection. *Proceedings of the National Academy of Sciences USA, 84*, 2727–2731.

Delbrück, M. (1949). *In Unités biologiques douées de continuité génétique (Publication CNRS)*, 33–35.

Delbrück, M. (1986). *Mind from matter*. Palo Alto, CA: Blackwell.

Dennett, D. (1984). *Elbow room*. Cambridge, MA: MIT Press.

Dennett, D. (1987). *The intentional stance*. New York: Basic Books.

Derrida, B., Gardner, E., & Zippelius, A. (1987). An exactly solvable asymmetric neural network model. *Europhysics Letters, 4*, 167–170.

Derrida, B., & Nadal, J.P. (1987). Learning and forgetting on a symmetric diluted neural network. *Journal of Statistical Physics, 49*, 993–1009.

Doe, C.Q., Hiromi, Y., Gehring, W.J., & Goodman, C.S. (1988). Expression and function of the representation gene *fushi tarazu* during *Drosophila* neurogenesis. *Science, 239*, 170–175.

Edelman, G.M. (1978). Group selection and phasic reentrant signaling: a theory of higher brain function. In G.M. Edelman and V.B. Mountcastle (Eds.), *The mindful brain: Cortical organization and the group-selective theory of higher brain function* (pp. 51–100). Cambridge, MA: MIT Press.

Edelman, G.M., (1985). Molecular regulation of neural morphogenesis. In G.M. Edelman, W.E. Gall, & W.M. Cowan (Eds.), *Molecular bases of neural development*. New York: Wiley.

Edelman, G.M. (1987). *Neural Darwinism*. New York: Basic Books.

Edelman, G.M., & Finkel, L. (1984). Neuronal group selection in the cerebral cortex. In G. Edelman, W.E. Gall, & W.M. Cowan (Eds.), *Dynamic aspects of neocortical function*. New York: Wiley.

Edelman, G.M., Gall, W.E., & Cowan, W.M. (Eds.) (1984). *Dynamic aspects of neocortical function*. New York: Wiley.

Edelman, G.M., & Mountcastle, V. (Eds.) (1978). *The mindful brain; Cortical organization and the group-selective theory of higher brain function*. Cambridge, MA: MIT Press.

Eimas, P.D. (1975). In L.B. Cohen & P. Salapatek (Eds.), *Infant perception: From sensation to cognition* (Vol. 2). New York: Academic Press.

Feigelman, M.V., & Toffe, L.B. (1987). The augmented model of associative memory asymmetric interaction and hierarchy of pattern. *International Journal of Modern Physics, B, 1*, 51–68.

Feldman, J.A. (1986). Neural representation of conceptual knowledge. *Technical report, Department of Computer Science, University of Rochester*, TRI89, June 1986.

Ferguson, C.A. (1985). Discovering sound units and constructing sound systems: It's child's play. In J.S. Perkell & D.H. Klatt (Eds.), *Invariance and variability in speech processes*. Hillsdale, NJ: Erlbaum.

Finkel, L.H., & Edelman, G.M. (1987). Population rules for synapses in networks. In G.M. Edelman, W.E. Gall, & M.W. Cowan (Eds.), *Synaptic function*. New York: Wiley.

Fodor, J. (1975). *The language of thought*. Cambridge, MA: Harvard University Press.

Fodor, J. (1983). *The modularity of mind*. Cambridge, MA: MIT Press.

Fodor, J., & Pylyshyn, Z. (1988). Connectionism and cognitive architecture: A critical analysis. *Cognition, 28*, 3–71.

Fraser, S.E. (1985). Cell interactions involved in neuronal patterning: An experimental and theoretical approach. In G.M. Edelman, W.E. Gall, & W.M. Cowan (Eds.), *Molecular bases of neural development*. New York: Wiley.

Fuster, J.M. (1980). *The prefrontal cortex*. New York: Raven.

Fuster, J.M. (1984). Electrophysiology of the prefrontal cortex. *Trends in Neuroscience, 1*, 408–414.

Gazzaniga, M.S. (1987). The dynamics of cerebral specialization and modular interactions. In L. Weiskrantz (Ed.), *Thought without language*. Oxford: Clarendon Press.

Georgopoulos, A.P., Schwartz, A.B., & Kettner, R.E. (1986). Neuronal population coding of movement direction. *Science, 233*, 1357–1460.

Geschwind, N., & Galaburda, A. (Eds.) (1984). *Cerebral dominance: The biological foundations*. Cambridge, MA: Harvard University Press.

Geschwind, N., & Galaburda, A.M. (1987). *Cerebral lateralization*. Cambridge MA: MIT Press.

Getting, P.A. (1981). Mechanism of pattern generation underlying swimming in *Tritonia*. I. Neuronal network formed by monosynaptic connections. *Journal of Neurophysiology, 46*, 65–79.

Ghering, W. (1985). Homeotic genes, the homeobox and the genetic control of development. *Cold Spring Harbor Symposium for Quantitative Biology, 50*, 243–251.

Goelet, P., Castellucci, V., Schacher, S., & Kandel, E. (1986). The long and the short of long-term memory: A molecular framework. *Nature, 322*, 419–422.

Goldman-Rakic, P. (1987). Circuitry of the primate prefrontal cortex and the regulation of behavior by representational knowledge. In V. Mountcastle & K.F. Plum (Eds.), *The nervous system: Higher functions of the brain, Vol. 5, Handbook of Physiology*. Washington, DC: American Physiological Society.

Goldowitz, D., & Mullen, R. (1982). Granule cell as a site of gene action in the weaver mouse cerebellum. Evidence from heterozygous mutant chimerae. *Journal of Neuroscience, 2*, 1474–1485.

Gombrich, E.H. (1960). *Art and illusion*. Oxford: Phaidon Press.

Gombrich, E.H. (1983). *L'écologie des images*. Paris: Flammarion.

Goodman, C.S., Bastiani, M.J., Raper, J.A., & Thomas, J.B. (1985). Cell recognition during neuronal development in grasshopper and *Drosophila*. In G.M. Edelman, W.E. Gall, & W.M. Cowan (Eds.), *Molecular bases of neural development*. New York: Wiley.

Gouzé, J.L., Lasry, J.M., & Changeux, J.P. (1983). Selective stabilization of muscle innervation during development: A mathematical model. *Biological Cybernetics, 46*, 207–215.

Grillner, S. (1975). Locomotion in vertebrates. Central mechanisms and reflex interaction. *Physiological Review, 55*, 247–304.

Grillner, S., Wallén, P., Dale, N., Brodin, L., Buchanan, J., & Hill, R. (1987). Transmitters, membrane properties and network circuitry in the control of locomotion in lamprey. *Trend in Neuroscience, 10*, 34–41.

Gutfreund, H. (1988). Neural networks with hierarchically correlated patterns. *Physical Review, 91*, 375–391.

Hamburger, V. (1970). Embryonic mobility in vertebrates. In F.O. Schmitt (Ed.), *The Neurosciences: Second study program*. New York: Rockefeller University Press.

Hawkins, R.D., & Kandel, E. (1984). Is there a cell-biological alphabet for simple forms of learning? *Psychological Review, 91*, 375–391.

Hebb, D.O. (1949). *The organization of behavior: A neuropsychological theory*. New York: Wiley.

Heidmann, A., Heidmann, T., & Changeux, J.P. (1984). Stabilisation selective de représentations neuronales par résonance entre "pré-représentations" spontanées du réseau cérébral et "percepts" évoqués par interaction avec le monde extérieur. *C.R. Acad. Sci. Paris* (série 3), *299*, 839–844.

Heidmann, T., & Changeux, J.P. (1982). Un modèle moléculaire de régulation d'efficacité d'un synapse chimique au niveau postsynaptique. *C.R. Acad. Sci. Paris* (série 3), *295*, 665–670.

Heit, G., Smith, M.E., & Halgren, E. (1988). Neural encoding of individual words and faces by the human hippocampus and amygdala. *Nature, 333*, 773–775.

Hökfelt, T., Holets, V.R., Staines, W., Meister, B., Melander, T., Schalling, M., Schultzberg, M., Freedman, J., Björklund, H., Olson, L., Lindk, B., Elfvin, L.G., Lundberg, J., Lindgren, J.A., Samuelsson, B., Terenius, L., Post, C., Everitt, B., & Goldstein, M. (1986). Coexistence of neuronal messengers: An overview. *Progress in Brain Research, 68*, 33–70.

Hopfield, J. (1982). Neural networks and physical systems with emergent collective computational abilities. *Proceedings of the National Academy of Sciences USA, 79*, 2554–2558.

Hopfield, J., & Tank, D.W. (1986). Computing with neural circuits: A model. *Science, 233*, 625–635.

Hubel, P., & Wiesel, T. (1977). Functional architecture of macaque monkey visual cortex. Ferrier Lecture. *Proceedings of the Royal Society (London) B, 198*, 1–59.

Huttenlocher, P.R., De Courten, C., Garey, L.J., & Vander Loos, H. (1982). Synaptogenesis in human visual cortex. Evidence for synapse elimination during normal development. *Neuroscience Letters, 33*, 247–252.

Innocenti, G.M., & Caminiti, R. (1980). Postnatal shaping of callosal connections from sensory areas. *Experimental Brain Research, 38*, 381–394.

Ito, M., Sakurai, M., & Tongroach, P. (1982). Climbing fibre induced depression of both mossy fibre responsiveness and glutamate sensitivity of cerebellar Purkinje cells. *Journal of Physiology (London), 324*, 113–134.

Jackson, H. (1932). In J. Taylor (Ed.), *Selected Papers* (Vol. 2). London: Hodder & Stoughton.

Jerne, N. (1967). Antibodies and learning: Selection versus instruction. In G. Quarton, T. Melnechuck, &

F.O. Schmitt (Eds.), *The Neurosciences*. New York: Rockefeller University Press.

Johnson, M.H., McConnell, J., & Van Blerkom, J. (1984). Programmed development in the mouse embryo. *Journal of Embryology and Experimental Morphology, 83* (Suppl.), 197–231.

Johnson-Laird, P.N. (1983). *Mental models*. Cambridge: Cambridge University Press.

Kandel, E.R., Abrams, T., Bernier, L., Carew, T.J., Hawkins, R.D., & Schwartz, J.H. (1983). Classical conditioning and sensitization share aspects of the same molecular cascade in *Aplysia*. *Cold Spring Harbor Symposium on Quantitative Biology, 48*, 821–830.

Kanter, I., & Sompolinsky, H. (1987). Associative recall of memory without errors. *Physical Review A, 35*, 380–392.

Kelos, S.R., Ganong, A.H., & Brown, T.H. (1986). Hebbian synapses in hippocampus. *Proceedings of the National Academy of Science USA, 83*, 5326–5330.

Kihlstrom, J. (1987). The cognitive unconscious. *Science, 237*, 1445–1452.

Kleinfeld, D. (1986). Sequential state generation by model neural networks. *Proceedings of the National Academy of Sciences USA, 83*, 9469–9473.

Kleinfeld, D., & Sompolinsky, H. (1987). Associative neural network model for the generation of temporal patterns: Theory and application to central pattern generators. Unpublished paper.

Kolb, B., & Whishaw, I. (1980). *Fundamentals of human neuropsychology*. San Francisco: Freeman.

Konishi, M. (1985). Bird songs: From behavior to neuron. *Annual Review of Neurophysiology, 8*, 125–170.

Lashley, K.S. (1951). *Central mechanisms in behavior*. New York: Wiley.

Lehkey, S.R., & Sejnowski, T.J. (1988). Network model of shape-from-shading: Neural function arises from both receptive and projective fields. *Nature, 333*, 452–454.

Levinthal, F., Macagno, E., & Levinthal, C. (1976). Anatomy and development of identified cells in isogenic organisms. *Cold Spring Harbor Symposium on Quantitative Biology, 40*, 321–332.

Lhermitte, F. (1983). "Utilization behavior" and its relation to lesions of the frontal lobe. *Brain, 106*, 237–235.

Lisman, J.E. (1985). A mechanism for memory storage insensitive to molecular turnover: A bistable autophosphorylating kinase. *Proceedings of the National Academy of Science USA, 82*, 3055–3057.

Little, W.A. (1974). Existence of persistent states in the brain. *Mathematical Bioscience, 9*, 101–120.

Llinás, R.R. (1987). "Mindness" as a functional state of the brain. In C. Blakemore & S. Greenfield (Eds.), *Mindwaves*. London: Basil Blackwell.

Lumsden, C., & Wilson, E.O. (1981). *Genes, mind and culture: The coevolutionary process*. Cambridge, MA: Harvard University Press.

Luria, A.R. (1973). *The working brain: An introduction to neuropsychology*. New York: Basic Books.

Macagno, F., Lopresti, U., & Levinthal, C. (1973). Structural development of neuronal connections in isogenic organisms: Variations and similarities in the optic tectum of *Daphnia magna*. *Proceedings of the National Academy of Science USA, 70*, 57–61.

McCarthy, R.A., & Warrington, E.K. (1988). Evidence for modality-specific meaning systems in the brain. *Nature, 334*, 428–430.

McCulloch, W.S., & Pitts, W.A. (1943). Logical calculus of the ideas immanent in nervous activity. *Bulletin of Mathematical Biophysics, 5*, 115.

Marr, D. (1982). *Vision*. San Francisco: Freeman.

Mariani, J., & Changeux, J.P. (1981a). Ontogenesis of olivocerebellar relationships: I – Studies by intracellular recordings of the multiple innervation of Purkinje cells by climbing fibers in the developing rat cerebellum. *Journal of Neuroscience, 1*, 696–702.

Mariani, J., & Changeux, J.P. (1981b). Ontogenesis of olivocerebellar relationships: II – Spontaneous activity of inferior olivary neurons and climbing fiber-mediated activity of cerebellar Purkinje cells in developing rats and in adult cerebellar mutant mice. *Journal of Neuroscience, 1*, 703–709.

Marler, P., & Peters, S. (1982). Development overproduction and selective attrition: New process in the epigenesis of bird song. *Developmental Psychobiology, 15*, 369–378.

Marshall, J.C. (1988). The lifeblood of language. *Nature, 331*, 560–561.

Massaro, D. (1975). *Experimental psychology and information processing*. Chicago: Rand McNally.

Mayr, E. (1963). *Animal species and evolution*. Cambridge, MA: Harvard University Press.

Mehler, J., Morton, J., & Jusczyk, P.W. (1984). On reducing language to biology. *Cognitive Neuropsychology*, *1*, 83–116.

Meinhardt, H., & Gierer, A. (1974). Application of a theory of biological pattern formation based on lateral inhibition. *Journal of Cell Science*, *15*, 321–346.

Merzenich, M.M. (1987). Dynamic neocortical processes and the origins of higher brain functions. In J.P. Changeux & M. Konishi (Eds.), *The neural and molecular bases of learning*, New York: Wiley.

Mézard, M., Nadal, J.P., & Toulouse, G. (1986). Solvable models of working memories. *Journal de Physique (Paris)*, *47*, 1457–1462.

Mitchinson, G. (1987). The organization of sequential memory: Sparse representations and the targeting problem. *Proceedings of the Bad Homburg meeting on Brain Theory*, 16–19 September, 1986.

Miyawaki, K., Strange, W., Verbrugge, R., Liberman, A., Jenkins, J., & Fujimura, O. (1975). An effect of linguistic experience: the discrimination of $|r|$ and $|l|$ by native speakers of Japanese and English. *Perception and Psychophysics*, *18*, 331–340.

Monod, J., & Jacob, F. (1961). General conclusions: Teleonomic mechanisms in cellular metabolism, growth and differentiation. *Cold Spring Harbor Symposium for Quantitative Biology*, *26*, 389–401.

Monod, J. (1970). *Le hasard et la nécessité*. Paris: Le Seuil.

Montarolo, P.G., Goelet, P., Castellucci, V.F., Morgan, T., Kandel, E., & Schacher, S. (1986). A critical period for macromolecular synthesis in long-term heterosynaptic facilitation in *Aplysia*. *Science*, *234*, 1249–1254.

Motter, B.C. Steinmetz, M.A., Duffy, C.J., & Mountcastle, V.B. (1987). Functional properties of parietal visual neurons: Mechanisms of directionality along a single axis. *Journal of Neuroscience*, *7*, 154–175.

Mountcastle, V. (1978). An organizing principle for cerebral function: The unit module and the distributed system. In G.M. Edelman & V. Mountcastle (Eds.), *The mindful brain: Cortical organization and the group-selective theory of higher brain function*. Cambridge, MA: MIT Press.

Nadal, J.P., Toulouse, G., Changeux, J.P., & Dehaene, S. (1986a). Networks of formal neurons and memory palimpsests. *Europhysics Letters*, *1*, 535–542.

Nadal, J.P., Toulouse, G., Mézard, M., Changeux, J.P., & Dehaene, S. (1986b). Neural networks: Learning and forgetting. In R.J. Cotteril (Ed.), *Computer simulations and brain science*. Cambridge: Cambridge University Press.

Nass, R.D., Koch, D.A., Janowsky, J., & Stile-Davis, J. (1985). Differential effects on intelligence of early left versus right brain injury. *Annals of Neurology*, *18*, 393.

Nass, R.D., Koch, D.A., Janowsky, J., & Stile-Davis, J. (1989). Differential effects of congenital left and right brain injury on intelligence (in press).

Nauta, W.J.H. (1971). The problem of the frontal lobe: A reinterpretation. *Journal of Psychiatric Research*, *8*, 167–187.

Nauta, W.J.H. (1973). Connections of the frontal lobe with the limbic system. In L.V. Laitiven & K.E. Livingston (Eds.), *Surgical approaches in psychiatry*. Baltimore, MD: University Pack Press.

Newell, A. (1982). The knowledge level. *Artificial Intelligence*, *18*, 87–127.

Niki, H. (1974). Prefrontal unit activity during delayed alternation in the monkey. I. Relation to direction of response. II. Relation to absolute versus relative direction of response. *Brain Research*, *68*, 185–196.

Nüsslein-Volhard, C., Frohnhöffer, H.G., & Lehmann, R. (1987). Determination of anteroposterior polarity in Drosophila. *Science*, *238*, 1675–1681.

Ojemann, G. (1983). Brain organization for language from the perspective of electrical stimulation mapping. *Behavioral and Brain Science*, *6*, 189–230.

Oster-Granite, M., & Gearhart, J. (1981). Cell lineage analysis of cerebellar Purkinje cells in mouse chimaeras. *Development Biology*, *85*, 199–208.

Parga, N., & Virasoro, M.A. (1985). Ultrametric organization of memories in neural network. *Journal de Physique Lettres*, *47*, 1857.

Peretto, P., & Niez, J.J. (1986). Collective properties of neural networks. In E. Bienenstock, F. Fogelman, & G. Weisbuch (Eds.), *Disordered systems and biological organization.* Berlin: Springer-Verlag.

Perrett, D.I., Mistlin, A.J., & Chitty, A.J. (1987). Visual neurons responsive to faces. *Trends in Neuroscience, 10,* 358–364.

Personnaz, L., Guyon, I., & Dreyfus, G. (1985). Information storage and retrieval in spin-glass like neural networks. *Journal de Physique Lettres, 46,* L359.

Petersen, S.E., Fox, P.T., Posner, M.I., Mintun, M., & Raichle, M.E. (1988). Positron emission tomographic studies of the cortical anatomy of single-word processing. *Nature, 331,* 585–589.

Piaget, J. (1979). *Behavior and evolution.* London: Routledge & Kegan Paul.

Pinker, S., & Prince, A. (1988). On language and connectionism: Analysis of a parallel model of language acquisition. *Cognition, 28,* 73–913.

Posner, M.I. (1980). Orienting of attention. *Quarterly Journal of Experimental Psychology, 32,* 3–25.

Posner, M.I., Petersen, S.E., Fox, P.T., & Raichle, M.E. (1988). Localization of cognitive operations in the human brain. *Science, 240,* 1627–1631.

Posner, M., & Presti, D.F. (1987). Selective attention and cognitive control. *Trends in Neuroscience, 10,* 13–17.

Price, D.J., & Blakemore, C. (1985). Regressive events in the postnatal development of association projections in the visual cortex. *Nature, 316,* 721–723.

Prince, A., & Pinker, S. (1988). Rules and connections in human language. *Trends in Neuroscience, 11,* 195–202.

Prince, D.A., & Huguenard, J.R. (1988). Functional properties of neocortical neurons. In P. Rakic & W. Singer (Eds.), *Neurobiology of the neocortex.* Chichester: Wiley.

Purves, D., & Lichtman, J.W. (1980). Elimination of synapses in the developing nervous system. *Science, 210,* 153–157.

Pylyshyn, Z. (1985). Plasticity and invariance in cognitive development. In J. Mehler & R. Fox (Eds.), *Neonate cognition.* Hillsdale, NJ: Erlbaum.

Rakic, P. (1988). Intrinsic and extrinsic determinants of neocortical parcellation: a radial unit model. In P. Rakic & W. Singer (Eds.), *Neurobiology of neocortex.* Chichester: Wiley.

Rakic, P., & Singer, W. (Eds.) (1988). *Neurobiology of the neocortex.* Chichester: Wiley.

Ramon y Cajal, S. (1909). *Histologie du système nerveux de l'homme et des vertèbrés* (2 vols.). Paris: Maloine.

Redfern, P.A. (1970). Neuromuscular transmission in newborn rats. *Journal of Physiology (London), 209,* 701–709.

Reiter, H.O., & Stryker, M.P. (1988). Neural plasticity without postsynaptic action potentials: Less-active inputs become dominant when kitten visual cortical cells are pharmacologically inhibited. *Proceedings of the National Academy of Science USA, 85,* 3623–3627.

Ribchester, R.R. (1988). Activity-dependent and -independent synaptic interactions during reinnervation of partially denervated rat muscle. *Journal of Physiology, 401,* 53–75.

Rockwell, A., Hiorns, R., & Powell, T. (1980). The basic uniformity in structure of the neocortex. *Brain, 103,* 221–224.

Roland, P.E., & Friberg (1985). Localization of cortical areas activated by thinking. *Journal of Neurophysiology, 53,* 1219–1243.

Rolls, E. (1987). Information representation, processing and storage in the brain: Analysis at the single neuron level. In J.P. Changeux & M. Konishi (Eds.), *The neural and molecular bases of learning.* Chichester: Wiley.

Rugg, M. (1988). Stimulus selectivity of single neurons in the temporal lobe. *Nature, 333,* 700.

Rumelhart, D.E., & McClelland, J.L. (1987). Learning the past tenses of English verbs: Implicit rules or parallel distributed processing? In B. MacWhinney (Ed.), *Mechanisms of language acquisition.* Hillsdale, NJ: Erlbaum.

Sasanuma, S. (1975). Kana and Kanji processing in Japanese aphasics. *Brain and Language, 2,* 369–383.

Schmidt, J. (1985). Factors involved in retinotopic map formation: Complementary roles for membrane recognition and activity-dependent synaptic stabilization. In G.M. Edelman, W.E. Gall, & W.N. Cowan (Eds.), *Molecular bases of neural development.* New York: Wiley.

Searle, J.R. (1983). *Intentionality: An essay in the philosophy of mind.* New York: Cambridge University Press.

Sejnowsky, T.J., Koch, C., & Churchland, P.S. (1988). Computational neuroscience. *Science, 241,* 1299–1306.

Sejnowsky, T.J., & Rosenberg, C.R. (1986). *NET-talk: A parallel network that learns to read aloud.* Technical report JHU/EECS-86/01. Department of Electrical Engineering and Computer Science, John Hopkins University.

Shallice, T. (1982). Specific impairments of planning. *Philosophical Transactions of the Royal Society of London B, 298,* 199–209.

Simon, H.A. (1969). *The sciences of the artificial.* Cambridge, MA: MIT Press.

Sompolinsky, H., & Kanter, I. (1986). Temporal association in asymmetric neural networks. *Physical Review Letters, 57,* 2861–2864.

Sperber, D. (1984). Anthropology and psychology: Towards an epidemiology of representations. *Man* (N.S.), *20,* 73–89.

Sretavan, D.W., Shatz, C.J., & Stryker, M.P. (1988). Modification of retinal ganglion cell axon morphology by frontal infusion of tetrodotoxin. *Nature, 336.*

Steinmetz, M.A., Motter, B.C., Duffy, C.J., & Mountcastle, V. (1987). Functional properties of parietal visual neurons: Radial organization of directionalities within the visual field. *Journal of Neuroscience, 7,* 177–191.

Stent, G. (1973). A physiological mechanism for Hebb's postulate of learning. *Proceedings of the National Academy of Science USA, 70,* 997–1001.

Stent, G. (1981). Strength and weakness of the genetic approach to the development of the nervous system. *Annual Review of Neuroscience, 4,* 163–194.

Stent, G. (1987). The mind–body problem. *Science, 236,* 990–992.

Stent, G.S., Kristan, W.B., Friesen, W.O., Ort, C.A., Poon, M., & Calabrese, R.L. (1978). Neuronal generation of the leech swimming movement. *Science, 200,* 1348–1356.

Stryker, M.P., & Harris, W.A. (1986). Binocular impulse blockage prevents the formation of ocular dominance columns in cat visual cortex. *Journal of Neuroscience, 6,* 2117–2133.

Stuss, D., & Benson, F. (1986). *The frontal lobes.* New York: Raven.

Taine, H. (1870). *De l'intelligence.* Paris: Hachette.

Tank, D.W., & Hopfield, J.J. (1987). Neural computation by concentrating information in time. *Proceedings of the National Academy of Science USA, 84,* 1896–1900.

Teuber, H.L. (1972). Unity and diversity of frontal lobe functions. *Acta Neurobiology Experiments (Warsz.), 32,* 615–656.

Thom, R. (1980). *Modéles mathèmatiques de la morphogènèse.* Paris: Bourgeois.

Thomas, R. (1981). On the relation between the logical structure of systems and their ability to generate multiple steady-states or sustained oscillations. *Springer Series in Synergetics, 9,* 180–193.

Toulouse, G., Dehaene, S., & Changeux, J.P. (1986). Spin glass model of learning by selection. *Proceedings of the National Academy of Science USA, 83,* 1695–1698.

Turing, A.M. (1952). The chemical basis of morphogenesis. *Philosophical Transactions of the Royal Society (London), 237,* 37–72.

Van Essen, D.G. (1982). Neuromuscular synapse elimination: Structural, functional and mechanistic aspects. In N.C. Spitzer (Ed.), *Neuronal development.* New York: Plenum.

Von der Malsburg, C. (1981). *The correlation theory of brain function.* Internal report 8–12 July 1981, Department of Neurobiology, Max Plank Institute for Biophysical Chemistry, Göttingen.

Von der Malsburg, C. (1987). Synaptic plasticity as basis of brain organization. In J.P. Changeux & M. Konishi (Eds.), *The neural and molecular bases of learning.* Chichester: Wiley.

Von der Malsburg, C., & Bienenstock, E. (1986). Statistical coding and short-term plasticity: A scheme for knowledge representation. In E. Bienenstock, F. Fogelman, & G. Weisbuch (Eds.), *Disordered systems and biological organization.* Berlin: Springer-Verlag.

Wilson, E.O. (1975). *Sociobiology*. Cambridge, MA: Harvard University Press.

Young, J.Z. (1964). *A model of the brain*. Oxford: Clarendon Press.

Young, J.Z. (1973). Memory as a selective process. *Australian Academy of Science Reports: Symposium on the Biology of Memory*, 25–45.

Zeki, S. (1988). Anatomical guides to the functional organization of the visual cortex. In P. Rakic & W. Singer (Eds.), *Neurobiology of neocortex*. Chichester: Wiley.

Zipser, D., & Andersen, R.A. (1988). A back-propagation programmed network that stimulates response properties of a subset of posterior parietal neurons. *Nature, 331*, 679–684.

Résumé

Comprendre les bases neurales de la cognition est devenu un problème abordable scientifiquement, et des modèles sont proposés dans le but d'établir un lien causal entre organisation neurale et fonction cognitive. Dans ces conditions, il devient nécessaire de définir des niveaux d'organisation dans l'architecture fonctionelle des systèmes de neurones. Les transitions d'un niveau d'organisation à l'autre sont envisagées dans une perspective évolutive: elles ont lieu avec différentes échelles de temps, et reposent sur la production transitoire de nombreuses variations et la sélection de certaines d'entre elles au cours de l'interaction avec le monde extérieur. Au cours du développement et chez l'adulte, cette évolution interne est de nature épigénétique: elle ne requiert pas d'altération du génôme. L'activité (spontanée ou évoquée) d'un réseau de neurones au cours du développement stabilise de manière sélective certaines synapses et en élimine d'autres, contribuant, de ce fait, à la mise en place de la connectivité adulte à l'intérieur d'une enveloppe de potentialités définies génétiquement. A un niveau supérieur, la modélisation de représentations mentales par des états d'activité de populations restreintes de neurones est réalisée par les méthodes de la physique statistique: la mémorisation de ces représentations est envisagée comme un processus de sélection parmi des "pré-représentations" variables et instables. Des modèles théoriques montrent que des fonctions cognitives comme la mémoire à court-terme ou la manipulation de séquences temporelles peuvent dépendre de paramètres physiques élémentaires. Une implémentation neuronale et sélectionniste des intentions est envisagée.

4

Seeking the neurobiological bases of speech perception*

JOANNE L. MILLER
Northeastern University

PETER W. JUSCZYK
CNRS et EHESS, Paris, and University of Oregon

Abstract

Miller, J.L., and Jusczyk, P.W., 1989. Seeking the neurobiological bases of speech perception. Cognition, 33: 111–137.

One of the most highly developed human abilities is communication by speech. Throughout the years, research on speech perception has demonstrated that humans are well adapted to extract highly encoded linguistic information from the speech signal. The sophisticated nature of these capacities and their early appearance during development suggest the existence of a rich biological substrate for speech perception. In the present paper, we describe some of these important capacities and examine research from different domains that may help illuminate the nature of their biological foundations.

Introduction

We take as the goal of a theory of speech perception an account of how the listener recovers the phonetic structure of an utterance from the acoustic signal during the course of language processing. Part of the theory and the specific concern of this paper is the nature of the biological mechanisms that underlie speech perception. What must be resolved in any theoretical account is how our biology allows us, as listeners, to perceive speech on-line as it is

---

*Support was provided by NINCDS grant NS-14394 (J.L.M.), NIH BRSG RR-07143 (J.L.M.), and NICHHD HD-15795 (P.W.J.). Order of authorship was determined by the flip of a coin. We thank Peter Marler and, especially, Peter D. Eimas, for their very helpful comments on previous versions of the paper. Requests for reprints should be sent to Dr. Joanne L. Miller, Department of Psychology, Northeastern University, Boston, MA 02115, U.S.A. or to Dr. Peter W. Jusczyk, Department of Psychology, University of Oregon, Eugene, OR 97403, U.S.A.

produced by a talker; and to do so with no apparent effort, for voices never before encountered, across changes in such factors as speaking rate and style and, to a remarkable extent, in the presence of noise and other sources of distortion.

Very little is currently known about the neurophysiological mechanisms that subserve speech perception. Nonetheless, findings from a variety of domains provide at least initial hints as to the form such mechanisms might take. The purpose of this article is to consider these findings. Our approach is as follows. In the first part of the paper we describe three fundamental characteristics of speech perception. For each we give an overview of the basic issues and illustrate with selected examples from the literature. In the second part of the paper we review findings that bear on possible underlying physiological mechanisms for speech perception, especially with respect to the three fundamental characteristics that provide our focus.

1. Three characteristics of speech perception

1.1. Complex relation between acoustic signal and phonetic segment

A fundamental characteristic of speech that has constrained theory construction over the past four decades concerns the apparent lack of isomorphism between the acoustic and phonetic levels of language. This lack of isomorphism can be construed as having two closely related facets, namely, the segmentation and invariance problems. Virtually every discussion of speech perception includes a characterization of these twin problems — attesting to their central importance — and we continue in the tradition, considering each in turn.

It is possible to describe the speech signal in terms of a temporal sequence of acoustic segments. These segments can be seen on a spectrographic display as a series of relatively homogeneous stretches of the signal, demarcated by rather abrupt discontinuities in spectral form that mark the boundaries between segments (Fant, 1973). The problem for any theory of perception is that these acoustic segments do not correspond in any straightforward manner to the perceived phonetic segments, the consonants and vowels of the utterance. This complexity in mapping from acoustic to phonetic levels of language takes two major forms (Liberman, Cooper, Shankweiler, & Studdert-Kennedy, 1967). First, a given acoustic segment typically contains information for more than one phonetic segment, such that there is parallel transmission of information about segmental identity. Second, the information for any given phonetic segment is typically spread over a series of acoustic segments, overlapping the information for nearby segments. This lack of a one-to-one relation between acoustic and phonetic segments is a direct consequence of the nature of speech production. Speakers do not produce speech one segment at a time, but rather the gestures for a given segment overlap those for segments nearby in time; that is, the segments are coarticulated.

We can illustrate the basic segmentation problem with a simple example from the literature involving the identification of fricative–vowel syllables, such as /si/. The syllable /si/ consists of two quite distinct acoustic segments: the initial frication portion and the subsequent periodic portion. But these two segments do not correspond in a one-to-one fashion with the perceived fricative /s/ and vowel /i/. A study illustrating this is provided by Yeni-Komshian and Soli (1981), who tested the perception of four fricatives, each paired with three vowels. The frication segments were excised from the full syllables and presented to listeners for identification. Not only could the listeners identify which fricative had been uttered but, to a considerable extent, which vowel – although the precise level of vowel identification depended on the particular fricative–vowel combination. The important point is that the frication segment contained, in parallel, information about both the consonant and the vowel. And since the primary information for vowel identity is the periodic portion of the syllable and not the frication, this example also illustrates how the information for a given phonetic segment — in this case the vowel — is spread across more than one acoustic segment.

Closely related to the segmentation problem is the invariance problem. The basic idea here is that there is no single invariant property in the acoustic signal that serves as the necessary and sufficient information for a given perceived phonetic segment (or phonetic feature). It has been known for some time that a given articulatory act results in an array of acoustic consequences, each of which appears to be perceptually relevant. Moreover, because of coarticulation any given acoustic property typically varies systematically as a function of the phonetic context, and listeners process speech so as to take account of this contextual variation (see Repp, 1982, for a review; see Stevens & Blumstein, 1981, and Fowler, 1986, for alternative conceptualizations of the issue).

A classic illustration of how multiple properties specify a phonetic segment involves the distinction between voiced and voiceless consonants in medial position, for example, the /b/–/p/ contrast in the words *rabid* versus *rapid*. In a recent paper reviewing this contrast, Lisker (1986) lists 16 acoustic properties that contribute to the perception of this distinction; seven pertain to speech prior to closure, three to the closure interval itself, and six to the speech following the closure interval. Numerous studies have shown that such multiple properties enter into a perceptual trading relation with one another: a change in one property can be perceptually offset with an appropriate change in another. Moreover, listeners are typically aware only of the resulting phonetic percept, not the specific settings of the properties (Fitch, Halwes, Erickson, & Liberman, 1980). At issue is how the processing system integrates quite diverse properties to yield a unified percept of a single segment.[1]

To illustrate a listener's sensitivity to contextual variation in phonetically relevant acoustic properties, consider the distinction between /ʃ/ (the 'sh' sound in 'ship') and /s/ in syllable-initial position. It is well established that the spectrum of the frication noise provides important information for the identification of a fricative as /ʃ/ or /s/, with the noise spectrum for /s/ being higher in frequency than that for /ʃ/. However, as Mann and Repp (1980) showed, the spectra for the two consonants are not invariant across phonetic contexts; for both /ʃ/ and /s/, there is a systematic lowering of the spectrum before the rounded vowel /u/ compared to the unrounded vowel /a/, presumably due to anticipatory lip rounding as the consonant is produced. Moreover, this context dependency is reflected in perception. When Mann and Repp asked listeners to identify frication noises varying in frequency as /ʃ/ or /s/, they began to hear /s/ at a lower frequency before /u/ than /a/. That is to say, they treated the frication noise not in an absolute manner but in terms of the context in which it occurred.

The picture that emerges is one of a complex, though systematic, relation between the acoustic properties of speech and the perceived phonetic structure of the utterance. The complexity derives from the nature of speech production and, indeed, the processes of production have been used to constrain theoretical descriptions of perception, most notably the motor theory of speech perception proposed by Liberman and his colleagues (e.g., Liberman & Mattingly, 1985).

1.2. Categorical representation of phonetic structure

The nature of the internal representation of speech also provides potential constraints on the mechanisms of speech perception. We focus on one aspect of this multi-faceted issue: the categorical nature of such representations.[2]

---

[1]The type of mental computations undertaken in this situation seems to fit well with that described by Fodor (1983) for input systems. He suggested that for computations that take place in such highly specialized and encapsulated systems, the perceiver has conscious access only to the representations derived in the final stages of processing, that is, in the present case, the phonetic percept.

[2]A closely related issue concerns the representational units of speech. Virtually every theory of spoken language processing assumes that the speech perception system provides some type of sublexical representation that is involved in lexical access. However, the nature of these representational units – for example, whether they are phonetic features, phonetic segments, diphones, or syllables – remains a matter of considerable debate. For further discussion of this issue, see Eimas et al. (1987) and Pisoni (1981).

The basic phenomenon, traditionally labeled 'categorical perception', was first reported in the late 1950s. The seminal study by Liberman, Harris, Hoffman, and Griffith (1957) provides a clear illustration. Liberman et al. used a speech synthesizer to create a continuum of syllables that varied in equal steps in the onset frequency of the second-formant (F2) transition. This property is sufficient to distinguish the three syllable-initial consonants /b/, /d/, and /g/, which differ from each other in place of articulation — the point of major constriction in the vocal tract during the production of the segment. Subjects participated in two tasks. In an identification task they labeled random presentations of the syllables from the series as /be/, /de/, or /ge/. Although the stimuli varied physically in equal steps across the acoustic continuum, subjects divided them into three quite discrete phonetic categories, with sharp boundaries between categories. Results from a discrimination task revealed further that the ability to differentiate stimuli from one another was a function of the phonetic categories to which they belonged: stimuli identified as belonging to two different categories were readily discriminated, whereas those identified as members of the same category were discriminated only slightly better than chance. This occurred, furthermore, even though the acoustic difference between the stimuli to be discriminated was kept constant. Thus although the stimuli formed a physical continuum, perception was not continuous, but categorical.

This early finding led to a very large literature – and much debate – on the conditions for categorical perception, its role in the speech perception process, and the nature of the underlying mechanisms (see Repp, 1984, for a comprehensive review). For our purposes, we focus on one aspect: the relative inability of listeners to distinguish within-category members. The early results were taken as evidence that categorization (at least for certain classes of stimuli, most notably stop consonants) was nearly absolute. The idea was that the processing system had very limited access to auditory information that could potentially be used to differentiate members of the same category. That is to say, the perceptual mechanism provided an initial representation containing only information about category identity.

It soon became clear, however, that the situation was far more complex. In particular, certain tasks revealed that even for dimensions relevant to the perception of stop consonants, putatively the most encoded of speech sounds (cf. Liberman et al., 1967), within-category information was not entirely stripped away during perception. To illustrate we consider an influential study by Pisoni and Tash (1974). Their stimuli were drawn from a /ba/–/pa/ series. Members of the series differed in voice-onset time (VOT), a complex property sufficient to distinguish the syllable-initial voiced consonant /b/ from its voiceless counterpart /p/. Subjects were presented pairs of stimuli drawn from the continuum for speeded judgment as to whether the two stimuli were phonetically the same (two /ba/'s or two /pa/'s) or different (one /ba/ and one /pa/). Two types of same trials were employed. In one, the two stimuli were acoustically identical; in the other they differed in VOT value. The interesting result was that it took subjects longer to respond "same" to the acoustically different pairs than to the acoustically identical ones, indicating that subjects were not responding solely on the basis of identity in phonetic category. Corroborating evidence for the use of non-phonetic, auditory information came from trials with stimuli from different categories: "different" responses were faster for pairs in which the acoustic difference between members of the two categories was larger. Data such as these provide strong evidence that at least under certain task conditions within-category information is available. Recent evidence suggests further that within-category information is not only available, but that the representation of this information is highly structured. Miller and Volaitis (in press) showed that listeners consistently judge some members of a category to be better exemplars than others and, importantly, which stimuli are judged best varies with context. These findings suggest that the perceptual mechanism must be capable of providing a representation that codes category identity but, at the same time, retains information about internal category structure.

1.3. Developmental course of speech perception: The initial state and beyond

Investigations into the perceptual capacities of young, prelinguistic infants have revealed a perceptual system that is not only highly sensitive to the acoustic differences that distinguish phonetic segments, but is highly sophisticated in its manner of functioning. We know that in the early months of life the system is already well suited to provide a discrete representation of the signal at a level that corresponds roughly to the phonetic segments that are heard by more mature listeners. With respect to the infant's sensitivity to acoustic differences, researchers over the past 20 years have found that infants between 1 and 4 months of age, and in some cases even younger, are able to distinguish acoustic differences that are sufficient to signal many, perhaps all, of the phonetic distinctions that exist in human languages (for reviews of this literature see Aslin, Pisoni, & Jusczyk, 1983, and Eimas, Miller, & Jusczyk, 1987).

With regard to the categorization of speech, infants have been shown to be capable of categorically perceiving the acoustic information for phonetic distinctions based on voicing, place of articulation, and manner of articulation. For example, Eimas (1974) showed that only those changes in the spectral characteristics of the formant transitions that signal a difference in place of articulation among stop consonants were discriminated; the same magnitude of change among members of a single category was not discriminated. Nevertheless, the categorization of speech by infants does not appear to be solely a function of a failure to discriminate; several studies (e.g., Miller & Eimas, 1983) have shown that in some cases it is possible for infants to discriminate the variation that exists within categories, albeit not nearly as well as similar differences that mark a change in category (cf. section 1.2). Moreover, as is true for adult listeners, the infant's mapping of stimuli along a continuum onto phonetically relevant categories is not invariant. The infant's categories are influenced by contextual factors such as speaking rate and by a sensitivity to the multiplicity of acoustic properties that specify a given phonetic distinction, resulting in perceptual trading relations (Eimas & Miller, 1980; Levitt, Jusczyk, Murray, & Carden, 1988; Miller & Eimas, 1983).

In related work on the categorization process, Kuhl (1980, 1985) has shown that 6-month-old infants are able to form categorical representations of vowels, /a/ and /i/ for example, and fricatives, such as /s/ and /ʃ/, when the individual segments varied in speaker and intonation in the former case and in speaker and vocalic environment in the latter. Moreover, in control studies, Kuhl as well as Katz and Jusczyk (1980) found that the categorization that was evidenced was not a result of learning specific responses to each speech pattern, but rather a consequence of the natural tendency to perceive speech in terms of phonetic categories or at least the forerunners of these categories.

Given the sophisticated manner in which speech is perceived well before infants are able to consistently produce the sounds of speech, and certainly well before they are able to comprehend speech, the mechanisms underlying the perception of speech would seem to strongly reflect our biological heritage, and perhaps even our species-specific inheritance (cf. Liberman & Mattingly, 1985). Further evidence for this conclusion comes from cross-language studies that have shown common categorization abilities among young infants despite considerable differences in the phonologies of the parental language. For example, infants from English-speaking, Kikuyu-speaking, and Spanish-speaking linguistic environments all show very similar voicing categories with similar boundary locations — commonalities in processing that are markedly absent in their parents (see Aslin et al., 1983, for a summary of this work).

Given the diversity in the phonologies of human languages and the similarities in the earliest representations of speech by infants, it must be the case that the initial processing characteristics of the infant come to be modulated by experience with the parental language. Werker and Tees (1984) have recently begun to map the course of this development for certain phonetic contrasts (see also Best, McRoberts, & Sithole, 1988). They showed that infants born into English-speaking families in western Canada could discriminate phonetic contrasts that were present in Hindi and Salish but not in English at 6 months of age, but that this ability diminished in the next two months and was very nearly gone by 12 months of age. Nor is it just phonetic information that appears to be modulated by experience with the parental language. Hirsh-Pasek, Kemler Nelson, Jusczyk, Wright, Druss, and Kennedy (1987) found that 6-month-old American infants are sensitive to acoustic markers of clauses for English sentences. However, subsequent studies (Jusczyk, Kemler Nelson, Hirsh-Pasek, Kennedy, & Schomberg, forthcoming) indicate that American infants are sensitive to acoustic markers of clauses in other languages, such as Polish, at 4½ months, but not at 6 months of age. But even this surprisingly early influence of experience may not mark the beginnings of the role of language on perception: Mehler, Jusczyk, Lambertz, Halsted, Bertoncini, & Amiel-Tison (1988) have shown that neonates prefer to listen to the speech of the parental as opposed to a non-parental language. In sum, a neurophysiology of speech must reflect both the constraints of genetics and the consequences of very early learning.

2. Biological underpinnings of speech perception

Attempts to explain perceptual phenomena by recourse to neurophysiological mechanisms are characteristic in all domains of perceptual research. However, the search for the neurophysiological bases for speech perception poses some interesting problems beyond those found in other sensory domains. For example, an important method for investigating the neurophysiological bases of sensory systems is the collection of anatomical and physiological data from animals. The neuronal responses of animals exposed to various types of stimuli serve as models for the response of the human nervous system to the same types of stimuli. For example, in the case of the visual system's response to such properties as shape, size, and color, an animal model is quite reasonable inasmuch as the animals involved are known to respond to these properties in much the same way as do humans.

Human language as conveyed by speech, however, may occupy a unique place in terms of its complexity, especially when compared to communicative systems in other species. Hence, it is difficult to know at what level one can reasonably extrapolate from neurophysiological responses of animals to speech to the presumed mechanisms that serve speech perception in humans. Furthermore, if there is a special language module involved in processing speech sounds, as some have suggested (e.g., Fodor, 1983; Liberman & Mattingly, 1985), then it is questionable whether detailed descriptions of the neurophysiological responses of animals will ever elucidate the mechanisms underlying human perception.

With these caveats in mind, we note that data collected from animals, both behavioral and neurophysiological, have played (and will undoubtedly continue to play) an important part in the effort to understand the biological bases for speech perception. Another important source of information, primarily from the study of brain-damaged patients, concerns the cerebral specialization for speech processing. In what follows, we review pertinent findings in these areas and point out connections between these findings and the three basic characteristics of speech perception we have reviewed.

2.1. Perception of species-specific calls by animals

Animal communication systems are acknowledged to be considerably simpler and less flexible than human languages. Nevertheless, once we turn our attention to issues concerning the way in which signals within such communication systems are recognized, it is clear that a number of the same issues arise that are encountered in the study of human speech perception (e.g., perceptual constancy across different individuals, segmentation of signals, relations between perception and production). In addition, investigations of the development of such species-specific communication systems afford an opportunity to explore the impact of experience on the underlying perceptual mechanisms. In particular, opportunities are available to perform the kinds of developmental interventions that are not permissible with human listeners.

Primate vocalizations are among the most sophisticated systems of communication observed in animals. Recent research on vocal perception in monkeys suggests a number of interesting parallels with human speech perception (e.g., see the papers in Snowden, Brown, & Petersen, 1982). In addition to providing information about motivational and emotional states, it has been shown that such vocalizations serve rudimentary semantic functions (e.g., Cheney & Seyfarth, 1982; Seyfarth, Cheney, & Marler, 1980a,b). For example, vervet monkeys respond to different calls with different behaviors. When hearing a snake call, a vervet will stand up and look down at the ground around it, whereas upon hearing a leopard call it will take to the trees. An eagle call evokes visual search of the sky above. Thus, monkey calls are like human speech sounds in that they not only carry information about such paralinguistic features as the sex, age, and emotional state of the individual, but also contain semantic-like information about the environment, an individual's future intentions and the like. In some species, such as the Japanese macaque, a vocal repertoire of more than 80 distinctive calls (some forming distinct categories, others variants within a category) has been noted (Green, 1975).

The wide variety of distinctive calls observed in certain monkey species raises questions concerning the relevant acoustic cues that are used to distinguish these calls and the ways in which such cues are perceived. An interesting series of studies has been conducted by Petersen and his colleagues (Beecher, Petersen, Zoloth, Moody, & Stebbins, 1979; Petersen, Beecher, Zoloth, Green, Marler, Moody, & Stebbins, 1984; Petersen, Beecher, Zoloth, Moody, & Stebbins, 1978; Zoloth, Petersen, Beecher, Green, Marler, Moody, & Stebbins, 1979). Much of their work centered on the perception of two types of calls produced by Japanese macaques. The calls studied were the smooth early high (SE) and the smooth late high (SL) coos. These calls had been distinguished by Green (1975) on the basis of their function and acoustic structure. Both calls are highly tonal, frequency-modulated (FM) signals. They are distinguished according to where the FM segment is located in the signal: for SEs, the FM segment occurs within the first two-thirds of the call, whereas for SLs, it occurs during the last third. However, there is considerable variation in the precise location of the FM segment, both across and within individual monkeys. In addition, the calls used as tokens varied in duration and extent of modulation, and were selected with fundamental frequencies that gave cues for perceptual classification in direct conflict with those provided by placement of the FM segment. Hence, in order to correctly identify a particular call, the monkeys must be able to normalize this variability to extract a constant percept.

Zoloth et al. (1979; and see Petersen, 1982) demonstrated that the monkeys do indeed display perceptual constancy of the sort observed for human speech. Several Japanese macaques were trained to perform a response to a single token from each call class. Then their ability to generalize to novel instances of the calls uttered by different individuals (some adult and some young) was measured by progressively enlarging the number of SEs and SLs that they were required to discriminate. The Japanese macaques responded correctly to the new tokens almost immediately. By comparison, monkeys who were not Japanese macaques required extensive training before they mastered the discrimination. This result suggested that the Japanese macaques were biologically prepared to attend to the FM segment in the face of distracting variation in fundamental frequency, whereas the comparison group of other monkey species was not.

Additional research in this area suggests further parallels between the way monkey calls and human speech sounds are processed. Petersen et al. (1984) showed that although comparison monkeys eventually learn to attend to the temporal location of the FM portion of the SE and SL calls, they appear to be using different neural processing mechanisms than do the Japanese macaques. In particular, tests for laterality revealed that only the Japanese macaques displayed a significant right ear advantage for processing the calls; the comparison group exhibited no significant ear advantage. This finding of a significant right ear advantage for processing species-specific calls seems analogous to the right ear advantage in humans often noted for speech stimuli (see section 2.4), which is taken as evidence for a left-hemisphere specialization for speech processing (e.g., Bradshaw & Nettleton, 1981; Studdert-Kennedy & Shankweiler, 1970; and see Petersen & Jusczyk, 1984, for further discussion of the animal–human parallels).

Primates are an obvious choice for investigating possible parallels in the development of perceptual systems for species-specific calls. However, data concerning the development of vocal call perception in primates are sparse. In contrast, numerous developmental studies have been undertaken with another group of animals that depend heavily on vocal communication, namely, birds. Studies in this area have not only focused on how environmental input impacts upon the perceptual system, but have examined links between perception and production.

In the perceptual domain a number of the earliest studies inferred characteristics about the development of the underlying mechanisms by assessing the effects of various types of sensory intervention on vocal output (e.g., Konishi & Nottebohm, 1969; Marler, 1970, 1984; Marler & Waser, 1977). These studies showed that perceptual input was necessary for certain species to produce the subtle acoustic patterns that are characteristic of the species-typical song pattern. Thus, when the young were raised with no opportunity to hear normal adult song of their species, sparrows developed abnormal song (Marler & Sherman, 1985). If they were deafened before singing had fully matured, the acoustic character of the mature species-typical song pattern was aberrant (e.g., Konishi, 1965a,b; Marler & Sherman, 1983). Other research in this area has explored the ability of birds raised in isolation to pick out the song patterns characteristic of their own species. It has been observed that during the critical period for song learning, if sparrows are given a choice of two recorded songs, one of their own species and the other of a different species from the same habitat, they will learn the appropriate song (Konishi, 1978; Marler & Peters, 1988, 1989). If presented with tape recordings of the alien song only, they reject them and produce the innate song of an untrained social isolate (Marler, 1970). However, if forced, by use of live avian tutors, songs of other species can be learned and reproduced (Baptista & Petrinovich, 1984, 1986). This demonstrates that sparrows have the motor ability to reproduce the songs of other species, even though they favor their own species song if given a choice. As to the underlying basis of the link between production and perception, Williams and Nottebohm (1985) recently reported intriguing evidence that motor neurons responsible in part for song production in the male zebra finch are also selectively tuned to sound patterns.

More detailed explorations of the basis of song learning have been undertaken recently by examining the responses of birds to various systematic manipulations of song patterns. Marler & Peters (1977, 1988, 1989) investigated the response of song sparrows and swamp sparrows to different aspects of song structure. The conclusion they drew is that the innate mechanisms that control learning in the two species are quite different. The swamp sparrow appears to possess a highly selective innate template for learning tuned only to song phonology, whereas the song sparrow is tuned to both phonology and syntax (Marler & Peters, 1988, 1989). Additional data from a study conducted by Dooling and Searcy (1980) suggest that the selectivity that is observed for swamp sparrow learning includes a strong perceptual component and is not solely a motor phenomenon. At 20 days of age, well before singing begins, swamp sparrows give evidence of discriminating their conspecific songs from those of other species. This particular finding that the birds are able to discriminate between different songs long before they begin to produce them is reminiscent of findings with human infants who give evidence of discriminating speech contrasts long before they produce them (see section 1.3).

Another interesting parallel from studies of young birds comes from the research of Gottlieb (1981) with Peking ducks and wood ducks. He found that ducklings only retained their normal innate responsiveness to the species-specific maternal call if they received exposure as an embryo to specific acoustic features of that call. The possibility that prenatal exposure to characteristics of the maternal vocalizations may play a role in shaping the later preferences of the young in a species has also received some consideration in recent studies of human infants. DeCasper and Spence (1986) reported that newborn infants prefer a story that was read aloud by their mothers during pregnancy to an unfamiliar story. Moreover, as noted earlier, Mehler et al. (1988) have reported that newborn infants prefer to listen to utterances in the parental language as opposed to ones in a foreign language.

The studies of song learning in birds are illustrative of what Gould and Marler (1987) have termed an innately guided learning process — the notion that many organisms are 'preprogrammed' by information in their genetic make-up to learn particular things and to learn them in particular ways. Given the remarkable abilities of human infants to process speech (see section 1.3), it also appears that speech perception might be a likely candidate for innately guided learning (see Jusczyk & Bertoncini, 1988). Hence, despite the vast differences that exist between birds and humans, similar forces may be at work in the way in which perceptual categories develop. Thus, efforts to understand a less complex system of communication such as birdsong may furnish insights into the way in which human speech perception develops.

2.2. Perception of speech by animals

One strategy for delimiting the mechanisms underlying speech processing has been to study whether non-human species are capable of perceiving the same sorts of distinctions as human listeners do, and in the same manner. The aim in selecting subjects who are presumably incapable of phonetic perception is to determine which aspects of speech perception can be accomplished by recourse to general auditory processing mechanisms (see Kuhl, 1986, for further discussion of this point). The basic idea is to provide an account of at least the earliest stages of speech perception in terms of the simplest and most general set of mechanisms possible and to avoid postulating special speech-processing mechanisms unless absolutely necessary.

The phenomenon that has received the most attention with respect to this strategy is that of categorical perception, discussed in section 1.2 (e.g., Kuhl & Miller, 1975; Kuhl & Padden, 1982; Morse & Snowden, 1975; Waters & Wilson, 1976). Many of the animal studies have focused on the voicing contrast, specified by VOT. This contrast was of interest because it has been suggested that perception of voicing differences may be mediated by general auditory mechanisms that are sensitive to the temporal order of acoustic events (e.g., Miller, Wier, Pastore, Kelly, & Dooling, 1976; Pisoni, 1977; but see Lisker, 1978; Summerfield, 1982). If so, then non-human animals might show evidence of perceiving the voicing contrasts in a manner similar to humans.

Kuhl and Miller (1975) investigated this possibility by examining the ability of chinchillas to perceive the voicing contrast that occurs between syllables such as /da/ and /ta/. They found evidence of a perceptual boundary at 33.3 ms VOT, a locus that agrees well with that noted for human listeners (35.2 ms). Moreover, Kuhl (1981) reported that the chinchillas were particularly able to discriminate fine differences in VOT in the region of the phonetic boundary. This finding of a peak in discriminability that corresponds to the location of the category boundary satisfies the criteria typically given for categorical perception (Studdert-Kennedy, Liberman, Harris, & Cooper, 1970).

Further parallels in the way in which humans and chinchillas perceive VOT differences were noted in a later study (Kuhl & Miller, 1978) wherein the VOT boundary shifted depending on the place of articulation value of the initial consonant. Thus, for the chinchillas the VOT boundaries for /ba/–/pa/ and /ga/–/ka/ continua were at 23.3 and 42.5 ms, respectively. These values did not differ significantly from those reported for human listeners. This finding of shifts in the location of the VOT boundary with changes in the context (in this case, place of articulation) is reminiscent of the types of context effects noted in section 1.1. It suggests that in some cases such effects may be a consequence of the way in which the mammalian auditory system processes complex acoustic signals.

A second phonetic contrast to receive attention in the animal studies on categorical perception is that of place of articulation. This contrast has been of particular interest because place differences seem to have no easily identifiable, invariant acoustic correlates corresponding to each place value (e.g., Liberman et al., 1967; but see Stevens & Blumstein, 1981). Working with monkeys, Kuhl and Padden (1983) found evidence for peaks of discriminability in the phonetic category boundary regions for a /bæ/–/dæ/–/gæ/ continuum, suggesting that they might have categorical perception for this series. Morse and Snowden (1975) also found some evidence that monkeys perceived place of articulation differences categorically; however, their data also indicated that the monkeys did make significant within-category distinctions. Moreover, Sinnott, Beecher, Moody and Stebbins (1976) found that humans discriminated between-category stimuli with shorter response latencies than they did within-category stimuli, but Old World monkeys showed no such effects. Thus, at the present time, one cannot give a definitive answer to the question of whether non-human species perceive place of articulation differences in a manner similar to humans.

In light of the mixed results observed for monkeys' perception of place of articulation differences, the results of a recent study with Japanese quail are particularly interesting. Kluender, Diehl, and Killeen (1987) reported that they were able to teach these birds, albeit only after several thousand trials, to correctly categorize syllables containing /b/, /d/ and /g/ in different vowel contexts. As noted earlier, there appears to be no simple acoustic features or patterns of features that distinguish these phonetic segments across vowel contexts. Nevertheless, the quail were somehow able to solve the invariance problem and arrive at the desired classification of the syllables. Kluender et al. concluded that "a theory of human phonetic categorization may need to be no more (and no less) complex than required to explain the behavior of these quail."

Although Kluender et al. have drawn a reasonable conclusion from their data, it must be borne in mind that the data do not show that the mechanisms by which humans and quail classify speech sounds are necessarily the same or even similar. In principle, there are many different ways to arrive at the same classification of a set of objects. Hence, the fact that the animals can achieve the same classification does not prove that they used the same means to do so as humans (for further discussion of this point see Jusczyk, 1986). As with any model of human behavior, how convincing an animal model of human speech perception is depends, in part, on the degree to which it is able to reproduce the finer points of behavior, including the errors that are made. In this sense, the differences that Sinnott et al. (1976) found between response latency patterns of humans and monkeys may be quite telling. Thus, despite the inherent limitations in using animal models, studies showing similarities and differences in the way animals perceive human speech sounds furnish useful information with respect to the mechanisms that may underlie some important speech perception phenomena.

2.3. Speech processing in the peripheral auditory system

A necessary step in understanding the nature of the mechanisms underlying speech perception is to determine what information from the speech signal is transduced and encoded by the nervous system. In particular, information about the precision with which the characteristics of the acoustic signal are registered by the auditory system helps to determine the plausible set of mechanisms that could play a role in speech processing. For example, if it could be shown that, at some level, the nervous system provides a common representation for the same speech sound uttered by different talkers, we would be considerably closer to an explanation for the basis of perceptual normalization.

Much of the information that we have about the possible neural encoding of speech signals comes from electrophysiological recordings made with animals. There is general agreement that at the level of the cochlea and the auditory nerve there is little difference in anatomy, physiology and, to some extent, psychoacoustic behavior among the mammals tested (e.g., Smoorenburg, 1987). Moreover, it appears that signal coding at peripheral levels of the mammalian auditory system is basically a process of separating stimuli into their frequency components. Consequently, animals might serve as a useful model for how speech information is represented at the periphery. A number of different coding schemes have been suggested. These schemes tend to fall into two broad categories: rate-place models and temporal pattern models.

Rate-place models (e.g., Evans, 1978; Kiang & Moxon, 1974; Sachs & Young, 1979) represent the spectral energy of sounds in terms of the neural discharge rate as a function of place along the basilar membrane. Neural fibers along the basilar membrane are said to be tuned in the sense that they have a characteristic frequency to which they show the greatest discharge rate. Fibers with characteristic frequencies that are near peaks in the spectrum of an incoming sound fire at higher discharge rates than do those fibers whose characteristic frequencies are between the peaks (Hashimoto, Katayama, Murata, & Taniguchi, 1975).

Temporal pattern models (Delgutte & Kiang, 1984; Young & Sachs, 1979) represent the stimulus spectrum in the fine-time patterns of spike activity in single neurons. The temporal coding comes about because the neural discharges are synchronized (or "phase-locked") to frequency components of the stimulus (Delgutte, 1986). Some of the temporal models (temporal-place models) constrain the processing of discharge patterns to fibers from within the same characteristic frequency regions on the basilar membrane (e.g., Srulowicz & Goldstein, 1983; Young & Sachs, 1979). Other models (temporal non-place models) combine timing cues of fibers with different characteristic frequencies (e.g., Carlson, Fant, & Granstrom, 1975; Delgutte, 1984). Both types of temporal pattern models differ from the rate-place models in that they depend strongly on the variations in the probability of discharge within intervals of 5–20 ms.

Both rate-place and temporal pattern models are able to provide adequate representations of certain types of speech information. However, as currently formulated, both types of models have serious limitations. The chief problem for rate-place models is the limited dynamic range of the neuronal response. The range from spontaneous firing rate to maximal firing rate of most auditory nerve fibers is between 30 and 50 dB, with the discharge thresholds restricted to a low-level range of about 30 dB SPL (Smoorenburg, 1987). This suggests that the discharge rates of most fibers will be saturated at stimulus levels of about 70 dB SPL, resulting in a loss of detailed spectral information for high sound levels that might well be necessary for the identification of certain vowels. In addition, the presence of background noise tends to flatten out the rate profiles of these fibers (Delgutte & Kiang, 1984; Sachs, Voigt, & Young, 1983). Nevertheless, it is possible that the auditory system is able to overcome these problems. Palmer and Evans (1979) noted the existence of a small population of fibers with dynamic ranges in excess of 50 dB, and Liberman (1978) noted an even smaller group with thresholds up to 80 dB SPL. Both types of fibers have low spontaneous discharge rates and may convey sufficiently detailed spectral information up to the highest stimulus levels (Delgutte, 1987; Smoorenburg, 1987).

The major obstacle for temporal pattern models is that they do not provide an adequate spectral representation for all classes of speech sounds. In particular, temporal coding schemes are not effective for sounds that have intense high-frequency components, such as fricatives and the bursts of stop consonants (Delgutte & Kiang, 1984). Moreover, data from cochlear implant patients appear to present problems for a model based purely on temporal patterning. Although the timing acuity of neural discharges in these patients is not below normal, frequency discrimination in these patients is about an order of magnitude worse than normal (Smoorenburg, 1987). At the current time, then, there is considerable lack of agreement about the nature of neural coding during the early stages of processing in the peripheral auditory system. It is of interest to note that despite this disagreement, there have been attempts to use auditory models as "front ends" of speech recognition devices. For example, Blomberg, Carlson, Elenius, and Granstrom (1986) studied several different auditory models, including one that employed a temporal pattern analysis routine. They found that auditory models did not always lead to a higher recognition rate than traditional speech analysis techniques such as those based on spectrographic analysis. Other critics (e.g., Delgutte, 1986; Kiang, 1986) have suggested that auditory models will not be feasible until much more is known about the central as well as peripheral auditory processing of speech sounds.

2.4. Speech processing in the central auditory system

Research on speech processing by the central auditory system is only in its early stages. What data exist come largely from studies of brain-damaged populations and thus raise questions about the extent to which the data gathered are indicative of normal processing. In addition, the use of animals to model central auditory processing of speech in humans poses some obvious difficulties, as noted earlier. Nevertheless, interesting findings have emerged.

One important issue in understanding the way in which the auditory system processes speech sounds is the extent to which the representation of the stimulus information is sharpened by the central nervous system. In the first central auditory processing center, the cochlear nucleus, the homogeneous population of neurons found in the peripheral system gives way to at least five separate systems of neurons operating in parallel (Cant & Morest, 1984; Warr, 1982). Young (1987) has pointed out that the subsystems making up the cochlear nucleus are sufficiently different to suggest that each is specialized to perform particular tasks in auditory processing. He cites as an example the way in which two of these subsystems, bushy cells and stellate cells, are well adapted to serve different aspects of auditory functioning.[3]

---

[3]Neuroanatomical separation of different types of auditory processing has been noted in other cases. For example, Knudsen & Konishi (1978) showed that processing sites for sound frequency and for location of the sound source in space, in the midbrain auditory area (MLD) of the barn owl (*Tyto alba*), are anatomically separated in a tonotopic region and a space-mapped region.

Bushy cells have small dendritic trees with few, if any, terminals and they appear to receive powerful input from a small number of auditory nerve fibers. The morphological and physiological characteristics of these cells suggest that they are designed to transmit precise temporal information to the principal cell groups in the superior olive, where comparisons of interaural arrival time are made (Caird and Klinke, 1983; Goldberg & Brown, 1969; Guinan, Guinan, & Norris, 1972). In contrast, stellate cells have long dendritic trees, they receive and integrate small inputs from many different auditory nerve fibers and produce a very regular discharge. Although the characteristics of these cells have not been fully explored, there is some suggestion that they may produce an improved rate-place representation of the spectra of complex stimuli (Young, 1987). Thus, by integrating information from high and low spontaneous rate fibers, the stellate cells may be able to provide a rate-place representation of vowel spectra that is stable over a wide range of sound levels.

Studies with brain-damaged subject populations have also been undertaken to delineate the locus of brain structures involved in speech processing. Over the years, dichotic listening experiments with normal subjects have suggested that different brain regions may be involved in different aspects of speech perception. For example, it is well known that most normal listeners show a right ear advantage (implying left-hemisphere processing) for stop consonants, but little if any advantage for vowel sounds (Shankweiler & Studdert-Kennedy, 1967; Studdert-Kennedy & Shankweiler, 1970; see also Bradshaw & Nettleton, 1981, for a recent review). However, such studies with normals can at best provide a gross estimate, in terms of the left or right hemisphere, of the possible locus of mechanisms involved in speech processing. Tests of patient populations with well-defined lesions would appear to be one means of providing more precise information about the possible locus of mechanisms involved in speech processing.

Unfortunately, the data available from those studies which have classified subjects according to lesion type do not provide a very consistent picture. Blumstein and her colleagues (Blumstein, 1981; Blumstein, Baker, & Goodglass, 1977; Blumstein, Cooper, Zurif, & Caramazza, 1977) explored the perception of place of articulation and voicing contrasts in several different patient populations including Broca's, Wernicke's, and conduction aphasics. Despite prior contentions that phonetic perception disorders underlie comprehension difficulties for Wernicke's aphasics (e.g., Luria, 1970), Blumstein and her colleagues did not find that this group was significantly impaired compared to the other patient populations. However, what is worse from the standpoint of pinpointing the mechanisms underlying speech perception is the fact that there were substantial individual differences among patients having the same type of disorder. Thus, although some patients of a particular type did show impaired performance on identification and discrimination tests, other patients with the same disorder performed the tasks normally.

Blumstein et al. (1977) also gathered data from brain-damaged subjects that bear on another important issue in speech perception, viz. the possible links between perception and production. Hence, they investigated whether patients with deficits in segmental perception might also show concurrent deficits in segmental production. In particular, they examined how the perception of voicing differences related to the production of voicing differences in a group of aphasic patients. They found that normal perception did not necessarily lead to normal production, nor did deficits in perception relate to the type or severity of the production errors. Blumstein et al. concluded that the perceptual and productive systems in adults are at least partially autonomous.

At first glance, the results that Blumstein et al. (1977) obtained concerning the relation between perception and production appear to conflict with findings reported with other methods. In particular, Lassen, Ingvar, and Skinhoj (1978) conducted a study using brain blood flow measures. In line with claims that patients with Wernicke's aphasia have an underlying speech perception deficit, Lassen et al. found that when subjects listened passively to speech, the greatest changes in blood flow were produced in Wernicke's area. The suggestion is that Wernicke's area is the primary area for speech perception. However, it should be noted that Lassen et al. did not explicitly measure segmental perception per se. Hence, the apparent discrepancy between their findings and those of Blumstein et al. may be attributable to the fact that more global aspects of comprehension involving the establishment of sound-meaning correspondences may be occurring in Wernicke's area.

Intriguing suggestions about possible links between the underlying mechanisms of perception and production come from studies involving the electrical stimulation of the cortex. This particular procedure was first used to localize language functions in patient populations by Penfield and his associates (Penfield & Jasper, 1954; Penfield & Roberts, 1959). More recently, Ojemann (1983) has reported results with this technique that suggest links between cortical sites affecting the perception and production of speech sounds (but see Frazier, 1983, and Studdert-Kennedy, 1983). In particular, Ojemann found that stimulation of certain sites in the frontal, temporal, and parietal pre-Sylvian cortex was implicated in both the production of orofacial movements and phoneme identification. Thus, stimulation of these areas not only disrupted facial mimicry, but also evoked errors in phoneme identification. Ojemann argued that these results suggest the existence of a cortical area that has the common properties of speech perception and the generation of motor output (cf. Williams & Nottebohm, 1985, section 2.1), and noted that this type of finding fits well with the assumptions of the motor theory of speech perception, as formulated by Liberman and his colleagues (Liberman & Mattingly, 1985).

3. Concluding remarks

From our discussion, it is apparent that a neurobiology of speech perception remains as yet a hope for the future — but, we believe, not an unreasonable one.

One reason for our optimism is that there is now considerable knowledge about the basic phenomena involved in the perception of speech. As we illustrated in our review, we now know many of the conditions under which the listener is able to obtain perceptual constancy, despite the lack of isomorphism between acoustic and phonetic levels of language. In effect, we know that it is the perceptual mechanisms that must provide the equivalence in perception, owing to the absence of invariance in the environment. We also know that the representation of the speech signal is multi-grained, containing information about acoustic–phonetic detail as well as more abstract information about phonetic category identity. Furthermore, we have learned that the mechanisms of perception are innately organized and functional very early in life, while also extremely sensitive to the properties of the parental language, as early as the first few days of life. We are also moving closer to understanding how such abilities develop in the course of acquiring the native language.

And our knowledge of speech perception goes considerably beyond the three characteristics that provided the focus for our review. To take just one example, there is now evidence that although segmental perception can be influenced by higher levels of language processing, most notably those involved in lexical access (e.g., Ganong, 1980), under certain conditions no such influence is seen (e.g., Fox, 1984; Miller & Dexter, 1988). At least to some extent, then, the mechanisms underlying speech perception operate as an autonomous system, or module (cf. Liberman & Mattingly, 1985). Thus we have, or so we believe, a reasonably detailed functional description, a necessary condition for pursuing a neurophysiological account.

A second reason for our optimism is that, as our review shows, hints about possible underlying mechanisms seem to be forthcoming from a variety of sources. There is currently much effort devoted to understanding how the peripheral auditory systems of animals process complex sounds and, given the apparent close correspondence across mammalian auditory systems at the periphery, this research should shed light on at least the earliest stages of speech processing by humans. In quite a different way, the success of neurophysiology in explicating the operation of specialized perceptual systems in non-human species, communicative and otherwise, is encouraging. For example, the research on birdsong has revealed much about how precise types of early experience influence song learning, and has begun to uncover the physiological bases of perceptual learning and the relation between perception and production. And we can point to the remarkable progress by Konishi and his colleagues in mapping the physiological mechanisms responsible for the specialized function of source localization in owls (e.g., Takahashi & Konishi, 1986). To the extent that speech perception is also accomplished by a specialized system, as some have argued (e.g., Liberman & Mattingly, 1985), the animal findings may provide important guiding analogies. We also note that although progress in specifying the locus of speech perception in the human brain has been slow, new techniques of brain imaging, which have already provided useful results in other areas of cognitive processing (Posner, Petersen, Fox, & Raichle, 1988), hold promise for the study of speech.

Finally, new developments in formal modeling may provide useful constraints in our research for the biological basis of speech perception. For example, working within a connectionist framework, McClelland and Elman (1986) have provided simulations of many speech perception phenomena, including the kind of context-dependent processing that is so pervasive in speech. It should be noted, however, that these models, while neurologically inspired at an abstract level (e.g., they involve massively parallel processing), do not take account in a detailed way of known properties of neural structure and function (cf. Changeux & Dehaene, this issue). There is, however, another class of model, recently developed by Edelman and his colleagues (Edelman, 1987), that is more firmly grounded in neurophysiological principles. Interestingly, a major goal of the latter models has been to show how the brain might be able to learn to categorize objects in the world without direct tuition, despite inherent variability in the environment. As we have seen in our review, categorization is basic to recovering the phonetic structure of an utterance, and a solution to the categorization problem would constitute a major step toward a neurobiological description of speech perception.

References

Aslin, R.N., Pisoni, D.B., & Jusczyk, P.W. (1983). Auditory development and speech perception in infancy. In M.M. Haith & J.J. Campos (Eds.), *Infancy and the biology of development. Vol. 2 of Carmichael's manual of child psychology* (4th edn.). New York: Wiley.

Baptista, L.F., & Petrinovich, L. (1984). Social interaction, sensitive phases, and the song template hypothesis in the white-crowned sparrow. *Animal Behavior, 32,* 172–181.

Baptista, L.F., & Petrinovich, L. (1986). Song development in the white-crowned sparrow: Social factors and sex differences. *Animal Behavior, 34,* 1359–1371.

Beecher, M., Petersen, M., Zoloth, S., Moody, D., & Stebbins, W. (1979). Perception of conspecific vocalizations by Japenese monkeys (*Macaca fuscata*). *Brain Behavior, 16,* 443–460.

Best, C.T., McRoberts, G.W., & Sithole, N.M. (1988). Examination of perceptual reorganization for nonnative speech contrasts: Zulu click discrimination by English-speaking adults and infants. *Journal of Experimental Psychology: Human Perception and Performance, 14,* 345–360.

Blomberg, M., Carlson, R., Elenius, K., & Granstrom, B. (1986). Auditory models as front ends in speech recognition systems. In J.S. Perkell & D.H. Klatt (Eds.), *Invariance and variability in speech processes.* Hillsdale, NJ: Erlbaum.

Blumstein, S.E. (1981). Perception of speech in aphasia: Its relation to language comprehension, auditory processing, and speech production. In T. Myers, J. Laver, & J. Anderson (Eds.), *The cognitive representation of speech* (pp. 245–253). Amsterdam: North-Holland.

Blumstein, S.E., Baker, E., & Goodglass, H. (1977). Phonological factors in auditory comprehension in aphasia. *Neuropsychologia, 15,* 19–30.

Blumstein, S.E., Cooper, W.E., Zurif, E., & Caramazza, A. (1977). The perception and production of voice-onset-time in aphasia. *Neuropsychologia, 15,* 371–384.

Bradshaw, J., & Nettleton, N. (1981). The nature of hemispheric specialization in man. *Behavioral and Brain Sciences, 4,* 51–91.

Caird, D., & Klinke, R. (1983). Cat superior olivary complex (SOC): The basis of biaural information processing. In R. Klinke and R. Hartmann (Eds.), *Hearing: Physiological bases and psychophysics* (pp. 216–223). Berlin: Springer-Verlag.

Cant, N.B., & Morest, D.K. (1984). The structural basis for stimulus coding in the cochlear nucleus of the cat. *Neuroscience, 4,* 1909–1923.

Carlson, R., Fant, G., & Granstrom, B. (1975). Two-formant models: Pitch and vowel perception. In G. Fant & M.A.A. Tatham (Eds.), *Auditory analysis and perception of speech* (pp. 55–82). London: Academic Press.

Cheney, D., & Seyfarth, R. (1982). How vervet monkeys perceive their grunts: Field playback experiments. *Animal Behavior, 30,* 739–751.

DeCasper, A.J., & Spence, M.J. (1986). Prenatal maternal speech influences newborns' perception of speech sounds. *Infant Behavior and Development, 9,* 133–150.

Delgutte, B. (1984). Speech coding in the auditory nerve II: Processing schemes for vowel-like sounds. *Journal of the Acoustical Society of America, 75,* 866–878.

Delgutte, B. (1986). Comment on a paper by D.H. Klatt. In J. Perkell & D.H. Klatt (Eds.), *Invariance and variability in speech processes* (pp. 320–322). Hillsdale, NJ: Erlbaum.

Delgutte, B. (1987). Peripheral auditory processing of speech information: Implications from a physiological study of intensity discrimination. In M.E.H. Schouten (Ed.), *The psychophysics of speech perception* (pp. 333–353). Dordrecht: Nijhoff.

Delgutte, B., & Kiang, N.Y.S. (1984). Speech coding in the auditory nerve: IV. Sounds with consonant-like dynamic characteristics. *Journal of the Acoustical Society of America, 75,* 897–907.

Dooling, R., & Searcy, M.A. (1980). Early perceptual selectivity in the swamp sparrow. *Developmental Psychobiology, 13,* 499–506.

Edelman, G. (1987). *Neural darwinism: The theory of neuronal group selection.* New York: Harper & Row.

Eimas, P.D. (1974). Auditory and linguistic processing of cues for place of articulation by infants. *Perception and Psychophysics, 16,* 513–521.

Eimas, P.D., & Miller, J.L. (1980). Contextual effects in infant speech perception. *Science, 209,* 1140–1141.

Eimas, P.D., Miller, J.L., & Jusczyk, P.W. (1987). On infant speech perception and the acquisition of language. In S. Harnad (Ed.), *Categorical perception* (pp. 161–195). New York: Cambridge University Press.

Evans, E.F. (1978). Place and time coding of frequency in the auditory system: Some physiological pros and cons. *Audiology, 77*, 369–420.

Fant, G. (1973). *Speech sounds and features.* Cambridge, MA: MIT Press.

Fitch, H.L., Halwes, T., Erickson, D.M., & Liberman, A.M. (1980). Perceptual equivalence of two acoustic cues for stop-consonant manner. *Perception and Psychophysics, 27*, 343–350.

Fodor, J.A. (1983). *The modularity of mind.* Cambridge, MA: MIT Press.

Fowler, C.A. (1986). An event approach to the study of speech perception from a direct-realist perspective. *Journal of Phonetics, 14*, 3–28.

Fox, R.A. (1984). Effects of lexical status on phonetic categorization. *Journal of Experimental Psychology: Human Perception and Performance, 10*, 526–540.

Frazier, L. (1983). Motor theory of speech perception or acoustic theory of speech production. *Behavioral and Brain Sciences, 6*, 213–214.

Ganong, W.F. (1980). Phonetic categorization in auditory word perception. *Journal of Experimental Psychology: Human Perception and Performance, 6*, 110–125.

Goldberg, J.M., & Brown, P.B. (1969). Response of biaural neurons of dog superior olivary complex to dichotic tonal stimuli: Some physiological mechanisms of sound localization. *Journal of Neurophysiology, 32*, 613–636.

Gottlieb, G. (1981). The roles of early experiences in species-specific perceptual development. In R.N. Aslin, J.R. Alberts, & M.R. Petersen (Eds.), *Development of perception: Psychobiological perspectives: Vol I, Audition, somatic perception, and the chemical senses.* New York: Academic Press.

Gould, J., & Marler, P. (1987). Learning by instinct. *Scientific American, 256*, 62–73.

Green, S. (1975). Communication by a graded vocal system in Japanese monkeys. In L.A. Rosenblum (Ed.), *Primate behavior. Vol. IV* (pp. 1–102). New York: Academic Press.

Guinan, J.J., Guinan, S.S., & Norris, B.E. (1972). Single auditory units in the superior olivary complex II: Locations of the unit categories and tonotopic organization. *International Neuroscience, 4*, 147–166.

Hashimoto, T., Katayama, Y., Murata, K., & Taniguchi, I. (1975). Pitch synchronous response of cat cochlear nerve fibers to speech sounds. *Japanese Journal of Physiology, 25*, 633.

Hirsh-Pasek, K., Kemler Nelson, D.G., Jusczyk, P.W., Wright, K., Druss, B., & Kennedy, L. (1987). Clauses are perceptual units for young infants. *Cognition, 26*, 269–286.

Jusczyk, P.W. (1986). Some further reflections on how speech perception develops. In J. Perkell & D.H. Klatt (Eds.), *Invariance and variability of speech processes* (pp. 33–35). Hillsdale, NJ: Erlbaum.

Jusczyk, P.W., & Bertoncini, J. (1988). Viewing the development of speech perception as an innately guided learning process. *Language and Speech, 31*, 217–238.

Jusczyk, P.W., Kemler Nelson, D.G., Hirsh-Pasek, K., Kennedy, L.J. & Schomberg, A. (forthcoming). Young infants' perception of acoustic correlates of clausal units in English and in Polish.

Katz, J., & Jusczyk, P.W. (1980). *Do six-month-olds have perceptual constancy for phonetic segments?* Paper presented at the International Conference on Infant Studies, New Haven, CT.

Kiang, N.Y.S. (1986). Comments on paper by Blomberg, Carlson, Elenius, and Granstrom. In J.S. Perkell & D.H. Klatt (Eds.), *Invariance and variability of speech processes* (p. 122). Hillsdale, NJ: Erlbaum.

Kiang, N.Y.S., & Moxon, E.C. (1974). Tails of tuning curves of auditory-nerve fibers. *Journal of the Acoustical Society of America, 55*, 620–630.

Kluender, K.R., Diehl, R.L., & Killeen, P.R. (1987). Japanese quail can learn phonetic categories. *Science, 237*, 1195–1197.

Knudsen, E.I., & Konishi, M. (1978). Space and frequency are represented separately in auditory midbrain of the owl. *Journal of Neurophysiology, 41*, 870–884.

Konishi, M. (1965a). Effects of deafening on song development in American robins and Black-headed grosbeaks. *Zeitschrift fur Tierpsychologie, 22*, 584–599.

Konishi, M. (1965b). The role of auditory feedback in the control of vocalization in the white-crowned sparrow. *Zeitschrift fur Tierpsychologie, 22*, 770–783.

Konishi, M. (1978). Ethological aspects of auditory pattern recognition. In R. Held, H.W. Liebowitz, & H.L. Teuber (Eds.), *Handbook of sensory physiology. Vol. VIII: Perception*. Berlin: Springer-Verlag.

Konishi, M., & Nottebohm, R. (1969). Experimental studies in the ontogeny of avian vocalizations. In R.A. Hinde (Ed.), *Bird Vocalizations* (pp. 29–48). London: Cambridge University Press.

Kuhl, P.K. (1980). Perceptual constancy for speech-sound categories in early infants. In G.H. Yeni-Komshian, J.F. Kavanagh, & C.A. Ferguson (Eds.), *Child phonology, Vol. 2: Perception* (pp. 41–66). New York: Academic Press.

Kuhl, P.K. (1981). Discrimination of speech by nonhuman animals: Basic auditory sensitivities conducive to the perception of speech-sound categories. *Journal of the Acoustical Society of America, 70*, 340–349.

Kuhl, P.K. (1985). Categorization of speech by infants. In J. Mehler & R. Fox (Eds.), *Neonate cognition: Beyond the blooming, buzzing confusion* (pp. 231–262). Hillsdale, NJ: Erlbaum.

Kuhl, P.K. (1986). Theoretical contribution of tests on animals to the special mechanisms debate in speech. *Experimental Biology, 45*, 233–265.

Kuhl, P.K., & Miller, J.D. (1975). Speech perception by the chinchilla: Voiced–voiceless distinction in alveolar plosive consonants. *Science, 190*, 69–72.

Kuhl, P.K., & Miller, J.D. (1978). Speech perception by the chinchilla: Identification functions for synthetic VOT stimuli. *Journal of the Acoustical Society of America, 63*, 905–917.

Kuhl, P.K., & Padden, D.M. (1982). Enhanced discriminability at the phonetic boundaries for the voicing feature in macaques. *Perception and Psychophysics, 32*, 542–550.

Kuhl, P.K., & Padden, D.M. (1983). Enhanced discriminability at the phonetic boundaries for place of articulation in macaques. *Journal of the Acoustical Society of America, 73*, 1003–1010.

Lassen, N.A., Ingvar, D.H., & Skinhoj, E. (1978). Brain function and blood flow. *Scientific American, 239*, 50–59.

Levitt, A., Jusczyk, P.W., Murray, J., & Carden, G. (1988). The perception of place of articulation contrasts in voiced and voiceless fricatives by two-month-old infants. *Journal of Experimental Psychology: Human Perception and Performance, 14*, 361–368.

Liberman, A.M., Cooper, F.S., Shankweiler, D.P., & Studdert-Kennedy, M. (1967). Perception of the speech code. *Psychological Review, 74*, 431–461.

Liberman, A.M., Harris, K.S., Hoffman, H.S., & Griffith, B.C. (1957). The discrimination of speech sounds within and across phoneme boundaries. *Journal of Experimental Psychology, 53*, 358–368.

Liberman, A.M., & Mattingly, I.G. (1985). The motor theory of speech perception revised. *Cognition, 21*, 1–36.

Liberman, M.C. (1978). Auditory nerve response from cats raised in a low noise chamber. *Journal of the Acoustical Society of America, 63*, 442–455.

Lisker, L. (1978). In qualified defense of VOT. *Language and Speech, 21*, 375–383.

Lisker, L. (1986). "Voicing" in English: A catalog of acoustic features signalling /b/ versus /p/ in trochees. *Language and Speech, 29*, 3–11.

Luria, A.R. (1970). *Traumatic aphasia*. The Hague: Mouton.

Mann, V.A., & Repp, B.H. (1980). Influence of vocalic context on perception of the [ʃ]–[s] distinction. *Perception and Psychophysics, 28*, 213–228.

Marler, P. (1970). A comparative approach to vocal learning: Song development in white-crowned sparrows. *Journal of Comparative and Physiological Psychology, 71*, 1–25.

Marler, P. (1984). Song learning: Innate species differences in the learning process. In P. Marler & H.S. Terrace (Eds.). *The biology of learning* (pp. 289–309). Berlin: Springer Verlag.

Marler, P., & Peters, S. (1977). Selective vocal learning in a sparrow. *Science, 198*, 519–521.

Marler, P., & Peters, S. (1988). The role of song phonology and syntax in vocal learning preferences in the song sparrow. *Melospiza melodia. Ethology, 77,* 125–149.

Marler, P., & Peters, S. (1989). Species differences in auditory responsiveness in early vocal learning. In S. Hulse & R. Dooling (Eds.). *The comparative psychology of audition: Perceiving complex sounds* (pp. 243–273). Hillsdale, NJ: Erlbaum.

Marler, P., & Sherman, V. (1983). Song structure without auditory feedback: Emandations of the auditory template hypothesis. *The Journal of Neuroscience, 3,* 517–531.

Marler, P., & Sherman, V. (1985). Innate differences in singing behaviour of sparrows reared in isolation from adult conspecific song. *Animal Behavior, 33,* 57–71.

Marler, P., & Waser, M. (1977). Role of feedback in canary song development. *Journal of Comparative and Physiological Psychology, 91,* 8–16.

McClelland, J.L., & Elman, J.L. (1986). The TRACE model of speech perception. *Cognitive Psychology, 18,* 1–86.

Mehler, J., Jusczyk, P.W., Lambertz, G., Halsted, N., Bertoncini, J., & Amiel-Tison, C. (1988). A precursor of language acquisition in young infants. *Cognition, 29,* 143–178.

Miller, J.D., Wier, L., Pastore, R., Kelly, W., & Dooling, R. (1976). Discrimination and labeling of noise-buzz sequences with varying noise-lead times: An example of categorical perception. *Journal of the Acoustical Society of America, 60,* 410–417.

Miller, J.L., & Dexter, E.R. (1988). Effects of speaking rate and lexical status on phonetic perception. *Journal of Experimental Psychology: Human Perception and Performance, 14,* 369–378.

Miller, J.L., & Eimas, P.D. (1983). Studies on the categorization of speech by infants. *Cognition, 13,* 135–165.

Miller, J.L., & Volaitis, L.E. (in press). Effect of speaking rate on the perceptual structure of a phonetic category. *Perception and Psychophysics.*

Morse, P.A., & Snowden, C.T. (1975). An investigation of categorical speech discrimination by rhesus monkeys. *Perception and Psychophysics, 17,* 9–16.

Ojemann, G. (1983). Brain organization for language from the perspective of electrical stimulation mapping. *Behavioral and Brain Sciences, 6,* 189–230.

Palmer, A.R., & Evans, E.F. (1979). On the peripheral coding of the level of individual frequency components of complex sounds at high sound levels. *Experimental Brain Research, Suppl. II,* 19–26.

Penfield, W., & Jasper, H. (1954). *Epilepsy and the functional anatomy of the human brain.* Boston: Little, Brown.

Penfield, W., & Roberts, L. (1959). *Speech and brain mechanisms.* Princeton, NJ: Princeton University Press.

Petersen, M. (1982). The perception of species-specific vocalizations by primates: A conceptual framework. In C. Snowden, C. Brown, & M. Peterson (Eds.). *Primate communication* (pp. 171–211). New York: Cambridge University Press.

Petersen, M., Beecher, M., Zoloth, S., Green, S., Marler, P.R., Moody, D.B., & Stebbins, W.C. (1984). Neural lateralization of vocalizations by Japanese macaques: Communicative significance is more important than acoustic structure. *Behavioral Neuroscience, 98,* 779–790.

Petersen, M., Beecher, M., Zoloth, S., Moody, D.B., & Stebbins, W.C. (1978). Neural lateralization of species-specific vocalizations by Japanese macaques (*Macaca fuscata*). *Science, 202,* 324–327.

Petersen, M.R., & Jusczyk, P.W. (1984). On perceptual predisposition for human speech and monkey vocalizations. In P. Marler & H.S. Terrace (Eds.), *The biology of learning* (pp. 585–616). New York: Springer-Verlag.

Pisoni, D.B. (1977). Identification and discrimination of the relative onset time of two-component tones: Implications for voicing perception in stops. *Journal of the Acoustical Society of America, 61,* 1352–1361.

Pisoni, D.B. (1981). *In defense of segmental representation in speech perception.* Research on speech perception: Progress Report No. 7, Bloomington: Indiana University.

Pisoni, D.B., & Tash, J. (1974). Reaction times to comparisons within and across phonetic categories. *Perception and Psychophysics*, *15*, 285–290.

Posner, M.I., Petersen, S.E., Fox, P.T., & Raichle, M.E. (1988). Localization of cognitive operations in the human brain. *Science*, *240*, 1627–1631.

Repp, B.H. (1982). Phonetic trading relations and context effects: New experimental evidence for a speech mode of perception. *Psychological Bulletin*, *92*, 81–110.

Repp, B.H. (1984). Categorical perception: Issues, methods, findings. In N.J. Lass (Ed.), *Speech and language: Advances in basic research and practice, Vol. 10*. New York: Academic Press.

Sachs, M.B., Voigt, H.F., & Young, E.D. (1983). Auditory nerve representation of vowels in background noise. *Journal of Neurophysiology*, *50*, 27–45.

Sachs, M.B., & Young, E.D. (1979). Encoding of steady state vowels in the discharge patterns of auditory-nerve fibers: Representation in terms of discharge rate. *Journal of the Acoustical Society of America*, *66*, 1381–1403.

Seyfarth, R., Cheney, D., & Marler, P. (1980a). Vervet monkey alarm calls: Semantic communication in a free-ranging primate. *Animal Behavior*, *28*, 1070–1094.

Seyfarth, R., Cheney, D., & Marler, P. (1980b). Monkey responses to three different alarm calls: Evidence of preditor classification and semantic communication. *Science*, *210*, 801–803.

Shankweiler, D., & Studdert-Kennedy, M. (1967). Identification of consonants and vowels presented to the left and right ears. *Quarterly Journal of Experimental Psychology*, *19*, 59–63.

Sinnott, J.M., Beecher, M.D., Moody, D.B., & Stebbins, W.C. (1976). Speech sound discrimination by monkeys and humans. *Journal of the Acoustical Society of America*, *60*, 687–695.

Smoorenburg, G.F. (1987). Discussion of the physiological correlates of speech perception. In M.E.H. Schouten (Ed.), *The psychophysics of speech perception* (pp. 393–399). Dordrecht: Nijhoff.

Snowden, C.T., Brown, C.H., & Petersen, M.R. (1982). *Primate communication*. New York: Cambridge University Press.

Srulowicz, P., & Goldstein, J.L. (1983). A central spectrum model: A synthesis of auditory nerve timing and place cues in monaural communication of frequency spectrum. *Journal of the Acoustical Society of America*, *73*, 1266–1276.

Stevens, K.N., & Blumstein, S.E. (1981). The search for invariant acoustic correlates of phonetic features. In P.D. Eimas & J.L. Miller (Eds.), *Perspectives on the study of speech* (pp. 1–38). Hillsdale, NJ: Erlbaum.

Studdert-Kennedy, M. (1983). Mapping speech: More analysis, less synthesis please. *Behavioral and Brain Sciences*, *6*, 218–219.

Studdert-Kennedy, M., Liberman, A.M., Harris, K.S., & Cooper, F.S. (1970). Motor theory of speech perception: A reply to Lane's critical review. *Psychological Review*, *77*, 234–249.

Studdert-Kennedy, M., & Shankweiler, D. (1970). Hemispheric specialization for speech perception. *Journal of the Acoustical Society of America*, *48*, 579–594.

Summerfield, Q. (1982). Differences between spectral dependencies in auditory and phonetic temporal processing: Relevance to the perception of voicing in initial stops. *Journal of the Acoustical Society of America*, *72*, 51–61.

Takahashi, T., & Konishi, M. (1986). Selectivity for interaural time difference in the owl's midbrain. *Journal of Neuroscience*, *6*, 3413–3422.

Warr, W.B. (1982). Parallel ascending pathways for lateral inhibition from the cochlear nucleus: Neuroanatomical evidence of functional specialization. *Contributions to Sensory Physiology*, *7*, 1–38.

Waters, R.S., & Wilson, W.A. (1976). Speech perception by rhesus monkeys: The voicing distinction in synthesized labial and velar stop consonants. *Perception and Psychophysics*. *19*, 285–289.

Werker, J.F., & Tees, R.C. (1984). Cross-language speech perception: Evidence for perceptual reorganization during the first year of life. *Infant Behavior and Development*, *7*, 49–63.

Williams, H., & Nottebohm, F. (1985). Auditory responses in avian vocal motor neurons: A motor theory for song perception in birds. *Science*, *229*, 279–282.

Yeni-Komshian, G.H., & Soli, S.D. (1981). Recognition of vowels from information in fricatives: Perceptual evidence of fricative-vowel coarticulation. *Journal of the Acoustical Society of America*, *70*, 966–975.

Young, E.D. (1987). Organization of the cochlear nucleus for information processing. In M.E.H. Schouten (Ed.), *The psychophysics of speech perception* (pp. 354–370). Dordrecht: Nijhoff.

Young, E.D., & Sachs, M.B. (1979). Representation of steady state vowels in the temporal aspects of the discharge patterns of populations of auditory-nerve fibers. *Journal of the Acoustical Society of America*, *66*, 1381–1403.

Zoloth, S., Petersen, M., Beecher, M., Green, S., Marler, P., Moody, D., & Stebbins, W. (1979). Species-specific perceptual processing of vocal sounds by Old World monkeys. *Science*, *204*, 870–873.

Résumé

L'une des capacités humaines les plus développées est la communication par la parole. Au cours des années, la recherche sur la perception de la parole a démontré que les humains sont bien adaptés à l'extraction d'informations linguistiques hautement codées à partir d'un signal vocal. La nature sophistiquée de ces capacités et leur apparence précoce au cours du développement suggèrent l'existence d'un riche substrat biologique permettant la perception de la parole. Dans le présent article, nous décrivons, quelques unes de ces importantes capacités et examinons des recherches dans différents domaines pouvant aider à éclaircir la nature de leurs fondements biologiques.

5

Perception and its neuronal mechanisms*

RICHARD HELD

Massachusetts Institute of Technology

Abstract

Held, R., 1989. Perception and its neuronal mechanisms. Cognition, 33: 139–154

A classic view of the relation between sensorineural activity and perception has assumed that the former is somehow transformed into the latter at some locus in the brain. This notion conflicts with the modern view that the activity of the nervous system is restricted to transmitting and processing information. It is suggested that the conflict may be resolved by considering perception as reflective activity rather than passive reception. This cognitive process entails information about the perceiving self and the general context and not merely the stimulus input. Some aspects of perception can be related to neuronal mechanisms and even to neuronal activity at specific loci. How is this done? By identifying the characteristics of the perceptual process and finding a necessary and sufficient neuronal mechanism that receives information about the stimulus input and can perform the implied computation. Examples are taken from the study of visual development in human infants.

Introduction

If we include the study of visual perception under the rubric of cognition then my first association to its biology is to the neuronal mechanisms that we customarily speak of as underlying perception. Traditionally, states of mind in general are thought to correspond to states of the brain although demonstrations of the relation are typically fraught with difficulties, both conceptual and empirical. Some of these are discussed below. The clearest cases alleged to demonstrate this relation come from study of sensory phenomena. The reasons for this are fairly obvious. The sense organs and their closely as-

*The preparation of this manuscript and research reported from the author's laboratory have been supported by grants from the National Institutes of Health (nos. 2R01-EY-1191, SP30-EYO2621, and BRSG 2SO-7RRO747-18) and the Educational Foundation of America. I have profited from discussions with Rachel Joffe Falmagne, my colleague from Clark University. Requests for reprints should be sent to Richard Held, Department of Brain and Cognitive Sciences, MIT, Cambridge, MA 02139, U.S.A.

sociated nerves are among the more accessible parts of the nervous system. Neuronal activation is demonstrably achieved by stimulation of the sense organ. Stimulation is, in turn, comprised of easily definable and controllable physical energies. Consequently, there is an information transmission route from stimulus to brain. One of the oldest approaches to relating mind, brain, and world is the discipline of psychophysics. The word expresses the relation between sensation and stimulation (Boring, 1942). Specific neuronal excitation caused by stimulation is, in accord with the classic viewpoint, correlated with a state of mind called a sensation.

Perception and the sensorineural substrate

During the nineteenth century it was apparently easy to believe that a correlation may be established between sensorineural and perceptual states. Knowing little about the neuronal processes left a great deal of latitude for speculation. Various claims about the relation were made and given the status of psychophysical axioms (Boring, 1942). They assert how properties of perception and neuronal state are to be related. Like processes correspond to like, unlike to unlike, similar to similar, ordered to ordered, and so on. In recent times, these axioms have been called linking propositions. A thorough discussion of their logic can be found in Teller (1984). As our knowledge of neural science has increased, conceptualization of the function of the nervous system has sharpened. Currently, everywhere one examines the nervous system for activities relevant to perception, or for that matter any other psychological process, there appears to be nothing other than the transmitting and processing of information in the form of action potentials, graded potentials, and transmitter dynamics. In what sense do these activities underlie perception? How are they to be correlated with perceptual states? Teller and Pugh (1983, p. 581) recently made an effort to do so and have written the following:

> Most scientists probably believe that there exists a set of neurons with visual system input, whose activities form the immediate substrate of visual perception. We single out this one particular neural stage, with a name: the bridge locus. The occurrence of a particular activity pattern in these bridge locus neurons is necessary for the occurrence of a particular perceptual state; neural activity elsewhere in the visual system is not necessary ... For if one could set up conditions for properly stimulating them [the bridge locus neurons] in the absence of the retina, the correlated perceptual state presumably would occur.

Assuming that the authors' "perceptual state" corresponds to their "immediate substrate of visual perception" and implies conscious perception, this statement has the following implication. If activity in the bridge locus neurons is necessary and activity elsewhere in the nervous system, other than the input to the bridge locus, is not, then activity in the bridge locus neurons is not only necessary but also sufficient for perception. This implication raises difficulties. How does neuronal activity in the isolated bridge locus neurons give rise to perception? This question can of course be raised about any activity in the brain said to have correlated perceptual states. But as a rule such statements are applied either to the brain as a whole or to some region of the brain whose structure and physiology are poorly established. For example, Teller (1984, p. 1243) in discussing cells of Area 17 refers to "the still more central sites which are now implicitly assumed to form the immediate neural substrates of conscious perceptions." Parenthetically, I suspect that as knowledge of the more central, and currently less well understood parts of the brain increases, the sites referred to will become more and more problematic as the neural substrate of conscious perception. The history of ideas about the function of the brain is replete with examples of how the loci of consciousness, as well as the seat of the will, have been excluded from those portions of the brain whose function has become understood (Fearing, 1970). Beginning at least with Descartes, the concept of the reflex and other mechanistic formulations of the relation between stimulus and response have, in principle, been attempts to exorcise mind from body. Modern neuroscience is proceeding to do so empirically, making necessary a reformulation of the concept of mind lest we lose it completely.

In any event, to assert, as Teller and Pugh appear to, that activity in an isolated region of the nervous system gives rise to a perception is mysterious. Furthermore, it seems to contradict that above-mentioned canon of neuroscience that all the nervous system does is transmit and process information. I doubt that the authors intended what their assertion seems to imply: that at the bridge locus there is a direct transformation from neuronal activity to conscious perception. I do believe that their writing illustrates the dilemma that can be created by the traditional mode of search for the neuronal correlates of perception. If neuronal processing is restricted to the transmitting and processing of information, then its relation to perception must be conceptualized in a manner different from the traditional one. How might this be done? In brief outline, I suspect that to perceive something implies a communication to oneself and/or others of a juxtaposition between that something and one's self cum body and sense organs. We perceivers have the ability to reflect upon our own actions in and upon the world, including our own bodies. We remember these reflections and come to think they are known only to ourselves, hence private, and belonging to the class of events we call our consciousness. In short, conscious perception is a conception we have of an act we perform and not a direct translation of sensorineural activity into mental events.

Returning to the relation between perception and the nervous system, I think that we must recognize that disembodied percepts do not occur. That is, we always perceive an object or event in some context and most of the time that context includes an observing entity (our bodily self), which we are aware of as participating in the perception. For example, when I see an identifiable object I inevitably localize it with respect to other objects including my own body. When I claim that I have a visual percept of an object I mean that it is my eyes oriented in my head with respect to my body, as well as other aspects of attention that enable me to obtain the object as percept. The percept is always embedded in an act of seeing. That inference also proceeds from the perennial observation that so often we see what we want to or expect to see. The surprising resemblance of processes of imagery to those of perception (Finke, 1986) may well be related to the embedment of the percept in the broader context of other processes. Perhaps the stimulus provides only certain constraints on these processes. Perception is said to be distinguished from imagery by the presence of such stimulus constraints. The imagery process can rearrange parts of objects into new configurations, whereas perception of objects is always canonical with at most a limited set of interpretations as in the case of ambiguous figures. Imagery is inventive and innovative compared to perception. One can even entertain the possibility that imagery, instead of being the pale ghost of perception, might be the primary process whose outcome we observe in a much constrained form in perception.

If the context is ubiquitous to perception, then it must entail its own correlative activity in the brain in addition to whatever brain process is systematically evoked by the stimulus. In other words, neuronal activity at the bridge locus of Teller and Pugh cannot by itself be responsible for a percept. When, if ever, are circumscribed regions of the brain (bridge loci?) critical for understanding perception? I submit that this may occur only when such a region is either transmitting or otherwise processing information that plays a crucial role in the perceptual process under consideration.

Illustrating such a role are the blind regions of the visual field (scotomata) that are produced by circumscribed lesions of the visual cortex in man. This area of the brain is thought to process and transmit visual information essential for conscious perception. Because of the extraordinarily complex structure and functioning of the brain, this role becomes more difficult to demonstrate as the search goes from peripheral processes that constitute bottlenecks in transmission, to more central ones where pathways multiply and alternative modes of processing are available.

How can neuronal mechanisms with functions restricted solely to transmitting and processing information be related to perception which we acknowledge to depend upon such activity? The bridge-locus approach, as discussed, creates a serious difficulty by short-circuiting the relation. Let us try another tack. Consider cases in which brain scientists feel reasonably comfortable with the assertion of a relation between knowledge of the nervous system and perception. What general properties do such relations exhibit?

Perhaps the best-known success of the traditional psychophysical program relating perceptual to sensorineural states is the explanation of color mixture. Beginning with work of Isaac Newton, it was established that the color of any one wavelength of light can be matched by a combination of three other wavelengths of appropriate intensities. How was this equivalence to be explained? Thomas Young attributed the equivalence to the existence of three broad-spectrum, photosensitive substances in the retina. The combination of the three wavelengths causes the same relative levels of excitation of the three photopigments as does the single matching wavelength. In other words, matching color perceptions are paralleled by matching levels of excitation in the receptor photopigments. Excitation of the combined photopigments results in equivalent neuronal signals representing the matching colors. The existence of these postulated photosensitive pigments has been confirmed and very recently genes specifying the pigments were discovered (Nathans, Thomas, & Hogness, 1986).

What properties of this explanation, as one among others, accounts for its success in relating psychophysical results to underlying neuronal activities? I believe that they are the following. First, specification of what equivalences are produced from stimulation defined by wavelengths (color matching). Second, an account of how they might be produced by a hypothetical model (trichromacy theory). And third, the identification of a real or plausible device (the spectral absorption curves of the three photopigments) that achieves those equivalences. More generally, they are clear specification of what must be accomplished, an abstract account of how it might be accomplished, and identification of real or plausible neuronal mechanisms for doing it. This account bears a resemblance to Teller's Analogy proposition (Teller, 1984). That proposition would link psychophysical to physiological data sets if their functions look alike. An example is the similarity of the scotopic spectral sensitivity curve and the absorption spectrum of rhodopsin. In my view, we must and the caveat that the validity of such arguments also rests on the extent to which the physiological process at issue is demonstrably involved in the path of information processing. It must have both an input and output. Such involvement is patently the case with rhodopsin, since it is another photopigment present at a receptor bottleneck in information transmission.

It is much more difficult to establish a necessary involvement in the case of more central brain mechanisms. Once past the bottleneck of the transduction phase, many of the neuronal paths for transmission of information converge, diverge, and otherwise proliferate (also, see Damasio, this issue). Specification of the transmission pathways and processing centers becomes difficult. It is then necessary to acquire knowledge about paths of transmission by neuroanatomical and physiological methods although psychophysical methods may also provide clues to the structure of these paths (Wolfe, 1986). In recent years the anatomical methods for tracing pathways through the central nervous system have multiplied and their sensitivity greatly increased. Furthermore, our knowledge of pathways within the visual system is perhaps the most advanced of any part of the nervous system. Complementary to this anatomical knowledge have been studies of the physiology of single cells responding to particular visual stimuli. Cells in the visual cortex respond optimally to stimulation by particular hues, oriented edges, areas of limited size, disparate edges in the two eyes and so on. These cells have become a favorite locus for inferring the processing of particular perceptual properties such as the above. An important contemporary example of this approach occurs in Hubel and Livingstone (1987) and Livingstone and Hubel (1987).

Advances in neuroanatomy have also given us important insights into the microcircuitry of the brain and the information processing that can be achieved by such circuitry. These discoveries have clarified old questions but raised new mysteries as to the function and meaning of the enormously complex tangle of connections that constitutes the brain. How are these neuronal mechanisms to be related to perception let alone other functions we attribute to the activity of the brain? The general problem is the focus of research of a large number of workers. The remainder of this paper will deal with what I believe is a case in point. In it I try to illustrate how the use of our knowledge of concomitant developmental change in perception, measured psychophysically, and brain mechanism can lead to a model relating the two spheres.

The developmental dimension

Study of the development of visual capacities offers an opportunity to relate changes in functions to changes in the underlying neuronal substrate. It adds another source of information – that derived from growth-produced, temporal change – to the task discussed above. During the last decade or so a number of laboratories, including my own, have concentrated their work on basic measures of vision in the human infant and the course of development that they reveal. Can these data be related to changes in the nervous system?

I believe the attempt is worth making provided that we accept the validity of a series of inferential steps. Our knowledge of the developing human nervous system is largely restricted to post-mortem neuroanatomical studies. The invasive techniques that have provided so much knowledge in research with animals are obviously out of the question. We know a lot about the developing nervous systems of some animals, including monkeys, whose neural equipment is said to resemble our own. Consequently, we must reason by analogy from animal to human nervous systems. Such analogies are reasonable, but not as convincing when both the behaviors under analysis and the developing neuronal mechanisms have been studied in the same animals. In the following I examine certain developmental data collected from human infants with the goal of speculating about the underlying neuronal mechanisms. This account will make no attempt to be exhaustive but rather may serve instead as an exemplar of the enterprise.

Consider the curves plotted in Figure 1. They show the early development in a typical infant of three kinds of visual acuity. The data, from which the

Figure 1. *Development of the three types of acuity in an idealized human infant. Acuity is measured in minutes of visual angle.*

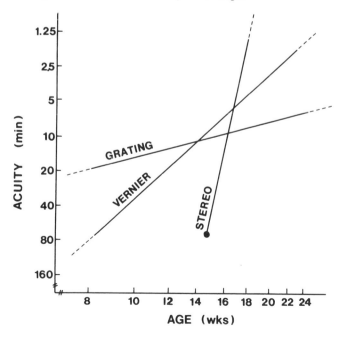

curves were drawn, were obtained by means of a two-alternative forced choice procedure. The infant was placed before one of the displays containing two paired stimuli of which Figure 2A, B, and C are examples. An observer viewed the infant's eyes and head through a peephole behind the display and within a few seconds of presentation decided which of the two stimuli the infant preferred to look at. Repeated trials with either varied bar width of a square-wave grating, varied stereodisparity, or varied vernier offset, allowed establishment of threshold measures for each of these acuities. The curves are idealized but could very well correspond to the fitted data of an average infant. The development of grating acuity is the slowest (this curve has least slope) of the three types. The curve shown is typical of measurements taken by the behavioral technique of preferential viewing (Dobson & Teller, 1978;

Figure 2.   *Paired stimuli for testing three types of acuity by the two-choice looking preference method.*

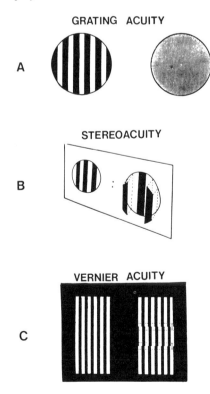

GRATING   ACUITY

A

STEREOACUITY

B

VERNIER   ACUITY

C

Gwiazda, Brill, Mohindra, & Held, 1978). Visual acuity has a measurable value at birth, rises rapidly during the first six months, and continues to increase in resolution through the first year of life (Gwiazda, Brill, Mohindra, & Held, 1980), finally reaching adult values (bar width between ½ and 1 minute) by a few years of age (Birch, Naegele, Bauer, & Held, 1980; Mayer & Dobson, 1980). What can be said about the neuronal mechanism underlying this change in resolution? Studies of the anatomy of the retina in infants reveal a considerable immaturity in the foveal and immediately surrounding central region (Abramov et al., 1982; Mann, 1964). Careful examination reveals that both the density of cone receptors in the fovea and the length of the outer segments of the cones themselves are fractions of the values found in adults (Hendrickson & Yuodelis, 1984). Calculations of both Wilson (1988) and Banks and Bennett (1988) argue that the changes in both length of cone outer segments and cone density together with growth of the eye can account for a many fold increase in acuity from birth to maturity. In effect the retina constitutes a bottleneck in information transmission, in principle not unlike that of the transduction of the wavelength information in light discussed above.

As shown in Figure 1, the curve of development of vernier acuity (the magnitude of the offset measured on the right) shows a more rapid rise than that of grating acuity (Manny & Klein, 1984; Shimojo, Birch, Gwiazda, & Held, 1984). It is presumably present and measurable at birth and continues to rise beyond the age which is plotted to an adult value of a few seconds. We were quite surprised to discover that vernier acuity is less than grating acuity during the first two months (Shimojo & Held, 1987). But we soon realized that our surprise resulted from a prejudice. Vernier acuity has been termed hyperacuity by Westheimer (1979) because the smallest offset that can be detected by an adult observer is considerably smaller than the smallest distance between receptors in the retina. As mentioned above, it is that distance which puts a limit on grating acuity. But although vernier acuity is hyperacute under some circumstances, it is not so either in early infancy or in the extreme periphery of vision (Westheimer, 1982).

How is this rapidly rising function to be dealt with in terms of neuronal mechanism? Vernier acuity is roughly an order of magnitude more sensitive than the separation of foveal cones. Consequently, it has been surmised that although the essential information must traverse the receptors, further processing must go on at higher levels (Zak & Berkley, 1986). Recently, some confirmation has come from the research of Stanley, Fleming, and Morgan (in press). Using the procedure developed by Shimojo et al. (1984), they demonstrated that infants suffering from intra-uterine growth retardation (reduced cranial capacity) have significantly higher vernier acuity thresholds than normals but the same grating acuity thresholds. In addition, the threshold of vernier acuity was negatively correlated with head circumference. They conclude that vernier acuity is cortically processed. Wilson (1986) has argued that hyperacuities, such as vernier acuity, can be accounted for by the activities of bar detector units resembling simple cells of the sort found in the visual cortex. These cells are made up of a central elongated region flanked on both sides by inhibitory regions. It is the influence of the inhibitory surround which fine tunes the spatial sensitivity of these units. This assertion can be understood intuitively by recognizing that the addition of an inhibitory surround to an excitatory region amplifies the effect of contrast at the border. If, as Wilson (1988) argues, the inhibitory surround is initially absent in the very young infant but develops rapidly during later months, then the rapid development of vernier acuity may occur concomitantly. Finally, Banks and Bennett (1988) have argued that the increase in resolution at the retinal level can have a magnified effect on vernier acuity that may account for its rapid rise.

Although we were surprised to discover that vernier acuity was less than grating acuity in very young infants, we were even more surprised when we followed the advice of a colleague, Dr. Joseph Bossom, who urged us to look for sex differences within our sample. After all, why should there be any significant sex differences during the first semester of infancy? Yet analysis revealed that during the fourth, fifth, and sixth months, females were significantly superior to males in vernier acuity (Held, Shimojo, & Gwiazda, 1984). This discovery prompted us to do a similar analysis with our extensive data on the development of grating acuity during the first year. We found no significant sex differences in these measurements (Held et al., 1984). The failure to find this difference serves as a control on the possibility that the difference is attributable either to non-visual factors, which are all very similar in both procedures, or to some other factor common to both tests of vision. In later experiments we have also found the same sex difference in the time of onset of stereopsis (Gwiazda, Bauer, & Held, in press) and binocular rivalry (see below): again females were significantly earlier. While at this time we can only speculate on the cause of this sex difference, it may serve as a marker that distinguishes between visual processes developing at different loci in the nervous system. One locus may be sexually differentiated, another not. Accordingly, if the limiting neuronal constraint on grating acuity is the sensitivity and spacing of the cone receptors of the retina while that of vernier acuity occurs at the cortical level, some factor may differentially affect these two loci. Elsewhere we have suggested that testosterone, present in male but not female infants, may be the critical factor (Held et al., 1984). Testosterone has been implicated as a neurotrophic factor by Geschwind and

Galaburda (1987), among others. It could serve in a particularly potent manner during the age range with which we are concerned because this is the period of most intense synaptogenesis in the human visual cortex during the entire postnatal life span (Huttenlocher, de Courten, Garey, & van der Loos, 1982). Recent experiments showing a correlation between blood plasma levels of testosterone and age of onset of mature binocularity have provided encouraging evidence for this hypothesis (Held, Bauer, & Gwiazda, 1988).

Tests for stereopsis, defined as detection of binocularly disparate stimuli, have been developed in a number of laboratories using a variety of techniques (Atkinson & Braddick, 1976; Birch, Gwiazda, & Held, 1982; Fox, Aslin, Shea, & Dumais, 1980; Held, Birch, & Gwiazda, 1980; Petrig et al., 1981). They all agree in showing that stereopsis has an abrupt onset in most infants at ages ranging between 2 and 6 months. This abrupt onset is marked by a heavy dot at the origin of the curve for stereoacuity showing in Figure 1. Tests for this onset have generally used the coarsest disparity (roughly one degree of visual angle) short of producing binocular rivalry. Although not shown in Figure 1, a very similar abrupt onset at the same approximate age has been found for detection of binocularly rivaling stimuli (Birch, Shimojo, & Held, 1983). At that age and thenceforth, when a non-rivaling stimulus is paired with a rivaling stimulus, the former is preferred as if to suggest that rivalry is aversive. Moreover, a number of other consequences of binocular and interocular interactions, including amblyopia resulting from esotropia, have their onsets at approximately the same age (Held, 1985). How are these data to be interpreted in terms of underlying neuronal mechanisms?

The abrupt onset of mature binocularity at an average age of several months stands out as a discontinuous process requiring its own special interpretation. We have speculated that this onset is dependent upon a visual cortex with a columnal structure (see Figure 3). These columns are defined in adult animals by the observation that the geniculocortical afferents which are laid out topographically in layer 4 show origins that alternate from one eye to the other (Figure 3B). In an argument developed elsewhere (Held, 1985) we point out that the age of achieving adult-like segregation in cat and monkey corresponds to the age of onset of mature binocularity measured behaviorally. Moreover, cells that respond selectively to binocularly disparate stimuli first appear at this age in the cat (Pettigrew, 1974). In man evidence for the developing segregation of the ocular dominance columns is fragmentary but not inconsistent with this age. But why should such segregation be relevant to the processing of information from the two eyes?

Prior to segregation it appears that the thalamocortical afferents originating from the two eyes overlap extensively and even synapse on the same cells in this layer (Figure 3A). That implies a loss of information about the eye of

Figure 3. *Development of the ocular dominance columns. A: Geniculostriate afferents from both eyes (R and L) synapse on the same cells in layer IV thereby losing information about the eye of origin. B: Geniculostriate afferents are segregated on the basis of eye origin (R and L) and consequently recipient cells in layer IV may send their axons to cells outside of that layer so as to synapse on cells which may be disparity selective.*
(From Held, 1985; reproduced by permission of the publishers, Erlbaum Associates, Hillsdale, N.J.)

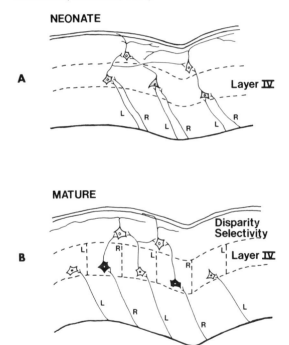

origin in further processing of binocular information. Consequently, unless the processing of binocular differences occurs in the very cells that receive the thalamocortical afferents, further analysis of these differences in order to extract disparity and produce interocular rivalry is precluded. For example, stereopsis requires computation of information from non-corresponding retinal loci. Interpreted anatomically this means that connections from each of the two eyes to disparity-sensitive cells must come from different columns in layer 4. If that information is not available then disparity detection is not

possible. Binocular rivalry entails a mutually inhibitory relation between ex-
citations originating from the separate eyes. In the absence of that information rivalry between stimuli in the two eyes is impossible. To test this model
of the non-segregated thalamocortical projection to layer 4, the following
prediction was generated.

One possible consequence of loss of the address of the eye of origin would
be a simple superposition of the central representations of the images on the
two retinas. Thus if a vertical grating is presented to the right eye and a
horizontal grating to the left eye, the superimposed representation of the
orthogonal gratings should appear like a plaid or grid-like figure. Rivalry is
ruled out. This suggests a simple test. We know that infants at any age prefer
to look at a grid over a grating and beginning at the same age of acquiring
stereopsis they prefer to look at a fused over a rivalrous stimulus. Consequently, we presented binocularly superimposed orthogonal grating stimuli
paired with binocularly superimposed parallel (hence fusible) gratings in a
two-choice looking preference arrangement. Prior to segregation of the columns, a grid-like structure should be seen and preferred to the fused grating.
However, once segregation is completed and binocularity is achieved, the
orthogonal grating stimuli should appear to rival and preference should shift
to the fused grating. The prediction was born out in an experiment carried out
in our laboratory (Shimojo, Bauer, O'Connell, & Held, 1986). The results
showed that at the approximate age of acquisition of stereopsis an initially
significant preference for the orthogonal gratings shifted to one for the parallel gratings. The shift occurred within an average time interval of two weeks.
This result not only clearly confirmed the abruptness of the transition to
adult-like binocularity, but it is also the first demonstration of a complete
reversal of an infant preference known to us. Moreover, we found that the
onset of this shift was significantly earlier in female than in male infants
(Bauer, Shimojo, Gwiazda, & Held, 1986). The result is an important confirmation of the conjecture that the male–female difference is to be found for
processing at the cortical level. The conjunction of inputs from the two eyes
necessary for binocular processing does not occur prior to the visual cortex.
In our laboratory we have also measured the development of stereoacuity
after the onset of coarse stereopsis (Birch et al., 1982; Held, Birch, &
Gwiazda, 1980). Stereoacuity is defined as the minimum detectable binocularity disparity. Disparity is the distance in visual angle between non-corresponding image points on the two retinas. Disparity is produced between the
images of objects that differ in distance from the eyes. Stereoacuity rises very
rapidly, as can be seen in Figure 1, such that within a few weeks from onset
of coarse stereopsis it approaches adult values within a couple of octaves.
The increasing values of stereoacuity imply increasingly fine tuning of the

disparity-sensitive neuronal mechanism, an implication consistent with both the development of inhibitory cortical circuitry and the increase of resolution at the retina as in the case of vernier acuity.

Having completed this account of an attempt to relate an aspect of perceptual development to its underlying neuronal mechanisms, we may consider what general implications may be drawn? The account relies principally on changes in the following sorts of neuronal processes:

(1) the initial filtering or sampling properties of the system as exemplified by the spatial dimensions of the retinal receptor array;
(2) the transmission of information as influenced by changing neuronal circuitry and possible hormonal influences; and
(3) the processing of incoming information by inhibitory circuitry and the development of such circuitry.

All of these changing neuronal processes imply changes in information-handling capabilities that can, at least in principle, be related to changes of the sort that we observe in perceptual functions. The logic of the procedure we have followed involves three steps: first, identifying the necessary and sufficient information that derives from stimulation; second, identifying the processing required for transforming that information into a form which satisfies the requirements of the perceptual task; third, identifying neuronal mechanisms that can, at least in principle, perform the transformation. These considerations allow us to correlate perceptual processes with neuronal mechanisms. They do not yet deal with the conscious aspect of perception. That requires specification of the task of perceiving, a cognitive process. If we shall ever be able to relate cognitive tasks with neuronal mechanisms, I suspect that it will be on the basis of such considerations. To the extent that cognitive processes can be rigorously specified and the computational capabilities of the nervous system understood, the two may be usefully related. If we can interpret perception in terms compatible with information transmission and processing in the nervous system, we shall have taken a major step toward that goal.

References

Abramov, I., Gordon, J., Hendrickson, A., Hainline, L., Dobson, V., & LaBossiere, E. (1982). The retina of the newborn human infant. *Science, 217*, 265–267.

Atkinson, J., & Braddick, O. (1976). Stereoscopic discrimination in infants. *Perception, 5*, 29–38.

Banks, M., & Bennett, P. (1988). Optical and photoreceptor immaturities limit the spatial and chromatic vision of human neonates. *Journal of the Optical Society of America A, 5*, 2059–2079.

Bauer, J., Shimojo, S., Gwiazda, J., & Held, R. (1986). Sex differences in the development of binocularity in human infants. *Investigative Ophthalmology Visual Science Supplement, 27*, 265.

Birch, E.E., Gwiazda, J., & Held, R. (1982). Stereoacuity development for crossed and uncrossed disparities in human infants. *Vision Research, 22*, 507–513.

Birch, E.E., Naegele, J., Bauer, J.A., Jr., & Held, R. (1980). Visual acuity of toddlers. *Investigative Ophthalmology Visual Science Supplement, 20*, 210.

Birch, E.E., Shimojo, S., & Held, R. (1983). The development of aversion to rivalrous stimuli in human infants. *Investigative Ophthalmology and Visual Science Supplement, 24*, 92.

Boring, E.G. (1942). *Sensation and perception in the history of experimental psychology*. New York: Appleton-Century-Crofts.

Dobson, V., & Teller, D. (1978). Visual acuity in human infants: A review and comparison of behavioral and electrophysiological studies. *Vision Research, 18*, 1469–1483.

Fearing, F. (1970). *Reflex action: A study in the history of physiological psychology*. Cambridge, MA: MIT Press.

Finke, R. (1986). Visual functions of mental imagery. In K.R. Boff, L. Kaufman, & J.P. Thomas (Eds.), *Handbook of perception and human performance, Vol II*. New York: Wiley.

Fox, R., Aslin, R.N., Shea, S.L., & Dumais, S.T. (1980). Stereopsis in human infants. *Science, 207*, 323–324.

Geschwind, N., & Galaburda, A.M. (1987). *Cerebral lateralization: Biological mechanisms, associations, and pathology*. Cambridge, MA: MIT Press.

Gwiazda, J., Bauer, J., & Held, R. (1989). Binocular function in human infants: Correlation of stereoptic and fusion-rivalry discriminations. *Journal of Pediatric Ophthalmology and Strabismus, 26*, 128–132.

Gwiazda, J., Brill, S., Mohindra, I., & Held, R. (1978). Infant visual acuity and its meridional variation. *Vision Research, 18*, 1557–1564.

Gwiazda, J., Brill, S., Mohindra, I., & Held, R. (1980). Preferential looking acuity in infants from two to fifty-eight weeks of age. *American Journal of Optometry and Physiological Optics, 57*, 428–432.

Held, R. (1985). Binocular vision: Behavioral and neural development. In J. Mehler & R. Fox (Eds.), *Neonate cognition: Beyond the blooming, buzzing confusion*. Hillsdale, NJ: Erlbaum Associates.

Held, R., Bauer, J., & Gwiazda, J. (1988). Age of onset of binocularity correlates with level of plasma testosterone in male infants. *Investigative Ophthalmology and Visual Science Supplement, 29*, 60.

Held, R., Birch, E.E., & Gwiazda, J. (1980). Stereoacuity of human infants. *Proceedings of the National Academy of Sciences (USA), 77*, 5572–5574.

Held, R., Shimojo, S., & Gwiazda, J. (1984). Gender differences in the early development of human visual resolution. *Investigative Ophthalmology and Visual Science Supplement, 25*, 220.

Hendrickson, A.E., & Yuodelis, C. (1984). The morphological development of the human fovea. *Ophthalmology, 91*, 603–612.

Hubel, D., & Livingstone, M. (1987). Segregation of form, color, and stereopsis in primate area 18. *Journal of Neuroscience, 7*, 3378–3415.

Huttenlocher, P.R., de Courten, C., Garey, L.J., & van der Loos, H. (1982). Synaptogenesis in human visual cortex: Evidence for synapse elimination during normal development. *Neuroscience Letters, 33*, 247–252.

Livingstone, M., & Hubel, D. (1987). Psychophysical evidence for separate channels for the perception of form, color, movement, and depth. *Journal of Neuroscience, 7*, 3416–3468.

Mann, I.C. (1964). The early stages of the formation of the primary optic vesicle. *The Development of the Human Eye*. New York: Grune & Stratton.

Manny, R., & Klein, S. (1984). The development of vernier acuity in infants. *Current Eye Research, 3*, 453–462.

Mayer, D.L., & Dobson, V. (1980). Assessment of vision in young children: A new operant approach yields estimates of acuity. *Investigative Ophthalmology and Visual Science, 19*, 566–570.

Nathans, J., Thomas, D., & Hogness, D.S. (1986). Molecular genetics of human color vision: the genes encoding blue, green, and red pigments. *Science, 232*, 193–202.

Petrig, B., Julesz, B., Kropfl, W., Baumgartner, G., & Anliker, M. (1981). Development of stereopsis and cortical binocularity in human infants: Electrophysiological evidence. *Science, 213*, 1402–1404.

Pettigrew, J.D. (1974). The effect of visual experience on the development of stimulus specificity by kitten cortical neurones. *Journal of Physiology, 237*, 49–74.

Shimojo, S., Bauer, J.A., O'Connell, K.M., & Held, R. (1986). Pre-stereoptic binocular vision in infants. *Vision Research, 26*, 501–510.

Shimojo, S., Birch, E.E., Gwiazda, J., & Held, R. (1984). Development of vernier acuity in infants. *Vision Research, 24*, 721–728.

Shimojo, S., & Held, R. (1987). Vernier acuity is less than grating acuity in 2- and 3-month olds. *Vision Research, 27*, 77–86.

Stanley, O.H., Fleming, P.J., & Morgan, M.H. (in press). Abnormal development of visual function following intra-uterine growth retardation. *Early Human Development.*

Teller, D.Y. (1984). Linking propositions. *Vision Research, 24*, 1233–1246.

Teller, D.Y., & Pugh, E.N., Jr. (1983). Linking propositions in color vision. In J.D. Mollen & L.T. Sharpe (Eds.), *Color Vision: Physiology and psychophysics.* London: Academic Press.

Westheimer, G. (1979). The spatial sense of the eye. *Investigative Ophthalmology and Visual Science, 18*, 893–912.

Westheimer, G. (1982). The spatial grain of the perifoveal visual field. *Vision Research, 22*, 157–162.

Wilson, H.R. (1986). Responses of spatial mechanisms can explain hyperacuity. *Vision Research, 26*, 453–469.

Wilson, H.R. (1988). Development of spatiotemporal mechanisms in the human infant. *Vision Research, 28*, 611–628.

Wolfe, J.M. (1986). Stereopsis and binocular rivalry. *Psychological Review, 93*, 269–282.

Zak, R., & Berkley, M.A. (1986). Evoked potentials elicited by brief vernier offsets: Estimating vernier thresholds and properties of the neural substrate. *Vision Research, 26*, 439–451.

Résumé

Il est généralement considéré à propos de la relation entre l'activité neurosensorielle et la perception que la première est en quelque sorte transformée en la seconde en un certain point du cerveau. Cette opinion est en contradiction avec l'idée plus récente que l'activité du système nerveux est restreinte à la transmission et au traitement de l'information. Il est suggéré que la contradiction puisse être résolue en considérant la perception comme une activité réfléchie plutôt que passive. Ce processus cognitif utilise des informations sur la perception et le contexte général et pas simplement sur le stimulus à l'entrée. Certains aspects de la perception peuvent être reliés à des mécanismes neuronaux et même à l'activité neuronale à des endroits spécifiques. Comment cela fonctionne-t-il? En identifiant les caractéristiques du processus de perception et en trouvant un mécanisme neuronal nécessaire et suffisant qui reçoit les informations concernant l'entrée du stimulus et peut accomplir les calculs impliqués. Des exemples sont pris à partir de l'étude du développement des capacités visuelles chez les enfants.

6

A view of the world through the bat's ear:
The formation of acoustic images in echolocation*

JAMES A. SIMMONS

Brown University

Abstract

Simmons, J.A., 1989. A view of the world through the bat's ear: The formation of acoustic images in echolocation. Cognition, 33: 155–199.

Echolocating bats perceive objects as acoustic images derived from echoes of the ultrasonic sounds they emit. They can detect, track, identify, and intercept flying insects using sonar. Many species, such as the big brown bat, Eptesicus fuscus, *emit frequency-modulated sonar sounds and perceive the distance to targets, or target range, from the delay of echoes. For* Eptesicus, *a point-target's image has a sharpness along the range axis that is determined by the acuity of echo-delay perception, which is about 10 ns under favorable conditions. The image as a whole has a fine range structure that corresponds to the cross-correlation function between emissions and echoes. A complex target – which has reflecting points, called "glints", located at slightly different distances and reflects echoes containing overlapping components with slightly different delays – is perceived in terms of its range profile. The separation of the glints along the range dimension is encoded by the shape of the echo spectrum created by interference between overlapping echo components. However,* Eptesicus *transforms the echo spectrum back into an estimate of the original delay separation of echo components. The bat thus converts spectral cues into elements of an image expressed in terms of range. The absolute range of the nearest glint is encoded by the arrival time of the earliest echo component, and the spectrally encoded range separation of additional glints is referred to this time-encoded*

*This research has been supported by contract no. N00014-86-K-0401 from the Office of Naval Research, by grant no. BNS 83-02144 and prior grants from the National Science Foundation, by NIMH Research Scientist Development Award no. 7-KO2-MH00521, by grant nos. 57 and 57A from the System Development Foundation, by a grant from the Whitehall Foundation, and by a University Research Instrumentation Program Grant from the Department of Defense. Numerous colleagues – including R.A. Altes, B. Escudié, M.B. Fenton, D.R. Griffin, A.D. Grinnell, W.M. Masters, D. Menne, A.J.M. Moffat, C.F. Moss, G. Neuweiler, H.-U. Schnitzler, A.M. Simmons, and N. Suga – have contributed to the ideas put forth here. I am grateful to Peter Eimas, Albert Galaburda, and the editors of *Cognition* for the invitation to write this article, part of which first appeared as a report to the Office of Naval Research in *Naval Research Reviews*. Reprint requests should be sent to James A. Simmons, Walter Hunter Laboratory of Psychology, Brown University, Providence, RI 02912, U.S.A.

reference range for the image as a whole. Each individual glint is represented by a cross-correlation function for its own echo component, the nearest of which is computed directly from arrival-time measurements while further ones are computed by transformation of the echo spectrum. The bat then sums the cross-correlation functions for multiple glints to form the entire image of the complex target. Range and shape are two distinct features of targets that are separately encoded by the bat's auditory system, but the bat perceives unitary images that require fusion of these features to create a synthetic psychological dimension of range. The bat's use of cross-correlation-like images reveals neural computations that achieve fusion of stimulus features and offers an example of high-level operations involved in the formation of perceptual "wholes".

Introduction

This paper describes a perspective on some fundamental aspects of spatial perception concerned with the relation between images that are perceived and their underlying neural representations. How are different dimensions or features of objects, which may be separately represented from stimuli by the brain, actually brought together to create a unified perception? This question is addressed here in a psychophysical and neuroethological analysis of a perceptual system found in bats – a group of animals that might seem exotic to most psychologists or cognitive scientists. Bats employ a kind of biological sonar system, called echolocation (Griffin, 1958), to orient themselves in their environment. Here I try to bring together what is known about how echolocating bats perceive distance and depth in their surroundings to illustrate principles emerging in the study of spatial perception. In the language of sonar, the distance to targets is target *range;* this discussion is concerned with the images that bats perceive along the target–range axis.

A neuroethological approach is a union of biological and psychological methods that arrives at a distinctive way of thinking about behavior and its mechanisms. It offers very practical examples of issues in cognition and neuroscience, being addressed in the context of understanding how particular animals acquire, process, and display specific kinds of information that they need for their daily lives. Both behavorial and anatomical/physiological data are taken as relevant for a neuroethological analysis, but their interpretation is disciplined by the advantages that derive from studying a system of behavior having known, direct significance for survival and evolution. The echolocation of bats may seem an unlikely place to seek knowledge about basic perceptual processes, perhaps because it seems so specialized in comparison with what many like to think of as the more general capabilities of the human mind and brain. However, this very specialization permits a close examination of the principles of perception because critical features of the representation and processing of information in stimuli are exaggerated by virtue of the importance of sonar for the lives of bats. Biological specialization and exaggeration bring with them scientific accessibility.

Echolocation and perception of target range

Bats are mammals, belonging to the order Chiroptera. Their lives are almost entirely nocturnal (Hill & Smith, 1984). Bats have evolved powered flight for locomotion and echolocation for orientation in darkness, and with this combination they achieve an unparalleled freedom of movement and action at night. Echolocation is a naturally occurring adaptation of the vocal and auditory systems that joins their capabilities to create a sonar system (Griffin, 1958; Novick, 1977). The bat's larynx and vocal tract act as the transmitter, while the ears and auditory system act as the receiver. An echolocating bat emits a series of brief, mostly ultrasonic sounds and perceives objects in its immediate environment from the echoes of these sounds that return to its ears (Busnel & Fish, 1980; Nachtigall & Moore, 1988). By reflecting sounds off objects, the bat in effect induces them to reveal their presence, location, and character as though the objects themselves were the source of the sounds.

The act of echolocation as practiced by bats requires an unusual degree of coordination of sound production and hearing, which makes it similar in some respects to human speech. Speech sounds lead to neural encoding of acoustic information that is transformed into higher-level cognitive representations of the objects and ideas conveyed in words and sentences. The bat's sonar sounds and their echoes lead to neural encoding of acoustic information that is transformed into higher-level representations of the spatial location and appearance of objects. In both instances, by a process that is not understood, the exercise of these representations gives rise to perception of the represented images. An integrative mechanism somehow *expresses* the information from various neural representations as a unitary perception. How is it that different dimensions of the information supplied by stimuli – which may be represented in different ways and in different places in the brain – can be brought together into a unified perception? The calculus of the emergence of perception from disparate neural representations presumably is founded on a neural substrate that links these representations. One example of a candidate mechanism of this sort has emerged from experiments on sound localization by barn owls – experiments that also proceed from a neuroethological viewpoint (Konishi, 1983). Recent experiments on the perception of complex sonar targets by echolocating bats provide an example of this integrative process in action, illustrating some of its properties and offering the hope that its neural basis can be identified from the clarity with which behavioral data define the underlying algorithms.

Not surprisingly, the auditory systems of bats are specialized for extracting and representing the spatial information about sonar targets conveyed to the bat by the acoustic features of echoes. This specialization is built upon auditory processes common to all mammals (Henson, 1970; Neuweiler, Bruns, & Schuller, 1980; Suga, 1973, 1988). Both the bat's sonar emissions and the echoes returning from neighboring objects stimulate the two ears, evoking a pattern of neural discharges that ascends the auditory pathways of the bat's brain. By a mixture of parallel and hierarchical interactions among neurons, bats represent, first, the acoustic features of echoes and, then, the spatial features of targets (Suga, 1988). The auditory representations of echoes and, through them, targets, lead to perception of images that must surely be expressed in spatial coordinates or are so readily transposed into spatial terms that they can routinely guide the bat's flight during the demanding task of capturing flying insects.

Interception of flying insects by sonar

There are over 700 species of echolocating bats, the majority of which make their living by feeding upon insects that are captured in flight after having been located by sonar. Several species that have been studied capture flying insects in a stereotyped interception maneuver that is similar, and thus amenable to comparison, across species. Although bats use their sonar to perceive all sorts of objects in their immediate vicinity – to navigate and detect obstacles to flight, for example – the use for which echolocation is most closely adapted is the detection, tracking, and identification of prey. As evidence for this close coupling of echolocation to pursuit of flying insects, the structure and the pattern of emission of sonar sounds are correlated in different species of bats with differences in the acoustic strategies they use for finding prey and with aspects of their flight morphology (Aldridge & Rautenbach, 1987; Fenton, 1984; Neuweiler, 1984). As a strategy, some types of bats emit constant-frequency (CF) sonar signals and rely upon Doppler shifts impressed on echoes by the wing-beats of insects to identify potential prey (Henson et al., 1987; Schnitzler, Menne, Kober, & Heblich, 1983), while others use the broad range of frequencies inherent in frequency-modulated (FM) sonar signals to "paint" acoustic images of targets (Ostwald, Schnitzler, & Schuller, 1988; Simmons & Stein, 1980). The acoustic conditions prevailing from moment to moment in each individual pursuit maneuver govern the pattern of emission of sonar sounds by the bat, indicating a high degree of behavioral adaptation to the perceptual requirements of each stage of the interception process (Fenton, 1984; Henson et al., 1987; Novick, 1977; Schnitzler & Henson, 1980; Simmons, Fenton, & O'Farrell, 1979). Furthermore, the representation of echo and target features in the bat's brain closely follows the structure of the bat's sonar sounds in the context of the interception maneuver (Neuweiler et al., 1980; Suga, 1988). The images that the bat actually perceives of targets depend upon the structure of the sonar sounds being emitted, and these in turn reflect the requirements of finding prey according to the acoustic strategy of each species (Neuweiler, 1984; Schnitzler et al., 1983; Simmons, Howell, & Suga, 1975; Simmons & Grinnell, 1988; Simmons & Stein, 1980). The quintessential behavior for which bats use their sonar is the pursuit of flying insects, and this process is the starting point for understanding how bats achieve spatial perception through sonar.

Figure 1 shows a diagram of the interception of a flying insect by an echolocating bat, based upon stroboscopic photographs and tape recordings of numerous pursuits by the little brown bat, *Myotis lucifugus,* and the big brown bat, *Eptesicus fuscus* (Griffin, 1958; Webster & Brazier, 1965, 1968); by the pipistrelle bat, *Pipistrellus kuhli* (Schnitzler, Kalko, Miller, & Surlykke, 1987); by the horseshoe bat, *Rhinolophus ferrumequinum* (Trappe & Schnitzler, 1982); by the mustache bat, *Pteronotus parnellii* (Henson et al., 1987; Novick & Vaisnys, 1964); and by two other species of *Pternonotus* (Novick, 1963, 1965). These species represent most of the different types of echolocation systems found among bats, and photographic studies establish that the interception maneuver for airborne prey appears to be substantially the same in all of them. The process of interception has several stages that are associated with the pattern of emission of sonar sounds and other aspects of the bat's behavior with respect to the target. For example, the bat regulates the rate of emission of its sonar sounds according to the progressively declining distance to the target (see "sound track" in Figure 1). The bat also follows the target's location by keeping its head pointed at the target as it approaches. Photographs of interceptions indicate that bats have a head-aim tracking accuracy of at least 5°. Experiments under controlled conditions with *Eptesicus fuscus* reveal that the tracking system probably is accurate to within 1–2° in the horizontal plane (Masters, Moffat, & Simmons, 1985), which corresponds to the sharpness of target images in this plane (Simmons et al., 1983). These tracking responses along the dimensions of distance and direction confirm that the bat is aware of the target's location in three dimensions throughout the interception maneuver.

The images that a bat perceives of the target throughout the pursuit ma-

Figure 1.   *Diagram of the interception maneuver by an echolocating bat. The bat and the insect are each shown as numbered images based on stroboscopic photographs taken at intervals of 100 ms. A thin dotted line connects corresponding images of the bat and the insect to show target range. The flight path of the bat provides a "sound track" of the bat's sonar signals, each of which is marked by a short bar perpendicular to the flight path at the location where the bat emitted the sound. The stages of pursuit are defined by the bat's behavior – the rate of emission of signals, the structure of the signals (see Figure 2), and its tracking of the target in various ways. (From Kick & Simmons, 1984)*

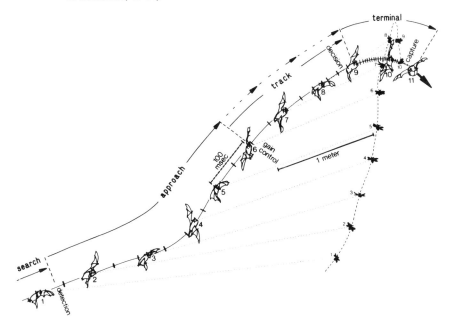

neuver depend first of all upon the characteristics of its sonar signals; these are the ultimate source of the echoes which give rise to the images. Figure 2 shows the sonar sounds emitted by the big brown bat, *Eptesicus fuscus,* as it intercepts a flying insect (Simmons, 1987). The sounds are illustrated here as spectrograms. (A spectrographic representation is useful because it visually conveys more information about the signals than other kinds of illustrations, such as their pressure waveforms or their overall spectra.) The spectrograms in Figure 2 show 34 numbered sounds that extend over a period of about $1\frac{1}{2}$

Figure 2. *A continuous spectrogram record of a sequence of sonar sounds emitted by the big brown bat,* Eptesicus fuscus, *during a pursuit maneuver. The time axis starts about 1½ seconds prior to capture and counts down to zero for the moment of capture. The pattern of emission of these signals largely defines the stages in the pursuit process. (From Simmons, 1987)*

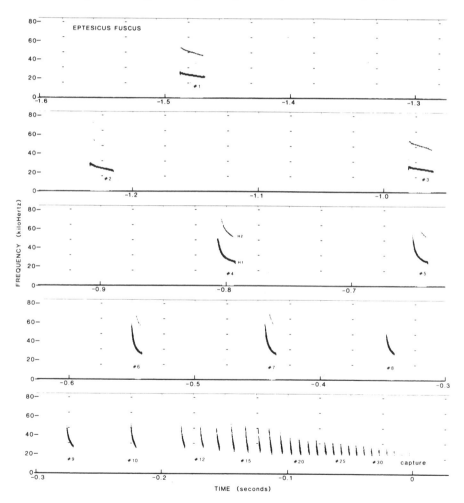

seconds leading up to the capture of the insect. Each sound yields a discrete image of the target to the bat, judging from the speed with which the bat updates its tracking behavior from sound to sound (Masters et al., 1985). The pursuit maneuver is guided by what must amount to a kind of acoustically derived motion-picture of the insect in relation to the attacking bat, with individual frames contributed by each echo in succession. The most notable features of these sounds are shown by the spectrograms: The sonar sounds are frequency-modulated (FM), sweeping downward in frequency from beginning to end; they are quite brief, each lasting only a few milliseconds; and they contain relatively high sound frequencies, from 20 kHz to over 60 kHz. Most of the sounds contain two prominent harmonics as well. The acoustics of field recording situations are not perfect – the higher frequencies in the bat's emissions are under-represented in Figure 2 due to absorption of sound by the atmosphere as the signal travels to the recording microphone (Griffin, 1971; Lawrence & Simmons, 1982; Pye, 1980). *Eptesicus* actually produces frequencies from 20 kHz to 100 kHz in most sounds, as is shown in the example in Figure 3.

   The first three sounds in Figure 2 sweep through a narrow range of frequencies from about 28 kHz to 22 kHz in the first harmonic and from 56 kHz to 44 kHz in the second harmonic (see caption for details). These are signals that the bat uses to search for targets when flying in an open area, and they are emitted at a regular rate of roughly five to ten sounds per second. When the bat detects the target and begins reacting to its presence, the sounds are emitted in a distinctive new pattern. The FM sweeps abruptly change from shallow to steep (compare sound no. 3 with sound no. 4 in Figure 2), so that after the target has been detected and pursuit is joined, the bandwidth of the sounds broadens considerably. During active pursuit the first harmonic sweeps from 50–60 kHz down to about 25 kHz, with the second harmonic sweeping from about 100 kHz down to 50 kHz. (See Figure 3, which was recorded with the microphone closer to the bat.) These broad FM sweeps introduced by the bat following detection of the target provide a wide range of frequencies with which to form sharp, information-rich images of the target (Simmons & Stein, 1980; Simmons et al., 1975). The bat's acoustic behavior during active pursuit documents that its attention is focused on the target – showing, for example, that the bat tracks the target's declining range by progressively shortening the interval between successive sonar emissions.

   The pursuit maneuver culminates in a brief burst of rapidly accelerating sonar emissions (beginning with sound no. 11 in Figure 2) and the actual capture of the target (see Figure 1). The species of bats studied so far reach out at the last moment to seize the insect in the wing or tail membrane (Webster & Griffin, 1962). The bat's use of its flight membranes to gather in

Figure 3.   *The spectrogram of a single echolocation sound emitted by* Eptesicus *during a discrimination experiment and recorded with a microphone located close to the bat's mouth. The full range of frequencies used by the bat is better represented here than in Figure 2. (From Simmons, Freedman, Stevenson, Chen, & Wohlgenant, 1989)*

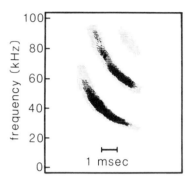

the target provides a valuable indication of the accuracy with which the bat has determined the target's location by the end of the maneuver. From multiple-flash photographs of interceptions, the bat appears to know the target's position in three dimensions to within about 1–2 cm at the moment of capture. Figure 4 shows a little brown bat, *Myotis lucifugus,* in the act of seizing a mealworm projected into the air. The coordination of the bat's reach with its wing towards the target's position in space is made obvious here. By dusting insects with flour before the bat is given the opportunity to capture them, and then measuring the extent of wing surface whitened from contact with targets at the moment of interception, the accuracy of the bat's reach also has been measured to be 1–2 cm (Trappe, 1982). Photographs such as Figure 4 show the bat's wing tip curled around the target in evident anticipation of capture, revealing that the target's range is known and used explicitly to guide this movement. The results of all these observations indicate that a mechanical accuracy of reaching to within 1–2 cm of the target's true position is sufficient to result in successful interceptions; no greater accuracy for determining the target's position in space is manifested or seems necessary in this aspect of the bat's behavior.

Since the primary use for echolocation is the detection, tracking, identification, and interception of flying insects, we can take the distance over which bats encounter and actively pursue prey to be the operating range of echolocation, at least for most practical purposes. This specifies the zone of space

Figure 4. *A stroboscopic photograph of the little brown bat,* Myotis lucifugus, *reaching out to seize an airborne mealworm (MW) with the tip of its left wing at the culmination of pursuit. The target is outlined to make it more visible against the highlight reflecting from the bat's wing. The shadow of the target falls on the bat's wing-tip. (Photo courtesy of F.A. Webster)*

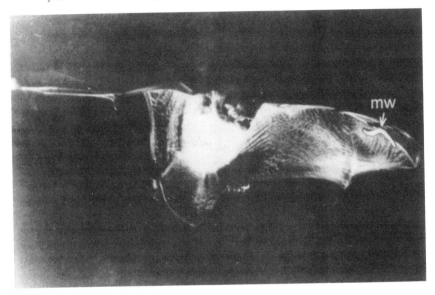

within which targets are perceived by the bat. Species of bats differ somewhat in the distances at which they first react to flying insects, but these distances seldom seem to be greater than a few meters (Fenton, 1984; Griffin, 1958). The largely ultrasonic sonar transmissions of bats occur at frequencies where the atmosphere is not an ideal medium for propagation over long distances. An appreciable fraction of the energy in echolocation sounds is absorbed by the air as the sound travels to and from the target (Griffin, 1971; Lawrence & Simmons, 1982; Pye, 1980). Furthermore, only a small fraction of the energy in the sound that strikes a target as small as an insect is reflected or scattered back in the direction of the bat to become a useful echo (Griffin, 1958; Neubauer, 1986; Pye, 1980). Consequently, the echoes eventually reaching the bat's ears are relatively weak under most circumstances. To combat the unfavorable acoustic conditions they often face, aerial-feeding insectivorous bats typically transmit very intense sounds for echolocation – sound pressures of 100–110 dB SPL (peak-to-peak) at distances of 10–20 cm from the mouth are common. Nevertheless, even these bats can be no further than a few meters from small targets if they are to receive echoes that are audible to them. For this reason echolocation is a relatively short-range mode of perception, at least for small targets. Even so, echolocation permits the bat to find flying insects in the dark, when they cannot be seen.

The distance at which bats can first detect small targets, and thus begin to actively pursue them, has been estimated from observation of interceptions and also measured directly in psychological tests. In laboratory experiments the big brown bat, *Eptesicus fuscus,* can detect a sphere with a diameter of 5 mm as far away as 3 m, and it can perceive a 20-mm sphere as far away as 5 m (Kick, 1982). The sonar echoes reaching the bat's ears from such small spheres at the maximum distance of detection have amplitudes approximately at the bat's threshold of hearing as measured in quiet conditions (Dalland, 1965). When bats are actually pursuing prey under natural conditions, they might not perform as well as they do in laboratory tests under quiet conditions, but observations of interceptions have shown that they certainly react to small insects and to targets such as 3- to 10-mm spheres at distances of about a meter (Griffin, 1958; Novick, 1977; Schnitzler et al., 1987; Webster & Brazier, 1965). (Part of the bat's reaction consists of changing the structure and repetition rate of its sounds as it detects and closes in on the object (see Figure 2). The bat's approach is characterized by a variety of target-tracking activities (see Kick & Simmons, 1984).) *Eptesicus fuscus* will react to individual mealworms thrown into the air when the target is as far away as 2 m (Webster & Brazier, 1968). Field observations reveal comparable distances of reaction to natural prey by other species of bats (Fenton, 1984).

The maximum operating range of echolocation by *Eptesicus fuscus* is 3–5 m, judging from the results of psychophysical tests (Kick, 1982). Most pursuits of insects probably are initiated at distances of 2–3 m. During pursuit, the bat adjusts the rate of emission of its sonar sounds in proportion to the declining range of the target. The bat must therefore perceive the target's distance more or less continuously throughout the interception process. At the time of capture, the coordination of the reach of the wing towards the target shows the culminating accuracy of distance determination to be at least 1–2 cm. For these responses to occur, the magnitude of target range must be represented explicitly in the bat's sonar receiver from the time the bat first reacts to the target's presence to the end of the maneuver. Some sort of display of target range for absolute ranges extending from a few centimeters out to several meters must exist in the bat's auditory system (see Suga, 1988).

The acuity of perception of target range

Bats perceive the distance to individual targets from the time-delay of echoes, and they can use echo delay to distinguish among targets located at different distances (Simmons, 1973). For a velocity of sound in air of 344 m/s, each centimeter of target range retards the arrival of echoes by about 58 μs, or 5.8 ms for each meter. (The total path traveled by the sound is twice the target's range – the distance is crossed once on the outgoing journey and once on the return journey.) Psychophysical experiments establish the complete equivalence of target range and echo delay for bats (Simmons, 1973). To the bat, perception of the distance to individual objects is essentially a matter of estimating the duration of the interval of time that elapses between production of sonar sounds and reception of echoes.

The earliest attempts to measure the target-ranging accuracy of bats used a two-choice discrimination procedure in which bats were trained to respond to the nearer of two simultaneously presented, flat-surfaced targets (one target on the bat's left, the other on the right). The difference in range between the targets was reduced in small steps until the bat could no longer reliably determine which was closer (Simmons, 1973). This seemingly straightforward method yielded about the same estimated accuracy of roughly 1–2 cm for several different species, including *Eptesicus fuscus*. The results were satisfying because they seemed to agree with the accuracy with which bats reached out to seize airborne targets at the end of the interception maneuver (see Figure 4). However, on each trial of the two-choice target-range discrimination experiment, the bat would move its head back and forth once or twice during one or two seconds to scan the target on the left and the right with its sonar sounds (Simmons & Vernon, 1971). These head movements introduced an artifact into the situation by changing the distance to each target, thus changing the path length traveled by echoes. Estimates of the size of the head-movement artifact were about a centimeter, which is comparable to the measured acuity of bats for target ranging. Echolocating bats might be able to perceive target range with greater acuity than 1–2 cm, but the ordinary two-choice procedure could never show it (Simmons & Grinnell, 1988).

One would like to know how accurately the bat under the best of conditions can determine target distance from the delay of echoes. As a test of the limiting target-ranging performance of the bat's sonar system, this provides an estimate of the sharpness of registration of images along the range dimension. It would indicate how acutely the bat displays target range *to itself*. For best results, the bat and the target should be kept stationary while the bat determines the delay of echoes because the distance to the target would shift if the bat or the target moved, disrupting the bat's own measurement of range, and, in turn, the experimental measurement of the bat's perceptual acuity (Simmons & Grinnell, 1988; Simmons & Stein, 1980). This requires putting the bat in a fairly artificial situation – after all, the bat and the targets that interest it are usually in flight – but the scientific question is itself an abstraction of what the bat does in nature.

The experimental procedure for measuring the limiting acuity of target ranging depends on the fact that the trained bat emits its sonar sounds at a higher rate (10–30 sounds per second) than it scans its head back and forth to examine targets (one or two cycles of head movement per second). During the fraction of a second between one sonar emission and the next, the bat's head remains in about the same place, so a change in delay *from one echo to the next* can be delivered without much of a movement artifact. The distance that the bat's head moves only adds up to substantial amounts over an interval of perhaps five to eight separate sounds (Simmons & Vernon, 1971). If the bat could be induced to detect and respond to a change in the delay of echoes from one sonar emission to the next, it should be possible to measure the smallest change in delay perceptible to the bat without such severe movement artifacts as were present in target-range discrimination experiments.

Figure 5 shows the experimental procedure for determining the bat's perceptual acuity for echo delay. The bat is trained to sit on a small, elevated Y-shaped platform, in an observing position about at the center of the Y, and to broadcast its sonar sounds in the direction of the left and right branches of the Y (Simmons, 1979; Simmons, Ferragamo, Moss, Stevenson, & Altes, in press). A microphone (*m*) that is sensitive to ultrasonic frequencies is placed at the end of each arm of the Y to pick up the bat's sonar emissions, and each microphone's recorded signal is conducted through an electronic *target simulator* to a loudspeaker (*s*). The electronic apparatus returns echoes to the bat from the loudspeaker after a predetermined delay to mimic the presence of a sonar target at a particular distance. (For details about the design of the target simulator and its calibration, see Simmons, Freedman, Stevenson, Chen, & Wohlgenant, 1989. Adaptation of this simulator to the jitter procedure is described in Simmons, Ferragamo, et al., in press). Different devices have been used in different experiments to produce the required electronic delay, including both analog and digital delay lines (Moss & Schnitzler, 1989; Simmons, 1979; Simmons, Ferragamo, et al., in press), but the principle of the simulator remains the same. With such a target simulator, one can expose the bat to stimuli that cannot be produced as echoes from real objects. The flexibility of electronic controls permits a direct measurement of the fine acuity of target ranging. The procedure is to alternate the arrival time of echoes back and forth from one value to another by changing

Figure 5.   *Diagram of the two-choice procedure and the electronic target simulator for studying the acuity of echo delay and target range perception by* Eptesicus. *The bat is trained to detect the target that jitters in range from* a₁ *to* a₂, *and the size of the jitter interval* (Δt) *is reduced in steps to measure the bat's threshold for perceiving the jitter. (From Simmons, Ferragamo et al., in press)*

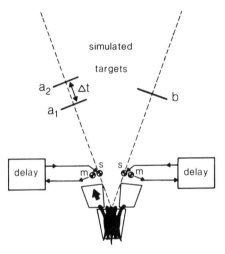

the electronic delay between one sonar sound and the next. The presence of jitter in echo delay (Δt in Figure 5) creates the effect of an artificial target that jumps back and forth from one distance to another on succeeding echoes (a_1 and a_2). The other channel of the simulator returns echoes with a constant delay, simulating a target (b) that is stationary at the mean range of the target that appears to move. The crucial feature of this apparatus is that the bat receives only *one stimulus echo* for each sonar transmission and must use several echoes in succession to determine which channel (left or right; changed randomly) returns the jittering echoes. The directional beam of the bat's sonar emissions (Simmons, 1969) selects one channel or the other for activation by switching on that channel which receives the stronger signal on any given emission. On any particular trial, if the bat aims its head (and its sounds) at the channel set to deliver jittering echoes, it receives echo a_1 on one sound and echo a_2 on the next. The delay of echoes alternates from a_1 to a_2 and back again in this fashion until the bat turns to the other channel or stops emitting sounds after making its choice. If the bat aims towards the other channel, it receives echo b for each emitted sound. In actual trials, the bats emit sounds up to 2 ms long that otherwise are similar to the one shown in Figure 3. A bat typically receives from six to ten echoes from the jittering side before making a choice. Because the bat can get only a single stimulus echo for each emission, it must remember the delay of one echo for comparison with the delay of the next echo to detect the jitter. The bat thus has to use a perceptual representation of each echo's delay to perform the task. In the particular experiment to be described below, the strength of the echoes was set at an amplitude 15 dB above the bat's detection threshold, which was separately measured for a single simulated target presented at the range of a_1 in a two-choice detection task (Kick & Simmons, 1984) with the same apparatus. For two bats, peak-to-peak echo sound pressures were 48 and 54 dB SPL, respectively.

In three different experiments conducted with the echo-delay jitter technique (Moss & Schnitzler, 1989; Simmons, 1979; Simmons, Ferragamo, et al., in press), the jitter has been presented around an average delay anywhere from 3–3.7 ms, which corresponds to simulated average distances of 52–64 cm to the "target" that appears alternately at range a_1 and range a_2. Each bat is trained with food as reward to detect the jittering echoes, usually by discriminating between the arm of the Y-shaped apparatus that produces jittered echoes and the arm that produces stationary echoes. For its response, the bat crawls onto the arm of the platform in the direction of the jittered echoes to receive its reward. The bat's responses to the correct and incorrect arms are totalled for blocks of trials in which a particular jitter value is presented. By reducing the size of the jitter from over 50 µs to only a fraction of a microsecond in small steps, one can determine the limiting acuity of echo delay perception by the bat.

Figure 6 shows the results of a jitter experiment to investigate the smallest detectable change in echo delay for *Eptesicus fuscus* (Simmons, Ferragamo, et al., in press). It was conducted after other experiments made it clear that this change must be smaller than a microsecond (Moss & Schnitzler, 1989; Simmons, 1979). The horizontal axis shows jitter values from zero to 60 ns (10^{-9} s), and the curves (60 trials per point) indicate that these bats can perceive echo-delay changes as small as 10–12 ns in the jitter task (for a 75% correct threshold criterion). It seems incredible that bats are able to perceive such small time changes, which correspond to changes of about 2 µm (10^{-6} m) in target range. A series of control experiments using different means of generating electronic echo delays yielded the same very small thresholds in the bat's behavior. (Other control experiments establish that the auditory cues for the jitter task are carried by the time of occurrence of neural discharges, and thus that echo spectral artifacts are not the true cues for such fine delay acuity. This is demonstrated by the fact that the bat's perception

Figure 6.   *A graph of the performance of two* Eptesicus *detecting jittering echoes in the two-choice task shown in Figure 5. The threshold falls around 10–12 ns for 75% correct responses using several different techniques for electronically delaying the sounds. The horizontal axis shows the size of the jitter interval (Δt). Each data point represents 60 trials. (From Simmons, Ferragamo, et al., in press)*

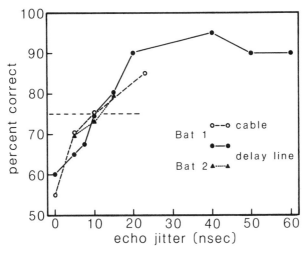

of echo-delay jitter is vulnerable to predicted shifts in perceived delay due to the known trade-off between the latency of neural discharges and stimulus amplitude (Simmons, Ferragamo, et al., in press; Simmons, Moss, and Ferragamo, 1989). Aside from the extraordinarily small size of the delay threshold, there is no obvious reason to doubt that the curves in Figure 6 reflect the bat's ability to determine the time of occurrence of sonar echoes, and thus target range, with great accuracy.)

Perception of target shape by FM bats

If a target-ranging accuracy of 1–2 cm is sufficient to effect capture of a flying insect (see Figure 4), why do bats have such a tremendous surplus of target-ranging acuity, from the centimeter range to the submillimeter, even micrometer, range? *Eptesicus* appears to have a limiting target-range acuity ten thousand times better than needed for seizing prey, which suggests that the bat may use the psychological dimension of delay or range to support other aspects of perception of targets than crude distance.

Discrimination of airborne targets

Echolocating bats cannot only use their sonar to detect and track small airborne objects, but they can also use it to identify targets as potential prey. Bats that emit CF sonar sounds are spectacularly successful at detecting flying insects from the rhythmic fluttering motions of their wings (Henson et al., 1987; Trappe & Schnitzler, 1982). This ability is based on unusual auditory specializations for detecting Doppler shifts in echoes – specializations that are manifested as early in the auditory system as the inner ear (Henson et al., 1987; Neuweiler et al., 1980). Several experiments suggest that bats which emit FM sonar sounds also are proficient at identifying targets (Griffin, Friend, & Webster, 1965; Webster & Brazier, 1965, 1968; Webster & Durlach, 1963), even determining whether targets have fluttering wings (Sum & Menne, 1988), but it is not so obvious just what auditory capacities they tap for doing so. The basis for target identification by FM bats resides in the computational capacities of the auditory system for creating images having spatial dimensions from sounds having acoustic dimensions. These computational "sound-to-space" modules cannot be seen in most kinds of anatomical/physiological experiments on auditory mechanisms, but their presence is readily evident from behavior. By their nature, most neurophysiological experiments are atomistic in perspective, providing data only on the cellular level of analysis in the brain, not on the performance that cellular systems can achieve. However, through pooling data from numerous neurophysiological experiments, some idea of the existence, if not the power, of the bat's imaging machinery emerges (Suga, 1988).

The ability of FM bats to discriminate among airborne targets on the basis of size and shape has been investigated in a series of experiments that brilliantly combine the bat's natural pursuit behavior with the requirements for stimulus control in psychophysical experiments. When presented with mealworms thrown into the air in a large room, a flying bat will capture and eat them. When presented with inedible targets such as plastic spheres or disks, the bat will soon learn to avoid them while still capturing mealworms. By alternating or mixing mealworms with various sizes and shapes of inedible targets in airborne discrimination tests, one can explore the bat's ability to identify targets using sonar (Griffin et al., 1965; Webster & Brazier, 1965, 1968; Webster & Durlach, 1963). In this adaptation of the bat's natural hunting behavior, the FM bats *Myotis lucifugus* and *Eptesicus fuscus* can distinguish mealworms from various sizes of spheres with considerable success. Bats more frequently capture spheres of similar size to mealworms than spheres of disparate size, as might be expected, but, with practice, some bats reach the point where they nearly always correctly capture mealworms and reject spheres of all sizes. Because mealworms are not spherically symmetrical, they reflect echoes that change according to the target's orientation to the incident sonar sound, while spheres reflect echoes of uniform characteristics from all orientations. To avoid having the bats simply use echo variability for discriminating airborne targets, disks similar in size to mealworms were substituted for spheres (Griffin et al., 1965). Disks reflect echoes that change according to the target's orientation, too. The disks turn and tumble in flight just as do mealworms, so the echoes from all the targets change from one emission to the next. The bats nevertheless proved able to discriminate several different-shaped disks from mealworms in this task.

From the successful performance of bats at airborne discrimination of mealworms from disks, one would expect echoes from the mealworm to be quite readily distinguishable from echoes from the disks. However, attempts to determine what features of echoes distinguish mealworms from disks, made at the time of the original experiments, yielded disappointing results. In these early studies, the echoes from mealworms and disks at different orientations were characterized by their amplitude spectra over the frequency range from about 20 to 100 kHz, the frequency region used for echolocation by *Myotis* and *Eptesicus* (Griffin, 1967; Griffin et al., 1965). Instead of dramatic differences between the echoes from mealworms and disks, there were only marginal differences, primarily in the variability of echo spectra along the frequency axis. The acoustic signature of "mealwormness" and "diskness" was not obvious in the echo data (Griffin, 1967). A more recent study of echoes from mealworms and disks has revealed a structure to the echoes that could have been the basis for the bat's discrimination (Simmons & Chen, 1989).

Figure 7 illustrates how the echoes from a mealworm (about 17 mm long when partially curled) and a disk (12.5 mm in diameter and 3 mm thick) differ at different target orientations. These targets are discriminated by *Myotis* with a high level of performance (Griffin et al., 1965). The diagram shows the incident sound (an impulse covering frequencies from 15 to 120 kHz) approaching the targets from the left, with the echo recorded from each target plotted beneath the target's outline. The echoes consist of one or more (usually two) prominent replicas of the incident impulse, with several secondary impulses present as well in the echoes from the mealworm. Starting at the bottom of the diagram, with the disk oriented facing the incident sound (designated 90° with respect to the plane of the diagram), the echo is virtually identical to the incident sound. As the disk rotates in steps of 30° towards the plane of the diagram, the echoes develop separate impulse-like components returned by the disk's leading and trailing edges. At 60° and 30° orientation, these two components in the echo from the disk are equally strong.

Figure 7. *A diagram of the echoes reflected by a disk and a mealworm at different orientations with respect to the incident sound (indicated at left). Angles are given relative to the plane of the page. The dual time and distance scale converts delay separations of echo components into target range separations. The range profile of the targets is represented by the time structure of the echoes. (From Simmons & Chen, 1989)*

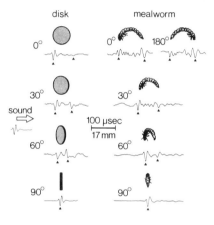

At 0°, where the incident sound catches the disk directly on its leading edge, the component in the echo due to the disk's trailing edge is very weak owing to its being occluded by the leading edge.

For the mealworm, the orientation of the target has a generally similar effect on the echoes in Figure 7, but with greater complexity in the waveform. At 90°, the mealworm's broadside reflection is basically a single replica of the incident sound, but at all other orientations the mealworm's head and tail produce distinct echo components. As the mealworm rotates from 90° to 60°, then 30°, and then 0°, the distance between the head and the tail is conveyed by the time separation of the echo components. In addition, the finer structure of the mealworm's body (legs, segments) adds smaller components to the echo that fill in the time between the components from the head and the tail. The disk, being bilaterally and radially symmetrical, is fully described by echoes from only 90° of rotation, but the mealworm is only approximately bilaterally symmetrical and reflects different echoes for a full 360° spherical set of orientations. These other orientations appear as a leftward or rightward rolling of the mealworm's body relative to what is shown in Figure 7. At most orientations of the mealworm not shown in Figure 7, the echoes also contain multiple impulse-like components similar to the echoes at 0°, 30° or 60°. The mealworm seems distinguishable from the disk on the basis of the impulse structure of its echoes over several different orientations. During the bat's approach to the targets in the airborne interception tests, it probably receives echoes covering a random sector of about 60° of rotation of the targets and thus can sample each target's reflectivity over a range of orientations within approximately a 60°-sector of each target's overall spherical reflectivity pattern (Griffin, 1967). If the bat can separately perceive the parts of a target that are closely spaced along the range axis, then it probably could use range profile as the basis for identifying the mealworm. (The overall amplitude of the echoes from mealworms and disks and their average reflectivities at different frequencies across different orientations do not differ significantly, so it seems unlikely that the bat perceives echoes as coming from mealworms or disks using general or orientation-independent echo characteristics – Simmons & Chen, 1989). To usefully distinguish mealworms from disks using range profile, the bat would need a range acuity of a fraction of a centimeter, perhaps even a fraction of a millimeter. The results of the echo jitter experiments demonstrate that bats in principle do have fine enough range acuity, so the question becomes whether bats actually can perceive the presence of multiple target components along the range axis. If the bat uses an auditory representation of echoes from which it can create images of targets comparable to the display of discrete impulse-like echo components in the waveforms shown in Figure 7, it should be able to identify the targets that produced the echoes. Each impulse-like echo component registers a reflecting point or surface within the target, called a *glint* (Altes, 1976), and the time separations of the impulses within the echo indicate the distances between the different glints in the target along the range axis. The impulse representation of echoes provides a display of the target's range profile in terms of the distribution of glints in range.

The spectral representation of target structure to FM bats

The impulses used as incident sounds in Figure 7 are short and can easily be seen as separate parts of the echo waveforms. Each impulse is only 10–15 μs long, while the echoes typically consist of several impulses distributed over a longer period of time. With such short incident sounds, the glint structure of the target is directly observable in the echo waveform. In contrast, the bat's sonar sounds are not impulses, they are FM signals that last for several milliseconds in most situations (see Figures 2 and 3). The time separation of the individual components of echoes from the mealworms and disks is much smaller than the duration of the bat's echolocation sounds. Accordingly, the waveforms of echoes reaching the bat from targets such as mealworms and disks consist, not of discrete impulses separated by short intervals of time, but of overlapping FM sounds that cannot easily be discerned separately by eye.

Figure 8 shows waveforms simulating echoes of a sonar sound emitted by *Eptesicus* and reflected by a series of complex targets having different range profiles. For simplicity, each target consists of two ideal (perfectly reflecting) glints separated in range by different amounts from zero to about 10 cm; echoes from these targets thus contain two replicas of the bat's incident sound separated by different intervals of time (Δt in Figure 8) from zero to 600 μs. The sonar signal giving rise to these echoes is about 2.5 ms long, so the components of the echoes overlap extensively. In Figure 8, the echo for zero time separation between the glints is simply a copy of the incident sound itself. (The echo components from two glints with no range separation simply add together to form an echo that has the same waveform as the incident sound.) For time separations of 5, 10, and 15 μs, the two echo components interfere with each other because they do not coincide exactly in delay. This interference primarily produces progressively greater amounts of cancellation of overall echo amplitude as the time separation increases (because the separation is smaller then the average period of the waves in the bat's signal, which is about 33 μs). The overall echo amplitude increases again going from a separation of 15 μs to a separation of 30 μs. For larger time separations, from 50 to 600 μs, the envelope or outline of the echo waveform becomes increasingly "choppy". The echo appears to be broken into segments as a result of the same interference that initially had its effect on the amplitude of the echo as a whole but that now selectively cancels some frequencies and reinforces others across the bandwidth of the FM sweeps in the signal (see Figure 3).

The presence and spacing of two distinct echo components in the two-glint echo waveforms in Figure 8 is not obvious, although it is obvious that the targets responsible for the echoes must be more complex than a single glint. Overlap of the echo components obscures the target's underlying range structure and transposes its acoustic manifestation from the time separation to the placement of notches in the spectrum (Beuter, 1980). The presence of the two components is conveyed by what appears to be the changing amplitude of the whole echo (0–30 μs in Figure 8), or by the echo's spectrum (50–600 μs in Figure 8). (Even for short separations of less than 30 μs, interference produces spectral notches; they just happen to be far enough apart in frequency that they appear to affect primarily the overall amplitude of echoes. The notches occur at frequencies half-way between spectral peaks defined by integer multiples of the reciprocal of the time separation of echo compo-

Figure 8.   *Waveforms of echoes of an* Eptesicus *sonar signal (2.5 ms long) reflected by a series of complex targets consisting of two glints separated by varying ranges. The glint separation is given in terms of the time separation of echo components. Each echo contains two components that overlap and interfere with each other according to their time separation.*

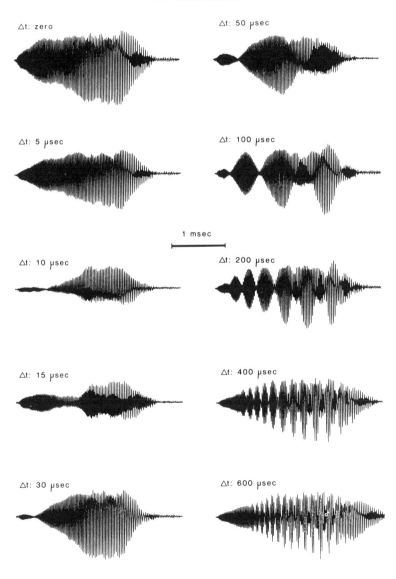

TWO-GLINT ECHOES

Figure 9.   *The spectrum of echoes reflected by the mealworm and the disk for different orientations (see Figure 7). The frequency separation of the notches in each spectrum is inversely related to the time separation of the impulse-like components of each echo. The range profile of the target thus is conveyed either by the echo's frequency structure or its time structure.*

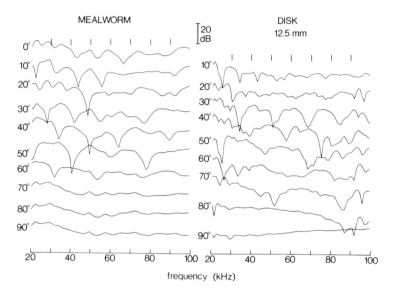

nents.) Presumably, for time separations shorter than about 350 μs, which approximates the integration-time of the hearing of *Eptesicus* for echoes (Simmons, Freedman, et al., 1989), a spectral representation substitutes for the seemingly more straightforward impulse representation of the structure of echoes from complex targets. For the individual echo components to again be rendered as visible parts of the overall echo waveform, the long FM signals used by *Eptesicus* would have to be compressed into much shorter impulses, such as those shown in Figure 7. This would be equivalent to converting the spectral notch representation back into a representation of time separations.

Figure 9 shows the frequency response of the mealworm and the disk as sources of echoes over the frequency range used for echolocation by *Eptesicus*. Target orientations are shown in 10° steps for the same plane of rotation as in Figure 7. These curves show the notches in the echo spectrum created by interference between the individual impulse-like components of the echoes in Figure 7 (Simmons & Chen, 1989). The location in frequency and the frequency separation of these notches is inversely related to the time separation of the echo components (see above; Beuter, 1980; Schmidt, 1988). The complicated, choppy appearance of the envelopes of the two-glint echoes shown in Figure 8 is a manifestation of these same interference patterns in the waveforms. In a FM bat like *Eptesicus*, the target's range profile probably is encoded by the auditory system in terms of these notches in the echo spectrum due to the almost complete overlap of the replicas of the bat's sonar sounds contained within echo waveforms. This is in contrast to the target's absolute range, which must be encoded directly in terms of the arrival time of echoes by the time of occurrence of nerve discharges (Bodenhamer & Pollak, 1981; Simmons, 1973; Simmons & Kick, 1984; Suga, 1988). (The sonar sounds of FM bats are kept short enough that echoes do not overlap with emissions and thus do not produce interference-related spectral cues for target range (Cahlander, McCue, & Webster, 1964).)

Discrimination experiments show that FM bats can perceive differences of a fraction of a millimeter in the range profile of targets (Habersetzer & Vogler, 1983; Schmidt, 1988; Simmons et al., 1974). The type of target developed for assessing this capability is a flat plastic plate with holes of uniform depth drilled part-way through its front surface. Bats are trained to choose beween a target with holes of one depth and another target with holes of a different depth. The front of the target and the bottoms of the holes provide two reflecting surfaces at different distances. Echoes from these reflecting surfaces overlap and create depth-related interference patterns similar to those shown in Figure 9. Figure 10 shows the spectra of echoes reflected by the targets used in a hole-depth discrimination experiment with *Eptesicus* to illustrate the bat's sensitivity to spectral cues. The 8.0-mm target was the standard, rewarded target (two different 8.0-mm targets, *A* and *B*, were used interchangeably to keep individual flaws in the machining of one target from becoming the bat's cue instead of hole depth), and it was paired with a series of targets having holes that were 6.5, 7.0, 7.2, 7.6, or 8.0 mm deep to determine the bat's discrimination threshold. *Eptesicus* is able to discriminate hole-depth differences of 0.6–0.8 mm, placing the threshold in spectral terms between the 7.2- and 7.6-mm spectra in Figure 10 (Simmons et al., 1974).

The interference notches in the echo spectra in Figure 10 show how good these targets are as models of the acoustic properties which distinguish mealworms from disks. From Figure 10, if the bats indeed did represent the range profile of the targets in terms of echo spectra, then they must be able to detect shifts of only a few kilohertz in the locations of the notches. As the hole depth changes, the notches in echo spectra move different amounts according to their frequency, with higher-frequency notches shifting more than lower-frequency notches. (Compare the sizes of the frequency shifts for

Figure 10. *The spectrum of echoes reflected by targets with holes of different depths in their front surfaces. The depth of the holes is represented by the location and spacing of the notches in the spectrum along the frequency axis. (From Simmons et al., 1974)*

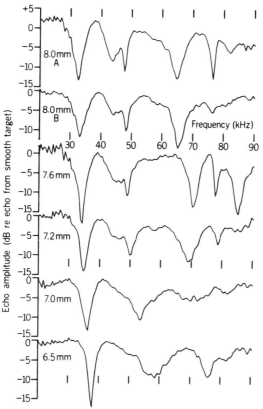

different notches in Figure 10.) It would be difficult to specify exactly the bat's threshold for detecting frequency shifts in the notches without having evidence that any one particular notch is relied upon by the bat. Probably *Eptesicus* perceives the shift in several notches together since it emits its sounds equally strongly at frequencies across the entire range illustrated in the spectra (see Figure 3). As a result, the bat's acuity for perceiving the range profile of targets is more economically stated in terms of the change in range or delay than in terms of frequency shifts (Simmons, 1987; Simmons & Stein, 1980), even though the auditory system may encode much of the required information spectrally when echoes are received at the inner ear. The range-profile thresholds for *Eptesicus* and several other FM bat species are similar at a fraction of a millimeter in range difference – at most a few microseconds in delay change (Habersetzer & Vogler, 1983; Schmidt, 1988; Simmons et al., 1974).

Acoustic images of complex targets

It seems likely that the spectrum of FM echoes from complex targets carries range-profile information to the bat. The first evidence for this is the overlap of echo components under the conditions that prevail in Figure 8 in relation to the 350-µs integration time of the bat's hearing for echoes (Beuter, 1980; Simmons et al., 1974; Simmons, Freedman, et al., 1989). The second evidence is an observed symmetry of threshold curves for discrimination data obtained by placing negative stimuli both above and below the positive stimulus from one species of bat (*Megaderma lyra*). This symmetry appears when the data are scaled and plotted for frequency intervals as opposed to time intervals (Schmidt, 1988). Both kinds of evidence depend upon interpretation, though. For example, the symmetry of threshold curves expressed in units of frequency assumes that the bat scales frequencies linearly, which may be approximately true for the species in question (*Megaderma*; Rubsamen, Neuweiler, & Sripathi, 1988) but probably not true for *Eptesicus fuscus* (Covey & Casseday, 1986; see below). What is needed is a direct experimental demonstration that the bat's perception of target shape can emerge entirely from its treatment of the notches in echo spectra, as distinct from the bat's ability merely to discriminate between echoes that differ in their spectra.

Eptesicus can detect changes in echo spectra that are small enough to be useful in discriminating among targets having different range profiles (Figure 10). However, does the bat perceive that the notches in echo spectra signify the presence of multiple components in echo waveforms, and, thus, multiple glints in the target? In other words, does the bat actually perceive a complex target as having reflecting points located at different ranges, or does the bat merely perceive it as being a "spectrally distinct" target at a single absolute range? If the latter, the bat ultimately represents the shape of targets entirely in terms of the spectrum of echoes. However, if the former, the bat ultimately represents target shape in terms of time separations related to range profile, using spectral information as part of the process of estimating them. That is, does the bat perceive images of targets that are organized along spatial or along acoustic dimensions? The experimental procedure used to address this question is a modification of what is shown in Figure 5 (Simmons, Moss, & Ferragamo, 1989). The same electronic target simulator used for echo jitter tests now delivers echoes to simulate the presence of a two-glint target (a_1 plus a_2) on one side of the two-choice situation and a single-glint target (b) on the other side. When the bat aims its sounds at one channel, it receives *both* echoes ($a_1 + a_2$) for each sonar emission. When it aims its sounds at the other channel, it receives only one echo (b). As in the jitter experiment, just one of the two channels is active for each emitted sound according to the aim of the bat's head, but the two echoes that were presented alternately are now presented together. Thus, echoes $a_1 + a_2$ are delivered together, but $a_1 + a_2$ *and* b never are delivered together on the same emission. This arrangement presents the bat with either the two-glint target or the one-glint target in a *sequential paradigm* controlled by the aim of the bat's head. For the bat to determine which target contains two glints, it must remember and compare their images. The time separation (Δt in Figure 5) of the echoes simulating the two-glint target is 100 µs, which corresponds to 17 mm. The two-glint target thus is a reasonable if simplified approximation to a mealworm or a disk in its range profile. Two *Eptesicus* were trained to discriminate the two-glint complex target from the one-glint simple target, being rewarded for choosing $a_1 + a_2$ instead of b. As before, echoes of the bat's sonar emissions were electronically delivered to the bat at delays corresponding to the desired ranges.

The two glints of the complex target were simulated at ranges of about 56.5 cm (glint a_1) and about 58.2 cm (glint a_2) by echoes delivered with delays of 3.275 and 3.375 ms, respectively. The single glint of the simple target (b) was presented *at a succession of different ranges* extending from nearer than a_1 to farther than a_2. In units of delay, the echoes for b appeared at delays from 3.1 to 3.4 ms in steps of 25 µs. The strategy of the experiment is to move the single glint along the range axis to determine where the bat perceives it to correspond with each of the parts of the complex target. The locations of b where the bat achieves poorer performance indicate the locations of the parts of the complex target along the range axis in the bat's images.

Figure 11A shows the results obtained with *Eptesicus* discriminating the two-glint target from the one-glint target. Here, the bat's performance – percentage errors – is being used as a continuous variable, without the imposition of an arbitrary 75% threshold criterion. The curves in this upper graph reveal that, as the echoes simulating target b are moved along the delay axis, the bat makes more errors in determining which is the correct target when the delay of b corresponds to either the delay of a_1 or a_2. (The amplitude of the echoes was the same as in the jitter experiment shown in Figures 5 and 6, and the same two bats were used.) Because the bat receives *only* the two-glint or the one-glint echoes for any particular sonar emission, it must

Figure 11. *Results of experiments with two* Eptesicus *(solid and dashed lines) discriminating a two-glint target from a single-glint target. (A) Performance when both glints are presented together. (B) Performance when the first glint is presented alone, with echoes filtered to mimic the presence of the second glint. (C) Performance when the two glints are presented separately, in alternation from one sonar emission to the next (jittering). The horizontal axis shows different delays for presenting echoes for target b. Each data point represents 50–75 trials. (From Simmons, Moss, & Ferragamo, 1989)*

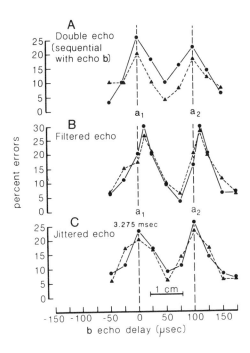

compare remembered images of the targets to make its choice. As Figure 11A shows, the bat actually seems to perceive the simulated complex target as composed of two reflecting points located at different ranges. The bat's image of the complex target evidently explicitly incorporates the location of a_1 and a_2 along the range axis, and the bat perceives these glints approximately at their objective ranges.

The results of the two-glint experiment involve the bat's perception of target range because the bat's performance changes with the range of b. Even though the bat's task is simply to determine which is the complex target, the results show that the bat's performance depends upon the placement of these glints in range. *Eptesicus* perceives the absolute range of the first glint, a_1, in the two-glint target and also the single glint, b, from the time-delay of their echo components since only the electronic delay of these echoes is available as a cue for the bat. (The echoes from the two simulator channels are always presented sequentially, so $a_1 + a_2$ can never overlap with b to create spectral cues, and the bat's emissions themselves are too short to overlap with any of these echoes.) The range of the second of the two glints in the complex target probably is encoded from the placement of notches in the spectrum of echoes from the two glints combined since their echo components overlap and occur together in the experiment. These echo components are only 100 μs apart, while the bat's sonar sounds are up to 2 ms long. The overlap creates spectral notches spaced 10 kHz apart (1/100-μs). In the frequency range used by *Eptesicus,* these notches appear at 25, 35, 45, 55, 65, 75, and 85 kHz. In Figure 11A, the bat evidently perceives an image of the target that expresses these spectral notches in terms of the equivalent underlying time separation of the echo components. In other words, *Eptesicus* perceives the second glint itself at its corresponding absolute range, in company with the nearer glint at its corresponding absolute range. When the echoes from b match the perceived range of those from a_1 or a_2, the bat's performance declines because the single glint partially masks each of the combined glints.

Transformation of echo spectra into time delays

In a second version of the two-glint experiment, only echo a_1 was presented (at its normal delay of 3.275 ms) whenever the bat aimed its head at the channel set to simulate the complex target. Echo b was presented at different delays, as before. Echo a_2 was deleted by simply switching off its delay line. However, echo a_1 was filtered through a set of six parallel band-pass filters to reproduce the same spectral notches that previously were created by over-lap of a_1 and a_2. (These filters were tuned to frequencies between the notches, and the slopes of their adjacent filter skirts adjusted to make the notches similar in depth to those caused by interference.) The results (Figure 11B) replicated the first two-glint experiment (Figure 11A), showing that *Eptesicus* perceives the filtered echo, a_1, with its filter-created notches, as though it consisted of two discrete echo components separated by 100 μs. The bat thus seems able to convert the shape of the echo spectrum into an estimate of the equivalent underlying time separation of summing and interfering echo com-ponents. It then uses this estimated time separation to perceive the range of the second glint relative to the first glint. The absolute range of the first glint is conveyed directly by the delay of a_1. In effect, the bat reconstructs an image of the range profile of the target from a combination of the time-delay and spectral composition of echoes. The spectral information adds to the image by providing for the reconstitution of the second glint.

A third experimental procedure was used to determine whether echo spectral information plays a role in shape discrimination besides being transformed into a time-separation estimate. The basis for this third stimulus regime is the jitter procedure used previously (Figures 5 and 6). The strategy is to present echoes for glint a_1 and echoes for glint a_2 at their appropriate delays (3.275 and 3.375 ms), but not to present them together. Time-delay cues are thus available to the bat to determine which channel delivers two delays rather than just one delay, but without any accompanying spectral cues generated by interference between the overlapping waveforms of a_1 + a_2 as in the first experiment (Figure 11A). Echo a_1 was alternated with echo a_2 from one sonar emission to the next using the jitter technique. Both a_1 and a_2 are presented, but never for the same sonar emission. The complex target now consists of a glint that jitters back and forth in range from one emission to the next. Echo b again is presented at various ranges, sequentially (depending on the bat's head aim) with the now jittering a_1 or a_2. For its reward, the bat must choose two glints separated by 17 mm (100 μs) without the spectral consequences of the direct mixing of their echoes. From the results (Figure 11C), the bats perceived the locations of the two glints as before. This is not surprising; in the jitter experiment they discriminate between jittering and non-jittering echoes, showing that they distinguish between different amounts of delay or range. However, this result establishes the equivalence of delay-encoded range information and spectrally encoded range information.

The significant finding in Figure 11 is that the percentage of errors made by the bats at the peaks of the curves is about the same for all three conditions. *Eptesicus* does not find it any easier to determine which is the two-glint target when spectral cues are available due to interference or to filtering than when only time-delay cues are available in the jitter condition. The spectrally estimated range profile of the complex target is perceived with the same level of performance as the two glints presented purely in terms of alternating echo delays, with no spectral cues at all. Thus, the spectrum of the echo appears to contribute no information about the shape of the target beyond what is used to estimate the equivalent delay separation of the overlapping echo components. Evidently *Eptesicus* converts sonar echoes entirely into a time-domain representation in the course of forming the acoustically derived spatial image of the target. Although spectral information is used to determine the presence of multiple glints, it evidently is destroyed as spectral information by this transformation.

In a strict sense, then, *Eptesicus* perceives the shape of a complex sonar target in terms of its range profile along a perceptual dimension or scale whose absolute values are derived from measurements of the arrival-time of echoes (Simmons & Stein, 1980). Multiple glints are somehow "entered" onto this scale from estimates of the location and spacing of spectral notches, but they are perceived with reference to absolute estimates of echo delay rather than as independent attributes of objects. Echolocating bats may only need to determine target range to within 1–2 cm for seizing prey in the wing or tail membrane (see Figure 4), but they would require substantially greater range acuity to support the range-based perception of target shape that is demonstrated in Figure 11. This could account for the "surplus" target-ranging acuity that bats exhibit in the jitter task (see Figure 6).

Computations which create the bat's acoustic images

The results shown in Figure 11 demonstrate unity in the images perceived by *Eptesicus*. These images are expressed along a single, synthetic, spatial, perceptual dimension created by combining two different auditory representations – one temporal, the other spectral. The bat's perceptions are organized along a spatial dimension that corresponds to the external world of targets, notwithstanding the fact that they are mediated by acoustic and auditory events taking place along dimensions of time and frequency. The convergence of two different kinds of auditory representations onto a common perceptual dimension justifies considering the outcome to be spatial rather than acoustic. A closer examination of the images of targets reveals features of this process of convergence.

Detailed structure of acoustic images of targets

The percentage-error peaks in Figure 11 for individual glints (either a_1 or a_2) appear to be about 50 μs wide at a level half-way down from the tip. This width is not the true outline of the bat's image of either glint but a consequence of the bat's head movements during experimental trials. As the bat scans the targets, it alters the position of its head and ears relative to the range of the target. (It must scan the targets because the electronic simulator requires that the bat's sounds be pointed at each channel separately before echoes from that channel are produced.) The echo jitter procedure (see Figure 5) was developed to remove head-movement artifacts from measurements of the bat's fine delay acuity, and this procedure provides a sharper picture of the true width and shape of the error peaks that mark the perceived locations of glints along the range axis. In effect, the jitter procedure can be used to trace the shape of the range image perceived by the bat without the blurring caused by the bat's movements (Altes, 1989; Simmons, Ferragamo, et al., in press; Simmons & Stein, 1980; Simmons & Grinnell, 1988). The curves demonstrating fine delay acuity in Figure 6 have a time axis only 60 ns in length. The same jitter discrimination paradigm used with the same bats over larger jitter intervals (Δt in Figure 5), extends the jitter data to cover a time span comparable to that covered by the two-glint data in Figure 11. Figure 12 shows jitter discrimination data collected over an interval of 50 μs (Simmons, Ferragamo, et al., in press). (Two different acoustic conditions are shown – 0° and 180° phase – for reasons that will be described

Figure 12. *Results of echo jitter discrimination experiments with two* Eptesicus *(circles and diamonds). The data are for larger jitter intervals than Figure 6. In the 0° phase condition (upper graph) the bats make significantly more errors at zero and around 30–35 μs, while in the 180° phase condition (lower graph) the bats make more errors around 15–20 μs and also around 45 μs. These regions of greater errors shift with the phase of echoes, indicating that the bats perceive phase. Each data point represents 60 trials. (From Simmons, Ferragamo, et al., in press)*

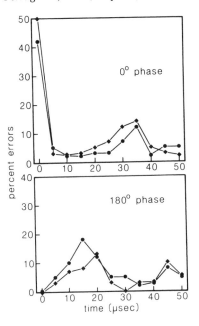

below.) The curves in the upper (0° phase) graph just extend the data from Figure 6 out to longer jitter intervals for the same two bats, but present the data as percentages of errors rather than correct responses to make them compatible with the data in Figure 11. The zero point on the time scale in Figure 12 is interpreted as though it corresponds to the zero point in Figure 11. The curves in Figure 11 show the bats making errors when echo b aligns with either echo a_1 or a_2. The curves in Figure 12 give a closer look at the shape of the right half of the curve for the a_1 peak from 0 to 50 µs without the intrusion of head-movement artifacts. The bats perceive the echoes for a_1 as located much more sharply at their objective delay than indicated in Figure 11. The width of the error peak for a_1 is about 2 µs wide in Figure 12. When sufficiently small time steps are used in the graph, the peak's true width, given (upside down) in Figure 6, is shown to be only about 20 ns. There is a smaller error peak located at 30–35 µs in the upper graph of Figure 12, indicating that the image of a_1 has a small ghost-like component located a short distance away from its objective position (Simmons, 1979; Simmons, Ferragamo, et al., in press). Since the curves in Figure 12 actually are symmetrical around their zero-time centers, the image of a_1 can be more fully described as consisting of a sharp primary point located at the objective range, with two weaker secondary points located about 6 mm (the equivalent of 30–35 µs in terms of range) nearer and farther than the primary point. Put in more general terms, the image of a single glint has a kind of fine structure along the range axis.

The primary and secondary parts of the image of a_1 revealed in the upper (0° phase) graph of Figure 12 are real in the sense that they are present as information in the sounds that reach the bat's ears, and the bat perceives them to exist. The primary part represents the best estimate of the time of occurrence of echoes in the jitter task. Secondary points originate in the bat's sonar signals themselves and constitute a preservation of phase ambiguity from the waveform of echoes into the resulting image (Simmons, 1979; Simmons, Ferragamo, et al., in press). This is illustrated by the upper (signal) graph of Figure 13, which contains a display of the combined time and phase composition of echoes, called the *cross-correlation function* between echoes and emissions. Briefly stated, the cross-correlation function provides an index of the time of occurrence of echoes relative to emissions that utilizes all of the frequencies contained in the echo to maximize the accuracy of the estimate (which is equivalent to minimizing the width of the error peak surrounding the estimate). Because the echoes are not infinite in bandwidth, the periodic repetition of cycles in the waveform at the "average" frequency of echoes inevitably introduces cyclic peaks into the cross-correlation function, as shown by prominent side-peaks in the upper graph of Figure 13. These

Figure 13. *Graphs comparing the cross-correlation function for echoes* (signal*) with a compound performance curve for the average percentage errors of three* Eptesicus *in the jitter discrimination task* (bat). *The 0° phase data are plotted on top of the 180° phase data, which are inverted to form a bidirectional error axis. The locations of the phase-sensitive error peaks correspond to the positive-going and negative-going peaks in the cross-correlation function.*

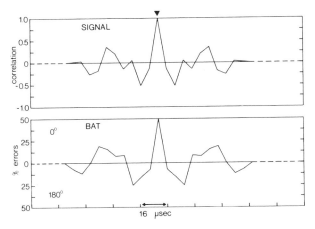

peaks intrude into the image, as shown in Figure 12. (See Woodward, 1964, and Van Trees, 1971, for details about the representation of information in radar or sonar echoes.) The bat perceives the secondary parts of the image of a single glint at points corresponding approximately to the 30 to 35-µs average periodicity inherent in the waveform of the echoes and the emissions.

Two-choice behavioral experiments yield data that can go from perfect performance (0% errors) to chance performance (50% errors). The scale of the data has a natural floor; it does not extend below zero. From Figures 12 and 13, *Eptesicus* evidently perceives secondary image components that correspond to the periodicity or positive (upward)-going waves of the cross-correlation function. If the bat's images incorporate the full cross-correlation function, including the negative (downward)-going waves, the two-choice procedure will fail to show this fact because negative percentage errors cannot happen. However, if the phase of one of the echoes in the jitter condition is inverted by 180° relative to the other (a_1 relative to a_2), the cross-correlation function itself for that echo is inverted so that the negative side appears on top. If the bat perceives each glint in terms of the full cross-correlation function of echoes, then to perform the jitter task will now require it to compare the positive side of this function for a_2 with the negative side of this function for a_1. Repeating the jitter discrimination experiment with a_1 inverted in phase should test the bat's ability to perceive the lower or negative waves of the cross-correlation function (Simmons, Ferragamo, et al., in press).

The lower (180° phase) graph in Figure 12 shows that *Eptesicus* makes errors in the jitter discrimination task at places that roughly correspond to the negative-going waves of the cross-correlation function in Figure 13. Data similar to those shown in Figure 12 are now available for three *Eptesicus* in the jitter task with phase-shifted echoes. By plotting the mean 0° phase curve for these three bats above an inverted 180° phase curve along a common time axis, the entire fine structure of the image of a single-glint target appears in the lower (bat) graph in Figure 13. This compound behavioral curve is a reasonable approximation to the entire cross-correlation function of echoes. The only aspect of the image not captured by the uniform 5-μs time steps used in Figure 13 is the exceedingly sharp 20-ns width of the primary part of the image around zero on the time axis. This is shown in Figure 6.

Even though a single glint is simply one point along the range axis, the bat's *image* of the glint contains a fine structure of multiple points along the perceptual equivalent of the range axis. The bat encodes the delay of echoes from a single glint, or from the first glint of a complex target, directly as an estimate of time (Simmons, Moss, & Ferragamo, 1989). The fine structure of the image, which Figure 13 shows as originating in the signals received by the bat, must occur because the bat's time-estimating mechanism preserves the relevant frequency and phase information in echoes (Simmons, Ferragamo, et al., in press). However, the bat encodes the delay of echoes from the second glint by representing the shape of the spectrum and then converting this representation into its equivalent estimate of time. Does the image of the second glint in a complex target have a fine structure, too? The error peaks for both a_1 and a_2 in Figure 11 are broadened by an artifact introduced by the bat's head movements. Figures 6 and 13 show that the image of a_1 is actually much sharper than it appears to be from Figure 11. If the head-movement artifact is removed from the data for a_2, does the image of a_2 have a fine structure comparable to that for the image of a_1?

The jitter discrimination procedure can be adapted to measure the true width of the error peak for a_2 as well as for a_1. In the jitter paradigm of Figure 5, the single glint a_1 is replaced by a double glint consisting of a_1 plus a_1' to determine the contribution of the second glint to the fine structure of the image. In the usual jitter procedure, each of the bat's emissions towards the jittering channel normally would produce only a_1 or a_2. Now each emission towards the jittering channel produces either the complex of $a_1 + a_1'$ or else just a_2, and these two possible stimuli alternate from one emission to the next. Each emission towards the non-jittering channel still produces b. (For reasons described below, the time separation of a_1 and a_1' is set to 10 μs, rather than to 100 μs as in Figure 11, producing a complex echo with a spectral notch at 50 kHz. The jittering echoes thus now simulate a two-glint target with a range separation of about 2 mm that alternates with a single-glint target.) The jitter interval itself is still the time separation of a_1 and a_2 (Δt in Figure 5), which is varied in small steps up to a value of 50 μs. As the jitter interval approaches the same value as the 10-μs separation of a_1 and a_1', the bat's performance curve traces out the shape of the image of the second glint. (The jitter experiment with $a_1 + a_1'$ was conducted for two phase conditions, too. In the 0° phase condition, $a_1 + a_1'$ and a_2 are all delivered to the bat with the same phase characteristics. In the 180° phase condition, $a_1 + a_1'$ are together inverted in phase by 180° relative to a_2.)

The results of the two-glint jitter experiment are best visualized in company with the cross-correlation functions for the echoes. Figure 14A–C shows a series of cross-correlation functions – for the first glint a_1 by itself, for the second glint a_1' by itself, and for the two-glint target, $a_1 + a_1'$. These cross-correlation functions are derived from representative *Eptesicus* sonar sounds recorded during the experiment. Figure 14D then shows the data from one *Eptesicus* in the jitter discrimination task with $a_1 + a_1'$ replacing a_1 alone. The horizontal time axis is the size of the jitter interval in the experiment. (The curve is compounded from percentage-error data for the 0° phase and 180° phase conditions of $a_1 + a_1'$ in the manner used for Figure 13.) The behavorial data contain two distinct upward-going peaks corresponding to the two glints, a_1 and a_1'. They are similar in height to the error peaks for the two glints in Figure 11A, indicating that no additional acoustic information seems to have been available to the bat just because the jitter procedure is used. For the bat, two glints are two glints, whether presented in the ordinary two-choice paradigm (Figure 11A), created by filtering echoes (Figure 11B), or incorporated into the jitter paradigm (Figures 11C and 14D). The peaks representing the glints in Figure 14D are narrower, however, due to the removal of head-movement artifacts by the jitter procedure.

Evidently the range of the second glint in a complex target is registered quite accurately in the image perceived by *Eptesicus* even though it is mediated by a spectral representation of echoes. This spectral representation is eventually expressed in terms of delay and referred to the delay of the echoes from the first glint. Consequently, the registration of the range of the first glint must be precise enough (see Figure 6) to support registration of the range of the second glint, because the bat's image of the complex target as a whole depends upon its estimate of the absolute range to the first glint.

Figure 14. *Graphs showing the cross-correlation function representing the image of (A) a single glint at range* a_1, *(B) a single glint at range* a_1', *(C) a two-glint target at ranges* a_1 *and* a_1', *and (D) the compound performance curve for* Eptesicus *(60 trials per data point) detecting a two-glint target* $(a_1 + a_1')$ *jittering with a single-glint target* (a_2). *The bat perceives an image of two glints that corresponds to the sum of the images of each glint taken separately. Because the first glint is represented temporally and the second glint is represented spectrally, the bat must fuse two separate auditory displays.*

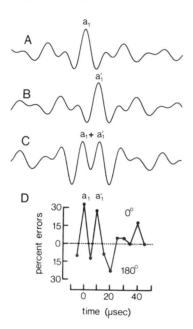

Perhaps this helps to explain why the bat is so phenomenally accurate at determining echo delay.

Eptesicus can perceive the echoes from two glints as being distinct in range even when they are as close together as 10 μs. The bat clearly perceives an image of a complex target that corresponds closely to the type of impulse waveform for echoes from mealworms and disks that appeared in Figure 7. Although the bat's FM sonar sounds are substantially longer than the 10-μs time-interval between the echo components reflected by the glints, the bat compresses individual echo components into much shorter, impulse-like components of the image. This compression is achieved by convergence of both time-domain and frequency-domain information onto a fundamentally time-domain display. *Eptesicus* thus has the perceptual machinery to distinguish between mealworms and disks using the range profile of the targets.

Fusion of time- and frequency-domain information into images

The reason that the two glints (a_1 and a_1') were placed only 10 μs apart in the jitter experiment was to bring the glints close enough together that the fine structure in the image of the first glint (see Figure 13) could mix with any fine structure that might be present in the image of the second glint. This mixing is illustrated by the cross-correlation function for the combined glints shown in Figure 14C. To a first approximation, *Eptesicus* perceives an image that corresponds to the cross-correlation function for the two glints combined. This is a very significant discovery, because each of these glints arises from a different sort of auditory representation – the first glint is encoded by the time of occurrence of the echo as a whole and the second glint is encoded by the spectrum of the echo. Figures 14C and D taken together demonstrate the unification of time- and frequency-domain components into a single range-axis image. This convergence proceeds approximately as a linear addition of the separate cross-correlation-like representations of the individual glints. The bat thus provides a rare glimpse of the calculus of perception in action as it fuses two differently represented elements into a single image.

This example of image formation by *Eptesicus* is specific enough that its neural substrate – the nature of the convergence operation in neural terms – ought to be accessible for physiological analysis. Extensive experiments on the mustached bat, *Pteronotus parnellii*, reveal that the dimension of target range and the dimension of echo spectrum are treated and displayed separately in the bat's auditory cortex (Suga, 1988). For representing range, *Pteronotus* computes a topographic neural map of echo delays that extends (in range units) from several centimeters to about 3 m. For representing the frequency axis of the spectrum, the bat uses the tonotopic (topographic frequency) map created by the "place" code of the organ of Corti for different frequencies of sound. These two classes of neural maps are segregated from each other in *Pteronotus*; they occupy different sites in the cortex. Neurons that are tuned to specific delays or to specific frequencies in these maps also respond selectively to a particular range of echo amplitudes. As a result, the bat in principle could represent the delay of echoes from the first glint in a complex target by the site of neural activity on the range map. The bat also could represent the separation of the first and the second glints from the shape of the spectrum by the distribution of activity across neurons tuned to different frequencies and amplitudes.

Pteronotus uses an echolocation system incorporating both CF and FM signals, which is different from *Eptesicus*, and it is not clear to what extent physiological results from *Pteronotus* can be generalized to purely FM bats such as *Myotis lucifugus* and *Eptesicus fuscus*. Physiological experiments with *Myotis* indicate that this FM bat computes an echo-delay or target-range map, too (Sullivan, 1982; Wong & Shannon, 1988). And, as in other mammals, the tonotopic representation created in the organ of Corti is conveyed through to the auditory cortex in *Myotis* (Suga, 1965; Wong & Shannon, 1988), so both delay (range) and spectral representations of echoes are present in the cortex. We have begun physiological experiments of this sort with *Eptesicus*, and our first observations confirm that the situation is comparable to that in *Myotis*. Significantly, although the delay and frequency maps have different axes, they are not spatially segregated in *Myotis* and *Eptesicus* as they are in *Pteronotus*. They overlap each other at the same site.

In principle, *Myotis* or *Eptesicus* could represent the range of the first glint in a complex target from echo delay along its neural target-range map, and it could represent the shape of the echo spectrum by the distribution of neural activity across the frequency and amplitude domains of its tonotopic map. The behavorial results in Figure 11 indicate that the neural representation of the shape of the spectrum of FM echoes can communicate with the neural representation of echo delay to create new delay information out of spectral notches. This "new delay information" leads to perception of the second glint in a complex target relative to the range of the first glint. The process of "communication" leads to addition of two cross-correlation functions in the resulting image. Registration of the second glint relative to the delay of echoes from the first glint is a specific process that has been demonstrated by showing the perceived location of the second glint to move with the first glint when the amplitude of echo a_1 changes. The latency of neural discharges depends upon stimulus amplitude, and, since the delay of echoes from the first glint is encoded by the timing of discharges, one can shift the apparent range of the target by changing echo amplitude (Simmons, Moss, & Ferragamo, 1989). Some neural interaction between the representation of echo delays and the representation of echo spectra computes the existence of the second glint along the range axis.

Eptesicus can quickly and effectively transform the location of notches in echo spectra into an estimate of the time separation of echo components. This amounts to executing a real-time Fourier transform to recover the cross-correlation function from echo spectra. The registration of the second glint relative to the first glint presumably means that the phase information implicit in the cross-correlation function must somehow be shared between the temporal and spectral representations that underlie the image perceived by the bat. For this transformation to occur, it would be convenient if the frequency axis of the spectral representation (the tonotopic axis) be scaled as the reciprocal of frequency, or period. (The resulting frequency scale is hyperbolic.) This would make equal increments along the frequency axis be equivalent to constant time steps rather than constant frequency steps. In principle, the locations of spectral notches then could be communicated directly from the tonotopic axis to the delay axis by lateral neural connections. Combined anatomical and physiological experiments have measured the tonotopic map at one site in the ascending auditory system of *Eptesicus* (the ventral nucleus of the lateral lemniscus – Covey & Casseday, 1986). The frequency scale found in *Eptesicus* is indeed approximately hyperbolic. (The reciprocal of frequency or period regression line for these data has a correlation coefficient of −0.99.) If this hyperbolic frequency scale is preserved up to the auditory cortex in *Eptesicus*, it could provide a neural substrate for organizing the connections that must create the range-axis image of the second glint in a complex target by transposing notches in echo spectra into an estimate of the time separation between the first and the second glints. It should be feasible to test this hypothesis by conducting physiological and anatomical studies of the auditory cortex in *Eptesicus*, with a view to determining what sorts of interactions might occur between the range and tonotopic maps, which overlie one another. Could the region of overlap of these maps be the place where the time- and frequency-domain elements of the acoustic images of targets become fused into a single perception?

Conclusion

Echolocating bats emit sonar sounds and perceive objects from the echoes of these sounds that return to the ears. Bats use sonar to guide their flight and to detect, identify, and track flying insect prey. Many species, such as the big brown bat, *Eptesicus fuscus*, use frequency-modulated (FM) signals for echolocation. These bats perceive acoustic images that represent objects along the dimension of distance, or target range. They determine the distance to individual targets from the delay of FM echoes. Although the target-range acuity minimally necessary to intercept airborne targets is 1–2 cm, *Eptesicus* can easily perceive target range differences of a fraction of a millimeter. The bat has a limiting range hyperacuity of 0.002 mm based on perception of echo delay changes as small as 10 ns. To have such extraordinarily fine acuity, bats must use the dimension of echo delay or target range to support more sophisticated aspects of acoustic imaging than merely determining target range.

Eptesicus perceives not only the distance to individual targets but also the distance to different parts of a complex target whose elements, called glints, are located at slightly different ranges. The distribution of a target along the range axis embodies much of its "shape" to the bat. An echo from a complex target contains components arriving after slightly different delays. Because the bat's FM signals (1–2 ms in duration) are much longer than the time separations of the echo components (up to several hundred microseconds), these components overlap and interfere with each other, creating a complex echo spectrum. The underlying time separations of echo components are represented by the shape of this spectrum. *Eptesicus* perceives a complex target in terms of its range profile by transforming the echo spectrum back into an estimate of differences in delay between echo components. The bat thus creates an image wholly defined along the range axis in perception. Spectrally represented range separations *within the target* are expressed with respect to the delay-represented absolute range *to the target*. The bat needs a high acuity for echo delay to support the "writing" of spectrally based estimates of range separations onto the range axis of images.

A target's image along the range axis corresponds to the cross-correlation function between sonar emissions and echoes. (This function represents all of the information contained in echo waveforms that is relevant to estimating echo delay.) The image of a single point-target is the cross-correlation function for a single echo component. Furthermore, the image of individual glints in a complex target each corresponds to the cross-correlation function for a single echo component. The bat evidently adds together the cross-correlation function representing the nearest glint, which is derived from the delay of the first component of echoes, to the cross-correlation function representing glints located further away, which are derived from the spectrum of echoes, to create a complete image of the target. This convergence of auditory temporal and auditory spectral processes is a specific example of the fusion of separately represented stimulus features into a unified perception. *Eptesicus* appears to represent frequency along a hyperbolic scale, which may facilitate the neural computations required to transform spectral shape back into estimates of range separation. The entire system of neural elements that work together to create spatial images from disparate stimulus representations may act as a "sound-to-space" module that gives the bat immediate perception of objects in their proper locations in a manner that is "transparent to the user", that is, to the bat. The output of this system is expressed very economically in the natural spatial dimensions of objects rather than in more cumbersome, intermediate acoustic dimensions.

References

Aldridge, H.D.J.N., & Rautenbach, I.L. (1987). Morphology, echolocation and resource partitioning in insectivorous bats. *Journal of Animal Ecology, 56,* 763–778.

Altes, R.A. (1976). Sonar for generalized target description and its similarity to animal echolocation systems. *Journal of the Acoustical Society of America, 59,* 97–105.

Altes, R.A. (1989). The ubiquity of hyperacuity. *Journal of the Acoustical Society of America, 85,* 943–952.

Beuter, K.J. (1980). A new concept of echo evaluation in the auditory system of bats. In R.-G. Busnel & J.F. Fish (Eds.), *Animal Sonar Systems* (pp. 747–761). New York: Plenum.

Bodenhamer, R.D., & Pollak, G.D. (1981). Time and frequency domain processing in the inferior colliculus of echolocating bats. *Hearing Research, 5,* 317–355.

Busnel, R.-G., & Fish, J.F., (Eds.) (1980). *Animal Sonar Systems.* New York: Plenum.

Cahlander, D.A., McCue, J.J.G., & Webster, F.A. (1964). The determination of distance by echolocating bats. *Nature, 201,* 544–546.

Covey, E., & Casseday, J.H. (1986). Connectional basis for frequency representation in the nuclei of the lateral lemniscus of the bat *Eptesicus fuscus. Journal of Neuroscience, 6,* 2926–2940.

Dalland, J.I. (1965). Hearing sensitivity in bats. *Science, 150,* 1185–1186.

Fenton, M.B. (1984). Echolocation: Implications for ecology and evolution of bats. *Quarterly Review of Biology, 59,* 33–53.

Griffin, D.R. (1958). *Listening in the dark.* New Haven: Yale University Press. (Reprinted by Dover Publications, New York, 1974, and by Cornell University Press, Ithaca, NY, 1986.)

Griffin, D.R. (1967). Discriminative echolocation by bats. In R.-G. Busnel (Ed.), *Animal sonar systems: Biology and bionics* (pp. 273–300). Jouy-en-Josas, France: Laboratoire de Physiologie Acoustique.

Griffin, D.R. (1971). The importance of atmospheric attenuation for the echolocation of bats (Chiroptera). *Animal Behaviour, 19,* 55–61.

Griffin, D.R., Friend, J.H., & Webster, F.A. (1965). Target discrimination by the echolocation of bats. *Journal of Experimental Zoology, 158,* 155–168.

Habersetzer, J., & Vogler, B. (1983). Discrimination of surface-structured targets by the echolocating bat *Myotis myotis* during flight. *Journal of Comparative Physiology, 152,* 275–282.

Henson, O.W., Jr. (1970). The ear and audition. In W.A. Wimsatt (Ed.), *Biology of bats,* Vol. II (pp. 181–263). New York: Academic Press.

Henson, O.W., Jr., Bishop, A.L., Keating, A.W., Kobler, J.B., Henson, M.M., Wilson, B.S., & Hansen, R.C. (1987). Biosonar imaging of insects by *Pteronotus p. parnellii,* the mustached bat. *National Geographic Research, 3,* 82–101.

Hill, J.E., & Smith, J.D. (1984). *Bats: A natural history.* Austin, TX: University of Texas Press.

Kick, S.A. (1982). Target detection by the echolocating bat, *Eptesicus fuscus. Journal of Comparative Physiology, 145,* 431–435.

Kick, S.A., & Simmons, J.A. (1984). Automatic gain control in the bat's sonar receiver and the neuroethology of echolocation. *Journal of Neuroscience, 4,* 2705–2737.

Konishi, M. (1983). Localization of acoustic signals in the owl. In J.-P. Ewert, R.R. Capranica, & D.J. Ingle (Eds.), *Advances in vertebrate neuroethology* (pp. 227–245). New York: Plenum.

Lawrence, B.D., & Simmons, J.A. (1982). Measurement of atmospheric attenuation at ultrasonic frequencies and the significance for echolocation by bats. *Journal of the Acoustical Society of America, 71,* 484–490.

Masters, W.M., Moffat, A.J.M., & Simmons, J.A. (1985). Sonar tracking of horizontally moving targets by the big brown bat, *Eptesicus fuscus. Science, 228,* 1331–1333.

Moss, C.F. & Schnitzler, H.-U. (1989). Accuracy of target ranging in echolocating bats: Acoustic information processing. *Journal of Comparative Physiology A, 165.*

Nachtigall, P.E., & Moore, P.W.B. (Eds.) (1988). *Animal sonar: Processes and performance.* New York: Plenum Press.

Neubauer, W.G. (1986). *Acoustic reflection from surfaces and shapes.* Washington, DC: Naval Research Laboratory.

Neuweiler, G. (1984). Foraging, echolocation and audition in bats. *Naturwissenschaften, 71*, 446–455.

Neuweiler, G., Bruns, V., & Schuller, G. (1980). Ears adapted for the detection of motion, or how echolocating bats have exploited the capabilities of the mammalian auditory system. *Journal of the Acoustical Society of America, 68*, 741–753.

Novick, A. (1963). Pulse duration in the echolocation of insects by the bat, *Pteronotus. Ergebnisse der Biologie, 26*, 21–26.

Novick, A. (1965). Echolocation of flying insects by the bat, *Chilonycteris psilotis. Biological Bulletin, 128*, 297–314.

Novick, A. (1977). Acoustic orientation. In W.A. Wimsatt (Ed.), *Biology of bats*, Vol. III. (pp. 73–287). New York: Academic Press.

Novick, A., & Vaisnys, J.R. (1964). Echolocation of flying insects by the bat, *Chilonycteris parnellii. Biological Bulletin, 127*, 478–488.

Ostwald, J., Schnitzler, H.-U., & Schuller, G. (1988). Target discrimination and target classification in echolocating bats. In P.E. Nachtigall, & P.W.B. Moore (Eds.), *Animal sonar: Processes and performance* (pp. 413–434). New York: Plenum Press.

Pye, J.D. (1980). Echolocation signals and echoes in air. In R.-G. Busnel & J.F. Fish (Eds.), *Animal sonar systems* (pp. 309–353). New York: Plenum Press.

Rubsamen, R., Neuweiler, G., & Sripathi, K. (1988). Comparative collicular tonotopy in two bat species adapted to movement detection, *Hipposideros speoris* and *Megaderma lyra. Journal of Comparative Physiology A, 163*, 271–285.

Schmidt, S. (1988). Evidence for a spectral basis of texture perception in bat sonar. *Nature, 331*, 617–619.

Schnitzler, H.-U., & Henson, O.W., Jr. (1980). Performance of airborne animal sonar systems: I. Microchiroptera. In R.-G. Busnel & J.F. Fish (Eds.), *Animal Sonar Systems* (pp. 109–181). New York: Plenum.

Schnitzler, H.-U., Kalko, E., Miller, L., & Surlykke, A. (1987). The echolocation and hunting behavior of the bat, *Pipistrellus kuhli. Journal of Comparative Physiology A, 16*, 267–274.

Schnitzler, H.-U., Menne, D., Kober, R., & Heblich, D. (1983). The acoustical image of fluttering insects in echolocating bats. In F. Huber & H. Markl (Eds.), *Neuroethology and behavioral physiology: Roots and growing points* (pp. 235–250). New York: Springer.

Simmons, J.A. (1969). Acoustic radiation patterns for the echolocating bats, *Chilonycteris rubiginosa* and *Eptesicus fuscus. Journal of the Acoustical Society of America, 46*, 1054–1056.

Simmons, J.A. (1973). The resolution of target range by echolocating bats. *Journal of the Acoustical Society of America, 54*, 157–173.

Simmons, J.A. (1979). Perception of echo phase information in bat sonar. *Science, 207*, 1336–1338.

Simmons, J.A. (1987). Acoustic images of target range in the sonar of bats. *Naval Research Reviews, 39*, 11–26.

Simmons, J.A., & Chen, L. (1989). The acoustic basis for target discrimination by FM echolocating bats. *Journal of the Acoustical Society of America, 86*.

Simmons, J.A., Fenton, M.B., & O'Farrell, M.J. (1979). Echolocation and pursuit of prey by bats. *Science, 203*, 16–21.

Simmons, J.A., Ferragamo, M., Moss, C.F., Stevenson, S.B., & Altes, R.A. (in press). Discrimination of jittered sonar echoes by the echolocating bat, *Eptesicus fuscus. Journal of Comparative Physiology A.*

Simmons, J.A., Freedman, E.G., Stevenson, S.B., Chen, L., & Wohlgenant, T.J. (1989). Clutter interference and the integration time of echoes in the echolocating bat, *Eptesicus fuscus. Journal of the Acoustical Society of America, 86*.

Simmons, J.A., & Grinnell, A.D. (1988). The performance of echolocation: Acoustic images perceived by echolocating bats. In P.E. Nachtigall & P.W.B. Moore (Eds.), *Animal sonar: Processes and performance* (pp. 353–385). New York: Plenum Press.

Simmons, J.A., Howell, D.J., & Suga, N. (1975). Information content of bat sonar echoes. *American Scientist, 63*, 204–215.

Simmons, J.A., & Kick, S.A. (1984). Physiological mechanisms for spatial filtering and image enhancement in the sonar of bats. *Annual Review of Physiology, 46*, 599–614.

Simmons, J.A., Kick, S.A., Lawrence, B.D., Hale, C., Bard, C., & Escudié, B. (1983). Acuity of horizontal angle discrimination by the echolocating bat, *Eptesicus fuscus. Journal of Comparative Physiology, 153*, 321–330.

Simmons, J.A., Lavender, W.A., Lavender, B.A., Doroshow, C.A., Kiefer, S.W., Livingston, R., Scallet, A.C., & Crowley, D.E. (1974). Target structure and echo spectral discrimination by echolocating bats. *Science, 186*, 1130–1132.

Simmons, J.A., Moss, C.F., & Ferragamo, M. (1989). *Journal of Comparative Physiology A.*

Simmons, J.A., & Stein, R.A. (1980). Acoustic imaging in bat sonar: Echolocation signals and the evolution of echolocation. *Journal of Comparative Physiology, 135*, 61–84.

Simmons, J.A., & Vernon, J.A. (1971). Echolocation: Discrimination of targets by the bat *Eptesicus fuscus. Journal of Experimental Zoology, 176*, 351–328.

Suga, N. (1965). Functional properties of auditory neurones in the cortex of echo-locating bats. *Journal of Physiology (London), 181*, 671–700.

Suga, N. (1973). Feature extraction in the auditory system of bats. In Moller, A.R. (Ed.), *Basic mechanisms in hearing* (pp. 675–744). New York: Academic Press.

Suga, N. (1988). Auditory neuroethology and speech processing: Complex-sound processing by combination-sensitive neurons. In Edelman, G.M., Gall, W.E., & Cowan, W.M. (Eds.), *Auditory function* (pp. 679–720). New York: Wiley.

Sullivan, W.E. (1982). Neural representation of target distance in auditory cortex of the echolocating bat *Myotis lucifugus. Journal of Neurophysiology, 48*, 1011–1032.

Sum, Y.M., & Menne, D. (1988). Discrimination of fluttering targets by the FM-Bat *Pipistrellus stenopterus? Journal of Comparative Physiology A, 163*, 349–354.

Trappe, M. (1982). Verhalten und Echoortung der Grossen Hufeisennase (*Rhinolophus ferrumequinum*) beim Insektenfang. PhD thesis, Universität Marburg.

Trappe, M., & Schnitzler, H.-U. (1982). Doppler-shift compensation in insect-catching horseshoe bats. *Naturwissenschaften, 69*, 193–194.

Webster, F.A., & Brazier, O.G. (1965). *Experimental studies on target detection, evaluation and interception by echolocating bats.* Technical Report No. AMRL-TR-65-172, Clearinghouse for Federal Scientific and Technical Information, Springfield, VA.

Webster, F.A., & Brazier, O.G. (1968). *Experimental studies on echolocation mechanisms in bats.* Technical Report No. AMRL-TR-67-192, Clearinghouse for Federal Scientific and Technical Information, Springfield, VA.

Webster, F.A., & Durlach, N. (1963). *Echolocation systems of the bat.* Lincoln Laboratory Report No. 41-G-3. Lexington, MA: MIT Lincoln Laboratory.

Webster, F.A., & Griffin, D.R. (1962). The role of the flight membrane in insect capture by bats. *Animal Behaviour, 10*, 332–340.

Wong, D., & Shannon, S.L. (1988). Functional zones in the auditory cortex of the echolocating bat, *Myotis lucifugus. Brain Research, 453*, 349–352.

Woodward, P.M. (1964), *Probability and information theory, with applications to radar*, 2nd Edn. New York: Pergamon Press.

Van Trees, H.L. (1971). *Detection, estimation, and modulation theory, Part III.* New York: Wiley.

Résumé

Les chauves-souris se repèrent par l'écho: elles perçoivent les objets sous la forme d'images acoustiques provenant des échos des ultra-sons qu'elles émettent. Elles peuvent détecter, reconnaître, identifier et intercepter des insectes volants en utilisant leur sonar. De nombreuses espèces, telle que la grande chauve-souris rousse, *Eptesicus fuscus*, émettent des sons en modulation de fréquence et évaluent la distance par rapport aux cibles à partir du temps de retour de l'écho. Pour l'*Eptesicus*, la distance de l'image d'un point cible est déterminée avec précision par le temps de retour de l'écho qui est d'environ 10 nanosecondes dans des conditions favorables. L'image toute entière possède une structure de champ correspondant à la fonction de corrélation croisée entre les émissions et les échos. Une cible complexe, avec des points réfléchissants appelés "lueurs" situés à des distances très légèrement différentes, et réfléchissant des échos contenant des composants se chevauchant avec des temps de retour légèrement différents, est perçue sous la forme d'un profil de distance. La séparation des "lueurs" sur l'étendue de la dimension du champ est codée par la forme du spectre de l'écho créé par interférence entre les composants de l'écho qui se chevauchent. Cependant, *Eptesicus* convertit le spectre de l'écho en retour en une estimation du temps de séparation original des composants de l'écho. La chauve-souris convertit ainsi le signal spectral sous la forme d'éléments d'une image exprimés en terme de distance. La distance absolue de la "lueur" la plus proche est codée par le temps d'arrivée du composant de l'écho dont le retour est le plus rapide, et la distinction des distances codées à partir du spectre pour les autres "lueurs" se fait à partir de cette distance de référence pour l'image toute entière. Chaque "lueur" individuelle est représentée par une fonction de corrélation croisée de son propre composant d'écho, le plus proche étant calculé directement à partir de son délai de retour alors que les suivants sont calculés par transformation du spectre de l'écho. La chauve-souris additionne ensuite les fonctions de corrélations croisées des "lueurs" multiples pour former l'image entière de la cible complexe. La distance et la forme sont deux caractéristiques distinctes des cibles et sont codées de façon séparée pour le système auditif de la chauve-souris, mais cette dernière distingue des images unitaires qui nécessitent la fusion de ces caractéristiques pour créer une dimension psychologique synthétique de distance. L'utilisation par la chauve-souris d'images à corrélation croisée met en évidence l'existence de systèmes neuronaux qui réalisent la fusion des caractéristiques des stimuli et donne un exemple des mécanismes de haut niveau impliqués dans la formation d'"entités" perceptuelles.

7

The neurobiology of learning and memory*

CARL W. COTMAN
GARY S. LYNCH
University of California, Irvine

Abstract

Cotman, C.W., and Lynch, G.S., 1989. The neurobiology of learning and memory. Cognition, 33: 201–241.

The study of memory is a great challenge, perhaps the greatest in biological sciences. Memory involves changes in a tiny fraction of an extremely large pool of elements, a conclusion that makes the task of finding those changes using current technologies formidable. What can be done about this roadblock to neurological investigations of learning? One response that has become particularly productive in recent years is to study learning or learning-like phenomena in relatively simple "model" systems. The idea is to extract basic principles from these models in which molecular and anatomical details can be studied and then to use these in analyzing learning in higher regions of the brain. In this article we discuss current progress and emerging concepts derived from the simple system approach using animal models.

Introduction

It has always been of interest to discover the mechanisms that transfer experience to memory. The ability to encode, catalogue, and recall a vast number of facts and experiences is one of the definitive characteristics of humans and one that distinguishes us as individuals. It is only appropriate then that the biomedical sciences should be concerned with the nature of the machinery in the brain that processes memory.

In this review, we discuss several recent approaches that have led to rapid progress in understanding the "how" and "where" of memory formation, and then consider the potential of these advances for treatment of clinical prob-

*This article is a revised and condensed version of a scientific review paper prepared by the authors for the National Conference on Learning Disabilities, Bethesda, MD, 12–13 January, 1987. Publication of Conference proceedings by the National Institutes of Health is in progress. The authors are grateful to Ms. Martina Klein for editorial assistance. Requests for reprints should be addressed to: Carl W. Cotman, Department of Psychobiology, University of California, Irvine, CA 92717, U.S.A.

lems. It will be useful to begin by considering the major questions and goals of the neurobiological analyses of memory. (1) Is learning a single phenomenon or can it be subdivided? (2) What is required of a neurobiological explanation of learning or, put another way, what answers do we require? (3) Why has the analysis of the substrates of memory been so difficult and are we approaching satisfactory answers?

What is learning?

Learning can be broadly defined as any lasting change in behavior resulting from previous experience. It may seem to be a single phenomenon but this is clearly not the case. Consider, for example, the difference between the memory involved in serving a tennis ball and that required to answer a question about the capital of the U.S.A. In the first instance, we are not really aware of the specific sequence of muscle movements that produces a successful result, while in the latter case, the information is conscious and clearly linked to a series of other facts and experiences. Thus there are at least two general categories: procedural, skill, or rule memory (playing tennis, typing, linguistic syntax) and fact or declarative memory (names, faces, semantic aspects of language). These distinctions are important because neuropsychological studies over the past ten years have shown that pathology can and often does affect memory in a selective fashion. Learning of fact memories appears to involve different, more easily disturbed, brain systems than those subserving skill memory. Neurobiological analyses of learning and memory that intend to explicate these phenomena as found in normal and brain-injured humans need to take cognizance of the multiple types of learning and memory, the differential effects of injury and disease upon them, and the need for appropriate animal models.

Why is the analysis of the neurobiology of learning so difficult? Interdependent variables and the subtle nature of the phenomenon

Learning and memory have proven to be among the most difficult subjects confronting the biological sciences. Despite years of intensive research, we still have not agreed upon a single explanation for most of the relevant phenomenology, and it is only recently that detailed hypotheses about specific aspects of memory have begun to appear. Part of the reason for this is that learning appears to require the coordination of physio-psychological variables that are not themselves part of the encoding and retrieval mechanisms; indeed, identifying these variables constitutes an important area of research and one that is pregnant with possibilities for clinical application. But the dependence of memory functioning on so many general variables makes it difficult to interpret results from the use of pharmacological and pathological approaches employed successfully in the study of non-memorial behaviors and physiologies. For example, it is often impossible to satisfactorily conclude that a drug has disturbed memory because it interrupted the synaptic chemistries related to storage as opposed to a more non-specific action on the "background" state needed for these chemistries to operate.

An additional and profound problem is that the changes required for learning are quite subtle and dispersed. This is suggested by the seemingly endless capacity of the brain for memory storage. By way of illustration, Standing (1973) presented college students with a series of photographs, each picture being observed for five seconds, and then tested the students for recognition the following day. He found that retention could be described as a mathematical function of the number of pictures observed and that this function held from 100 to 10,000 pictures. Feldman (1981) had made an estimate of how much information would have to be encoded in storage to recognize this number of complex pictures – the answer is on the order of 10^{11} "bits". This capacity is barely within the range of the largest computers. Also note that the memory processing of the students did not slow as ever more data were added to memory.

These observations lead inevitably to the idea that memory involves changes in a tiny fraction of an extremely large pool of elements, a conclusion that makes the task of finding those changes using current technologies formidable, if not impossible. What can be done about this roadblock to neurobiological investigation of learning? One response that has gained increasing popularity in recent years is to study learning or learning-like phenomena in relatively simple "model" systems. The idea is to extract basic principles from these models in which molecular and anatomical details can be studied and then to use these in analyzing learning in the higher regions of the brain.

The present review is concerned with ongoing attempts to develop neurobiological explanations of memory and in particular their potential relevance to cognitive disorders in humans. Such a description would have to incorporate three levels of information: (1) key brain regions: the location of these regions in the brain associated with the storage, retrieval, and processing of different types of memory; (2) synaptic mechanisms: the nature of the stable modifications that actually encode memory and the type of mechanisms that produce these modifications; and (3) memory "circuits" in brain: the characteristics of the circuitries contained within learning-related brain structures and how these characteristics are linked to the phenomenologies observed at the other levels of analysis. Recent successes in the first part of this program (finding plausible molecular processes) have encouraged the idea that a neurobiological description of memory, with considerable predictive and explanatory power, can now be achieved.

We begin by analyzing the issue of how different brain regions contribute to different aspects and types of learning. We focus on efforts to develop animal models to study the different forms of memory identified in humans and to reproduce specific clinical syndromes.

Next we discuss theories about the actual substrates of memory, and turn to the cerebral cortex to consider recent efforts to develop paradigms for detecting learning-induced changes. Studies in both very young and adult animals are summarized in which simple forms of learning can be directly correlated with changes in identified neurons and synapses.

To further analyze the circuitry of memory formation, we then move to work on invertebrates, as well as discussing studies analyzing conditioning in the far more complicated but still well-defined circuitries found in the brain stem of mammals. We then conclude with studies on early learning and its implications in producing long-term changes in CNS circuitry that impact upon subsequent behavior.

"Circuits" for fact or declarative memory

From experimental work reviewed below, we see that learning of some type occurs in even very simple nervous systems and that memory storage is found at several levels of the mammalian brain. Yet there is much evidence pointing to the conclusion that the encoding of data and episodes in humans is crucially dependent upon the cortex and the structures lying immediately beneath it in the forebrain. The vast neocortex in man (comprising some 80% or more of the whole brain) is such an attractive candidate for the repository of memories that most researchers assume that it plays this role. Specific areas of cortex generate so much of human behavior that it seems almost inevitable that the memories needed for those behaviors are also found in its folds. Moreover, the capacity of memory points to cortex as the storage site. But subcortical regions are also critical, at least to the encoding and retrieval aspects of memory, if not to its actual storage. Lesions in the hippocampal region of humans produce a surprisingly selective anterograde amnesia in which patients are unable to store new information, but still retain the greater part of their pre-injury memories. Work on primates, and very recently rats, has also succeeded in identifying a vital function for hippocampus in the formation of new fact memories. Despite these observations, there is still no satisfactory theory of how the hippocampus and certain other subcortical areas (e.g., amygdala, midline thalamus) contribute to the encoding of experience, presumably in neocortex.

Key brain areas in human cognition: definition of "memory" circuits

Amnesia is characterized by an impaired ability to acquire new information and by difficulty in remembering at least some information that was acquired prior to its onset. Our knowledge of memory formation in humans is based largely on the study of human amnestic syndromes.

At least two areas of the brain appear to be critical in memory formation: the medial temporal lobe region (including the hippocampal formation, amygdala, and temporal stem) and the regions surrounding the third ventricle (including the dorsomedial nucleus of the thalamus and mammillary bodies). Medial temporal lobe amnesia is reported to occur following surgical resection of the medial temporal lobes (Scoville & Milner, 1957), following encephalitis (Drachman & Adams, 1962; Rose & Symonds, 1960), following occlusion of the posterior cerebral artery (Benson, Marsden, & Meadows, 1974), and after hypoxic ischemia (Squire, 1986; Volpe & Hirst, 1983). Midbrain diencephalic amnesia is reported to occur in patients with Korsakoff's syndrome (Butters & Cermak, 1980; Talland, 1965; Victor, Adams, & Collins, 1971) and as a result of tumor in the third ventricle (Williams & Pennybacker, 1954). While both syndromes result from damage to limbic structures, the anatomical relatedness of these two types of amnesia is still unclear. Considerable insight has been obtained, however, through the study of a small number of individuals in which severe anterograde amnesia (inability to learn new things) has occurred in the absence of other cognitive deficits. These cases are discussed below.

The first case is that of subject "H.M." (Corkin, 1968; Scoville & Milner, 1957). In 1953, H.M. received a bilateral resection of the medial temporal lobes (including the anterior two-thirds of the hippocampal formation, hippocampal gyrus, amygdala, and uncus) in an effort to relieve severe epileptic seizures. Since that time, he has been unable to learn new facts and forgets daily events almost as fast as they occur. For example, H.M. cannot learn a list of words, even after many repetitions, and is unable to recognize faces he has seen many times in the past 30 years. His memory deficit extends to both verbal and non-verbal material and involves information acquired through all sensory modalities.

However, despite H.M.'s inability to store new information in the form of factual data, his ability to develop perceptual-motor skills appears to be normal. He successfully learned a mirror tracing task and a complex cognitive puzzle at a rate comparable to controls (Milner, 1968). His speed and accuracy increased in spite of the fact that he had no recollection of having previously performed the tasks. H.M. also successfully acquired the cognitive skills required for optimal solution to the Tower of Hanoi puzzle (Cohen, 1984). The second case is that of the subject N.A. (Kaushall, Zetin, & Squire, 1981; Teuber, Milner, & Vaughan, 1968). In 1960, N.A. received a penetrating brain injury with a miniature fencing foil, producing a lesion in the left dorsomedial thalamic nucleus (Squire & Moore, 1979). Since that time, N.A. has exhibited a severe anterograde amnesia primarily for verbal material, which is consistent with the left-hemisphere localization of his lesion. Nevertheless, he has an intelligence quotient of 124, can make accurate predictions of his own memory abilities, and, like H.M., has no noticeable impairment of the higher cognitive functions. Studies have also revealed that, as with H.M., N.A.'s ability to acquire perceptual-motor skill is unimpaired (Cohen & Squire, 1980). A similar finding has recently been reported for patients with Alzheimer's disease (Eslinger & Damasio, 1986). These findings have led to the suggestion that memory for facts (declarative memory) and memory for perceptual-motor skills (procedural memory) are distinct entities, which involve different areas of the brain.

Different brain structures appear essential for fact versus rule memory
The fact that H.M. and N.A. are impaired in their ability to form some memories but not others is one piece of evidence supporting the distinction between what are known as fact (declarative) and rule (procedural) memories. Fact memory refers to memories of things that can be "declared", such as word lists, faces and numbers. Rule memory refers to memories associated with the acquisition of skills or "procedures". Hence, while H.M. and N.A. are impaired in their ability to form declarative memories, their procedural memory abilities are intact. This suggests that the processes which underlie the formation of these two types of memory are functionally and anatomically distinct, and that medial temporal lobe and mid-diencephalic structures are involved specifically with declarative memory processes.

Memory deficits in primates versus man: close correlations
Primate models have been particularly useful for understanding the severe amnestic syndromes observed following medial temporal lobe injury in humans. Normal monkeys were trained to perform a delayed non-matching to sample (DNMS) task, a task also sensitive to human amnesia (Malamut, Saunders, & Mishkin, 1978; Murray & Mishkin, 1984; Zola-Morgan, Squire, & Mishkin, 1982). The task consists of two trials. On the first trial, the monkey displaces the junk object to obtain a food reward. On the second trial, which can be presented many minutes or even hours later, the monkey

is presented with the original object together with a novel object, and must displace the novel object to obtain a food reward. Subsequent trials use different pairs of junk objects taken from a large set of several hundred objects. Acquisition of this task requires that the animal be able to distinguish the objects, recall which was previously presented, and recall the rule that it must displace the novel object to obtain the reward. After being trained to a criterion of 90 correct choices in 100 trials, animals received: (1) bilateral ablation of the hippocampal formation; (2) bilateral ablation of the amygdala; (3) ablation of both the hippocampal formation and the amygdala; or (4) no lesion. Although results from different laboratories are somewhat variable, the combined destruction of both the hippocampal formation and amygdala produced a much greater deficit than either hippocampal or amygdala destruction alone (complete destruction of either the hippocampus or the amygdala produced little or no deficit, even when using intertrial intervals lasting several hours). In particular, performance dropped from 90 percent correct responses with delay intervals of a few seconds to near-chance scores after delays of only a minute or two. These results suggest that the animal is unable to recall which of the two objects had been previously presented.

To further characterize the deficits associated with medial temporal lobe amnesia, monkeys with amygdala and hippocampal lesions were also tested for their ability to perform a delayed matching to sample (DMS) task and an object discrimination task (Malamut et al., 1984). The DMS task is exactly the same as the DNMS task described above, except that animals must now choose the more familiar object of the pair to receive a reward. The object discrimination task requires animals to recall which objects of a pair of objects had been baited on previous trials and to choose the baited object to get a reward. For example, 20 object pairs are presented in a series and one object from each pair is baited. Each day, the same object pairs are presented in the same order, and the same objects are baited. Improved performance requires that the animals recall which object in each pair was baited on previous trials. This task is similar to the DMS task in that the associative learning strategy involved (choosing the previously baited object) is the same for each task.

It was predicted that animals that were impaired on the DMS task (testing "data" memory) would not be able to remember which objects had been previously baited and hence would perform at chance level on the object discrimination task (testing "procedural" memory). Surprisingly, however, animals with combined amygdala/hippocampal lesions were not impaired in the object discrimination task and in fact could learn visual discrimination habits about as quickly as controls, even with 24-hour intertrial intervals.

The above findings have been interpreted as evidence for two fundamentally different, anatomically distinct, memory systems. One system is thought to serve both recognition and association and to utilize a cortico-limbo-diencephalic circuit. This system is used to perform the delayed non-matching to sample task and is presumed to be impaired in patients with medial temporal lobe amnesia. The other system thought to mediate the retention of stimulus–response connections is thought to involve a cortico-striatal circuit. This system is used to perform the object discrimination task and is thought to be preserved in amnestic subjects. Further evidence that performance of the object discrimination task and the DNMS task involve two functionally and anatomically distinct memory systems stems from the fact that infant monkeys (3–4 months old) successfully learned to discriminate long lists of object-pairs about as quickly as adult monkeys, whereas their ability to learn the DNMS task matured much more slowly (Bachevalier & Mishkin, 1986).

The primate models discussed above suggest that severe temporal lobe amnesia will result only following the combined destruction of both the hippocampal formation and the amygdala. Destruction of either structure alone produced either a small deficit (hippocampus) or no deficit at all (amygdala). However, a recent case study suggests that selective hippocampal damage alone may produce a severe memory impairment in humans. This case is discussed below.

R.B. was a postal worker who, at the age of 52, suffered a severe ischemic episode (Zola-Morgan, Squire, & Amaral, 1986). Until his death five years later, he exhibited a marked anterograde amnesia on tests of both verbal and non-verbal memory functions. He could not recall a passage of prose 20 minutes after having heard it or read it, and he could not draw a diagram from memory 20 minutes after having previously drawn it. In addition, he frequently depended on his wife to tell him what had occurred and reported that, if he spoke to his children on the phone, he did not remember anything about it the following day. This deficit occurred against a background of little, if any, retrograde amnesia, and no sign of other cognitive impairment.

After R.B.'s death, histological analysis revealed a circumscribed, bilateral lesion of hippocampal subfield CA1, extending the full length of the hippocampus. Area CA1 is a region from which major hippocampal efferents emerge, the loss of which effectively isolates a large part of the hippocampal formation. Although minor cells loss was observed in the globus pallidus, the right postcentral gyrus, and the cerebellum, it was concluded that the only damage that could reasonably be associated with the memory deficit was the hippocampal lesion. This finding suggests that selective injury to the hippocampal formation alone can result in severe anterograde amnesia deficits in humans.

Summary

The data from neuropsychopathological studies of human amnestics demonstrate that memory formation processes can be localized to specific structures and circuits in the brain. Animal models have been useful for studying the relationship between specific structures and the formation of specific types of associative memories. Primate models have been particularly useful since the type of memory deficits observed are similar to those seen in humans with medial temporal lobe amnesia. As a result of these studies, a better understanding of the anatomy of memory formation processes in humans is beginning to emerge. Such studies will ultimately lead to a more accurate and precise understanding of the mechanisms by which human associative memories are formed.

Analysis of data memory and learning ("cognition") in rodent models

The discoveries that different neural systems in humans and primates mediate different aspects of memory illustrate the need for rodent behavioral tests that sample simple forms of cognition-linked learning and that respond appropriately to lesions in the hippocampus, amygdala, and dorsomedial nucleus of the thalamus. Most research is conducted with small animals, especially rodents and rabbits. These animals have a sophisticated olfactory system compared to their other sensory systems. Recent data indicate that the learning of olfactory cues in rodents may be a reliable means to probe cognitive-type learning in rodents. In a sense, it makes use of the rodent's strengths and man's weaknesses to compare central memory processing systems in both.

Olfaction is a common language for animals and humans

The study of human cognitive processes has most often been based on the use of verbal stimuli, not because of an interest in linguistics, but rather because words are excellent stimuli for probing memory processes: they are simple, identifiable, discrete, vast in number, and can be understood equally well by experimenter and subject. Olfactory stimuli are also simple, identifiable, discrete, and numerous, and therefore possess many of the advantages of words. They are, in a sense, a common vocabulary for animals and humans. Olfaction thus provides an opportunity for using laboratory animals to study cognitive processes that are also comparable in a very real sense to those experienced by humans.

Olfactory cues directly access memory-related brain structures

The olfactory cortex itself is but two neurons removed from the odor receptors in the nasal epithelium (Figure 1). The olfactory cortex directly

Figure 1.   *Two olfactory pathways through the telencephalon. The olfactory bulbs (at the front of the brain) generate the massive lateral olfactory tract, which innervates the contiguous pyriform and entorhinal cortices. The first of these projects into the dorsomedial nucleus of the thalamus, a structure that in turn innervates the frontal cortex. The entorhinal cortex produces the perforant pathway, a major efferent of the hippocampal formation (adapted from Lynch, 1986; reproduced by permission of the publishers, MIT Press, Cambridge, Mass.).*

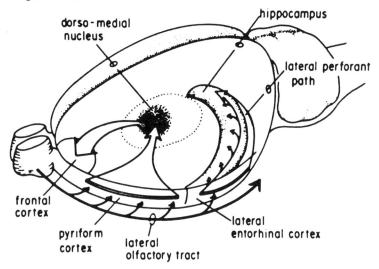

innervates the hippocampus, the amygdala, and the dorsomedial nucleus/ frontal cortex system. The olfactory system thus provides a remarkably direct access to the temporal lobe and midline thalamic regions that are linked by clinical and experimental evidence to memory processing in humans and animals. The nature of olfaction and the evolutionary conservatism of its underlying anatomy allows us to use the same tests in rats and humans. The likelihood that neurobiological discoveries can be transferred to humans is therefore greatly increased.

These anatomic features suggest that olfaction can be used to detect dysfunction in brain systems crucial to memory and cognition. There is experimental evidence for this possibility from patient H.M., who, as mentioned previously, exhibits an anterograde amnesia resulting from damage to the hippocampus and surrounding structures. He is profoundly impaired on even very simple smell identification tasks. Severe olfactory deficits have also been reported for amnestic individuals suffering from Korsakoff's syndrome. As discussed below, Lynch, Cotman and coworkers have found that patients diagnosed as being in the early stages of Alzheimer's disease also have a selective and dramatic impairment in olfactory functioning.

Olfactory memories in rodents appear to follow predictions of cognitive learning deficits in man

Fact memories in humans are aquired rapidly and stored in a system of enormous capacity. This observation proved to hold for odor memories in rats as well (Staubli, Fraser, Faraday, & Lynch, 1987). More important, lesions that separate the olfactory cortex from the hippocampus produce anterograde amnesia that matched the amnesia seen in humans with hippocampal lesions. Thus the rats appeared to learn new odors when several exposures were closely spaced in time, but they exhibited no memory of this training when tested one hour later (Staubli, Ivy, & Lynch, 1985a). This amnesia does not include memories formed before the lesions (Staubli, Fraser, Kessler, & Lynch, 1986b), much in the way that patients with temporal lobe/hippocampal dysfunction retain the greater part of their pre-injury memory store. Other experiments have shown that lesions of the dorsomedial nucleus and frontal cortex produce severe impairments in odor learning (Eichenbaum, Shedlack, & Eckman, 1980; Slotnick & Katz, 1974), possibly by cutting the links between sensory input and appropriate responses. These studies provide a very simple behavioral test that appears to measure a form of data memory that requires the hippocampus for encoding.

In addition, the circuitries underlying the behavior on these tests are sufficiently defined and simple in design to permit neurobiological experimentation. It has proven possible, for example, to use electrical stimulation of the inputs to the olfactory cortex in the place of odors as sensory cues (Mouly, Vigouroux, & Holley, 1985; Staubli, Roman, & Lynch, 1985b), and then follow the physiological events that accompany learning. There is evidence that much of what has been learned in simple systems is directly applicable to fact learning in the cortex.

The extreme conservatism of the olfactory system raises the possibility that tests that detect damage or circuit dysfunction in rats can also be used in humans. Initial efforts have already yielded some interesting clinical results. The olfactory cortex is now thought to be one of the earliest sites affected by Alzheimer's disease, and tests found to be effective in detecting damage to the cortex in rats did indeed prove to discriminate patients thought to be in the early stages of Alzheimer's from age-matched controls (Kesslak et al., 1988). It would indeed be intriguing to test subjects with learning disabilities or odor learning problems and determine if any observed deficits correspond to impairments found in rats with lesions or subjected to pharmacological manipulations.

Summary
Initial results indicate that many features of olfactory memory in rats match quite well with those used to define what cognitive psychologists refer to as "data" memory. Memory deficits after hippocampal damage in rats resemble the rapid forgetting of new information described for humans with hippocampal and temporal lobe damage. These types of models should prove useful in linking animal studies with studies of humans.

Plasticity mechanisms in cortical networks

Neuroscientists from the late nineteenth century to the present have assumed that the storage process involves events and alterations occurring in the synaptic contacts between cells. Long-term changes in the functional strength of connections would certainly affect the operation (and hence information processing) of brain networks, and the enormous number of synapses in the human brain provides a reasonable explanation for the astonishing capacity of memory.

The fact that not all events that trigger responses in the brain are learned leads to the conclusion that certain distinct patterns of activity are needed to elicit the memory-encoding processes. The brain utilizes a host of rhythms in its ongoing activity and it is tempting to imagine that some subset of these are learning signals. As we shall see, recent experiments have provided evidence that this suspicion is correct.

Investigation into the transient chemical events involved in storage constitutes one of the largest and most active areas of research in all of neuroscience. We can assume that the pertinent chemistries are triggered by unusual physiological events which, once activated, produce very long-lasting changes restricted to specific synapses. The identification of chemical processes which fulfill these requirements is difficult and the presence of such chemistries is rare. However, increasingly specific hypotheses are being advanced and there is reason to hope that one or a combination of others will indeed define the "chemistry of memory". The consequences of success in this area would be profound; beyond its scientific value, the identification of the chemistries that promote memory would open the way for the development of drugs directed at facilitating learning in impaired individuals.

It is also possible to make some reasonable guesses about the nature of the stable changes that are used to encode memory. Synapses, like all components of the neuron, are composed of lipids and proteins that are continuously being broken down and replaced. Since memory can last for years and the chemical constituents of the synapses clearly do not, most theorists assume that the enduring modifications associated with memory involve anatomical changes. It has been known for over a decade that the adult brain can grow new synapses in response to injury, but it is only recently that physiologically induced rapidly developing structural modifications have been observed. Whether these effects are indeed the same or similar to those occurring during a learning episode constitutes one of the pressing issues for contemporary research.

LTP in hippocampus as a component of learning
Long-term potentiation (LTP) is an extremely stable form of synaptic facilitation produced in the hippocampus (and elsewhere) by very short periods of high-frequency stimulation. LTP exhibits a number of properties expected of a learning mechanism and it is widely suspected that its substrates are used in behavioral learning. Recent studies have provided a remarkable picture of how LTP is induced and thereby describe a specific hypothesis concerning the origins of memory. Pharmacological studies have confirmed that drugs that block a receptor critical for LTP induction also cause a severe anterograde amnesia in rats; this constitutes the first (to our knowledge) instance in which neurobiological research pointed to a potent memory-blocking drug.

Characteristics of hippocampal long-term potentiation. As noted in the introductory sections, learning theorists generally assume that the actual encoding process involves particular patterns of activity acting upon a limited number of synapses resulting in a stable, perhaps structural, change in those synapses. Since any given learning episode affects a small number of contacts and these are widely dispersed, one cannot follow the synaptic events associated with specific memories. However, one could ask the question of whether particular patterns of stimulation do in fact produce the type of effects expected of a learning device. The answer to this is yes.

Brief periods (<1 s) of high-frequency stimulation delivered to pathways in the hippocampus cause an increase in synaptic strength that can last for weeks (Bliss & Gardner-Medwin, 1973). Subsequent experiments showed that this long-term potentiation effect has the proper characteristics to make it an excellent candidate as a process by which memories are formed:
(1)   rapid induction;
(2)   extreme persistence;
(3)   synapse specificity; induction of LTP in one group of synapses in a dendritic field does not increase the strength of neighboring contacts (Anderson, Silfvenius, Sundberg, & Sveen, 1980; Dunwiddie & Lynch,

1978; Lynch, Dunwiddie, & Gribkoff, 1977). This is a feature that is assumed by virtually every neurobiological theory of memory;
(4) requires convergent activity by a group of synapses onto the same cell (McNaughton, Douglas, & Goddard, 1978); again many "computational" theories of memory postulate that storage requires convergence;
(5) optimal pattern for induction corresponds to a naturally occurring brain rhythm ("theta") that appears when an animal is exploring its environment (Larson, Wong, & Lynch, 1986).

Causes and substrates of long-term potentiation. Studies from a number of laboratories have provided a satisfactory account of the events that trigger LTP; considerable progress has also been made in uncovering the modifications that maintain the potentiation. These findings, when considered together, provide a surprisingly detailed picture of how memory might be produced in the mammalian forebrain. Here we list only the major events in the LTP sequence: (1) brief bursts of activity in a collection of input axons with the bursts at five per second for a second or more (Larson et al., 1986). This pattern corresponds to firing patterns of hippocampal cells under some circumstances; (2) transient suppression of inhibitory responses with maximum suppression at 200 ms after each burst; this causes successive bursts at five per second to elicit longer post-synaptic responses (Larson & Lynch, 1986); (3) prolonged responses activate a peculiar type of receptor (the N-methyl-D-aspartate receptor; NMDA) linked to an ion conductance channel that is blocked under normal conditions (Larson & Lynch, 1986); blockade of these receptors prevents the induction of LTP (Figure 2; Collingridge, Kehl, & McLennan, 1983; Harris, Ganong, & Cotman, 1984; Morris, Anderson, Lynch, & Baudry, 1986); (4) elevation of internal calcium levels in the region of the synapse in the target cell; buffering of internal calcium prevents the occurrence of LTP (Lynch et al., 1983); (5) modification of the numbers of synaptic contacts and possibly alterations in existing contacts (Chang & Greenough, 1984; Lee, Schottler, Oliver, & Lynch, 1980; Wenzel & Mathies, 1985). The structural changes (step (5) above) correlate with the magnitude of the LTP effect and appear to be quite stable; they provide a simple explanation for the extreme persistence of the effect.

The five-step sequence described above does not explain how calcium produces anatomical reorganization, a crucial point for any theory of learning. Calcium has been linked to morphological reorganization and alterations in the surface chemistry of simple cells (e.g., blood platelets and red blood cells; see Siman, Baudry, & Lynch, 1986) and it is not unreasonable to assume that the processes it uses in these cases are also operative in the brain. One candidate mechanism involves a calcium-activated protease (calpain) that de-

Figure 2. NMDA *receptor antagonist (AP5) blocks long-term potentiation (LTP).
(A) LTP in a control preparation. Note the long-lasting increase in response
after high-frequency stimulation (arrow). (B) LTP does not develop in the
presence of D-AP5. The trace plots the peak amplitude of the synaptic
potential recorder extracellularly (data from Harris et al., 1984).*

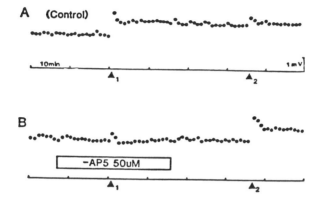

grade cytoskeletal proteins that are integral to the structure of the synapse
(see Lynch & Baudry, 1984, for review). Activation of this enzyme repro-
duces in synaptic membrane fractions a specific biochemical change (increased uptake and/or binding of glutamic acid) that is found after the induction of LTP (Lynch, Halpain, & Baudry, 1982; Siman, Baudry, & Lynch,
1985). The great advantage to this hypothesis is that calpain's effect (partial
breakdown of structural proteins) is irreversible and likely to affect anatomy
of the synaptic region; however, it seems likely that other calcium-dependent
enzymes (e.g., the protein kinases) also are transiently activated during the
induction of LTP and modulate the effects of calpain (see Akers et al., 1986).

Links between LTP and learning. The description of how LTP might be
elicited in behaving animals is sufficiently detailed in that it predicts that
certain drugs should influence the learning process. One of these predictions
has been recently confirmed.

When infused into the cerebral ventricles, antagonists of the NMDA receptor produce a profound impairment in the ability of the rats to learn spatial
locations (Morris et al., 1986), a data memory list that is reasonably resistant
to a host of other pharmacological treatments. Moreover, this anterograde
amnesia is highly selective; past memories are not disrupted and the animals
are still able to learn simple visual discrimination problems (Morris et al.,

1986). Behavorial studies growing out of LTP research have strengthened the idea that the substrates of potentiation are used by the brain to encode new data, and emphasize again the point that different forms of memory may involve different chemical mechanisms.

Other studies have shown that inhibitors of the calcium-sensitive protease calpain also disrupt spatial learning as well as the very simple task of learning and remembering that one of two odors leads to a reward.

From recent autoradiographic studies, it appears that NMDA receptors are most concentrated in the hippocampus and are widely distributed in different regions of the cerebral cortex. Their distribution may predict the locus of circuits throughout the brain where LTP may occur with learning.

Correlates of learning in cortical circuitries: environmental influences on synapses

The basic structure of the brain is laid down during development and, once formed, is usually thought of as being fixed throughout life. As noted in previous sections, however, the number and/or pattern of synapses may serve as a substrate for at least certain forms of learning and synapses may also change with use. Can environment, the composite influences of learning, experience, and use produce measurable affects on brain structure? If so, to what degree? It is now clear that the environment and even learning of skills impacts on brain structure throughout life, and particularly during development.

Neuron structure responds to the environment.   Behavioral experience influences the number of dendritic spines and size of the dendritic tree in the cortex and cerebellum. For example, mice raised for 17 days in an environment where they could exercise and be as active as they liked showed an increase of 23% in the number of spines on the dendrites of Purkinje cells beyond that of mice housed in cages with only enough space to allow access to food and water (Pysh & Weiss, 1979). Similar results were obtained in young monkeys. Likewise, rats raised in an "enriched" environment showed an increase in dendritic branching in the occipital cortex (Uylings, Kuypers, Diamond, & Eltman, 1978) relative to rats raised in an "impoverished" environment. Whether the increase in the number of synapses per neuron is due to an additional synapse formation or due to the stabilization of existing synapses is not yet clear. Changes in dendritic morphology have also been observed with aging (experience?) in both rodents and humans. Interestingly, dendritic structure often becomes more elaborate with age, perhaps reflecting life-long experience encoded into neuronal structure.

Structural changes are most easily produced in young animals; however, similar though less pronounced alterations occur in adults. Recently, for

Figure 3. *Mean number of branches at each order of bifurcation from the apical dendrite for combined groups. Trained group includes hemispheres opposite trained forelimbs. Non-trained group includes both hemisphere of controls and hemispheres opposite non-trained forelimbs. **p <.0001, *p <.001, by analysis of variance.*
(From Greenough et al., 1985; reproduced by permission of the publishers, Academic Press, Orlando, Fla.)

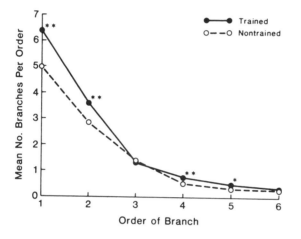

example, Greenough, Larson, and Withers (1985) demonstrated that motor training could directly remodel the apical dendrites of layer V pyramidal cells in the motor cortex of adult rats. Rats have a preferred paw, much like man has a preferred hand. Normal apical dendritic branching of layer V pyramidal neurons is greater on the side opposite the preferred paw. After 16 days of training to use the non-preferred paw, branching was greater on the side opposite the preferred paw (Figure 3). The experience changed dendritic structure and probably, therefore, synapse patterns. In the experiments of Greenough et al. (1985) the enhanced dendritic branching may have been produced by learning, increased use, or both.

Synapses may be lost and replaced ("turnover") throughout life. Structural changes in the number and pattern of synapses have long been suggested as a plausible mechanism for improved performance with use and from learning and memory. Indeed, recent basic evidence on synapse turnover adds new strength to this hypothesis.

Synapse turnover, defined as the loss and replacement of synapses by non-damaging stimuli, appears to be an ongoing process in at least some areas of the mammalian nervous system. In fact, if learning involves synaptic growth, turnover must occur because we are always learning. Synapse turnover has been well documented in the peripheral nervous system, including the parasympathetic innervation of the ciliary muscle (Townes-Anderson & Raviola, 1978) and the innervation of skeletal muscles by motor neurons (Barker & Ip, 1966), and at sensory nerve endings (Burgess, English, Horch, & Stensaas, 1974). In the mature central nervous system, perhaps the most remarkable example of stimulus-evoked synapse turnover occurs in the hypothalamus and neurohypophysis (see Hatton, 1985). Water deprivation, lactation, or late pregnancy and parturation cause the glial processes and pituicytes to withdraw, which results in (a) the appearance of synaptic contacts between adjacent magnocellular neurons in the supraoptic nucleus, and (b) access of the axon endings to the perivascular space in the neurohypophysis (Hatton, 1985). These events, which are totally reversible, result in increased water retention in the kidneys or a rise in mammary pressure (for review, see Cotman, Nieto-Sampedro, & Harris, 1981; Cotman & Nieto-Sampedro, 1984).

Summary
Synapse turnover may be the basic mechanism in neuronal remodeling caused by environment. Although relatively little is known about the relationship between synapse turnover and behavior, it seems logical to assume that the ability of the brain to alter its synaptic circuitry in response to stimuli is somehow related to the adaptive abilities of the nervous system. In this sense, synapse turnover is probably involved in improved performance and ongoing learning and memory processes. Learning may accelerate or slow the process and thereby adjust neuronal connectivity. Indeed, as shown by work on the LTP paradigm, changes in synaptic number can be rapidly induced in the adult brain.

Can differences in the structure of the mature brain created during development be correlated with learning? Very little data are available for animal models at present if lesion studies and genetic studies are excluded. One pertinent study, however, is that of Lippe, Schwegler, and Driscoll (1984). These investigators noted that the rate of two-way avoidance learning in rats and mice is inversely correlated with the size of the intra- and infrapyramidal mossy fiber projection in the hippocampus. In other words, rats that are good learners have a small mossy fiber projection, whereas rats that are poorer learners have a larger mossy fiber projection. Furthermore, this relationship is maintained following experimental manipulation of the mossy fiber projection by thyroxine treatment. Thus, rat pups obtained from a line of good learners and injected with thyroxine show an increase in mossy fiber projections and a decrease in their rate of learning as adults. The fact that learning ability is predictable on the basis of mossy fiber anatomy attains special significance in view of age-related increases in mossy fiber terminals in the hippocampus and dentate gyrus of humans (Cassell & Brown, 1984).

Memory circuits in skill of procedural learning

Simple systems in vertebrate brains

In order to study the vertebrate brain, simple learning paradigms involving brain regions and circuits that can be potentially defined must be used in order to realize an analysis with the precision and definition of the invertebrate work. Several models have now been developed where great progress toward this end has been made.

Recent evidence suggests that a memory trace for classical conditioning is localized in discrete areas of the brain. The most complete data are from studies on eyelid conditioning (McCormick et al., 1982a, b). Eyelid conditioning exhibits the same basic laws of learning in a wide range of mammalian species, including humans, and is prototypical of classical conditioning of striated muscle responses (Gormezano, 1972; Hilgard & Marquis, 1940; Prokasy, 1972; Rescorla, & Wagner, 1972). This simple form of learning proved valuable for analysis of theoretical issues in learning (Wagner, 1981) and is particularly well suited for neurobiological analysis (Thompson et al., 1976; Disterhoft, Kwan, & Low, 1977). It is the first example in the vertebrate brain where the basic circuitry has been defined and where the focus of memory storage (the elusive "engram") has been identified.

Classical conditioning of eyeblink: the first illustration of the essential memory circuit

The model uses a simple, well-characterized and robust form of associative learning: rabbits are trained in a simple Pavlovian task – classical conditioning of the nictitating membrane (NM) and eyelid response. Eyelid conditioning consists of a brief sound (a tone) followed by a puff of air to the eye. After a number of pairings of tone and air puff, the eyelid develops a learned closing response to the tone before the air puff comes. This is a simple adaptive response that protects the eye. Rabbits and humans learn the task equally well.

The paradigm is a standard classical conditioning design. A 350-ms auditory conditioned stimulus (CS) is paired with a 100-ms air puff to the cornea (unconditioned stimulus = UCS), which elicits nictitating membrane (NM) extension and eyelid closure. The UCS overlaps the last 100 ms of the tone

CS. Intertrial intervals are approximately 1 min, and 120 trials are usually given a day. Two types of responses occur during classical conditioning: (1) the unconditioned reflex response (UR) and (2) the classically conditioned eyelid/NM response (CR). Presentation of the UCS (airpuff) by itself elicits the unconditioned response or the UR. Pairing the CS (tone) with the UCS (airpuff) will ensure that after a few pairings the CS alone comes to elicit a response, called the CR, which is similar if not identical to the response formerly elicited by the UCS, i.e. the animal has learned a stimulus–response (CS–UR) relationship. Learning induced by classical conditioning produces the change in behavior that the experimenter records as CR to the CS.

Key brain areas implicated in the changes.   To understand the physiological substrate of the memory trace it is important to identify those brain regions which are essential for the acquisition and retention of the conditioned response. Strong evidence from the use of lesions, electrophysiological recordings, electrical microstimulation, and microinfusion of drugs support the view that the memory trace for the eyeblink response is localized rather than being widely distributed in the brain.

Where is memory for such a simple learned response stored? Rabbits with the neocortex and hippocampus removed can learn the NM/eyelid response relatively normally (Thompson, Berger, & Madden, 1983). The mapping of electrophysiological responses throughout the brain in rabbits have provided important clues. Learning-related increases in activity are prominent in certain regions of the cerebellum (both in cortex and deep nuclei), in certain regions of the pontine nuclei, and in the red nucleus (McCormick & Thompson, 1984). Several regions of the cerebellar cortex and deep nuclei were found where neurons develop patterned changes in firing frequency that precede and predict the occurrence and form of the learned behavioral response (CR) within trials; that is, the pattern of increased neural activity in these areas of the cerebellum formed a "model", in time, of the learned NM/eyeblink response to the tone, but not the reflex eyeblink to the airpuff (Figure 4).

Lesions ipsilateral to the trained eye in any of several locations of the cerebellum and related circuits (interpositus nucleus, the middle cerebellar peduncle, the pontine nuclear region and the dorsal accessory olive) permanently abolish the CR but have no effect on the UR (except lesions of the interpositus). None of these lesions prevent learning by the contralateral side (Lavond, Hembree, & Thompson, 1985; McCormick et al., 1982b).

Cerebellar cortical lesions cause only a transient loss of the CR; all lesioned animals eventually relearn (Lavond, Steinmetz, Yokaitis, & Thompson, 1986). It has been suggested that multiple parallel cortical (and interpositus)

Figure 4. *Histograms of unit-recording of the dentate–interpositus nuclei in one animal. The animal was first given random, unpaired presentations of the tone and airpuff and then trained with two days of paired training. Each histogram is an average over the entire day of training indicated. The upper trace represents movement over the NM, with the "up" being closure. Each histogram is 9 ms in duration. Note that these neurons develop a model of the CR, but not the UCR, during learning.*
(From McCormick & Thompson, 1984; reproduced by permission of the publishers, Oxford University Press, New York, N.Y.)

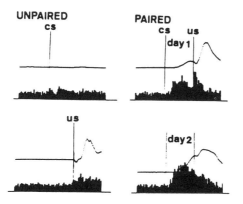

sites for the memory trace might exist. Collectively, these data suggest that the essential memory trace for this conditioned reflex is located in the cerebellum. The cerebellum has been suggested before as a possible locus for certain kinds of memory traces associated with learned movements.

The cellular and molecular mechanisms await discovery now that the site(s) have been identified. It remains to be determined if other training paradigms will share common features of this circuit. An important next step is to elucidate the cellular mechanisms involved in this form of learning.

At present the cellular mechanisms involved in this form of learning have only begun to be described. High concentrations of GABA and GABA receptors have been located in the nucleus interpositus. Microinjections of bicuculline methiodide, a GABA antagonist, selectively and reversibly abolished both the behavioral CR as well as the increment in neuronal firing usually observed in the nucleus interpositus during NM conditioning (Mamounas, Madden, Barchas, & Thompson, 1983). This finding suggests that bicuculline produces its selective abolition of the CR through blockage of inhibitory GABAergic synaptic transmission that is, in some way, essential

for generation of the learned response. What other specific chemical processes play a role in classical conditioning of the NM/eyelid response still needs
to be elucidated. Little is known about the duration or the neurobiology of
the changes underlying the learning of the CR.

*Classical conditioning of forearm position: synaptic plasticity and growth in
learning*
The neural mechanisms involved in learning of a motor response after
repeated trials are of fundamental importance. Unlike simple fact (cognitive)
tasks, learning of motor skills such as riding a bike and balancing usually
requires repeated trials over a considerable period of time. Inherent in such
learning is the need to learn a particular body response in reaction to one or
more sensory stimuli. The most detailed studies, which have been made in
the red nucleus of the cat by Tsukahara and coworkers, are concerned with
the mechanisms of classical conditioning of limb position. The results of these
studies illustrate that new synapse formation appears to occur with conditioning and that the same plastic growth reactions also occur after injury to
mediate functional recovery. Thus, the same mechanisms appear to serve a
range of adaptive capacities.

Nature of system and paradigm.   The essential circuitry involved in the
control of forearm position in the cat is simple and well defined (Figure 5;
Tsukahara, 1986). Sensory information from the forearm travels via the spinal
cord and the interpositus nucleus to the red nucleus. The red nucleus in turn
drives the motor neurons controlling the forearm flexor muscle (biceps bran-
chi). The red nucleus is the key integrative center. In addition to input from
the cerebellum, the red nucleus receives input from the cerebral cortex. The
red nucleus appears to be essential in avoidance conditioning since lesions
there abolish conditioned forearm flexion when a tone conditioned stimulus
(CS) is paired with forearm electric shock as an unconditioned stimulus (US;
Smith, 1970).
    What is the nature of the synaptic change that occurs upon conditioning?
In order to aid in the identification of the primary site of conditioning, outflow from the red nucleus was restricted to the cortical rubral pathway by
lesioning other corticofugal (outflow) pathways below the red nucleus
(Tsukahara, Oda, & Notsu, 1981). This experimental procedure eliminated
the contribution of the pyramidal tract as well as cortico-ponto-cerebellar and
other corticobulbar fibers in reflex. The training procedure involved pairing
a subthreshold CS to the cerebral peduncle with an electric shock (US) to
the forearm. After pairing the CS–US in close temporal association, an initially ineffective CS elicited flexion of the forelimb. The CS preceded the US

Figure 5.   *Associative learning mediated by the RN. (A) Arrangement of experimental set-up. (B) Change in performance. Abscissa, day after onset of training, CS–US interval of 100 ms. After day 11, the stimulus sequence was reversed to US–CS with an interval of 900 ms (modified from Tsukahara et al., 1981; reproduced by permission of the publishers, Oxford University Press, New York, N.Y.).*

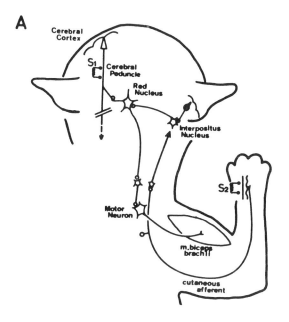

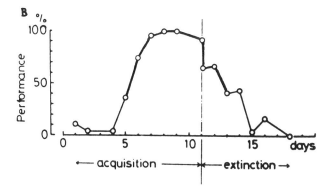

by 60–200 ms over about 120 trials per day. At the end of the training session, the flexion responses were tested by changing the CS intensity, and the relationship between the performance score and applied current was determined. Training required several days, consistent with motor learning of skills. Initially, stimulation of the cerebral peduncle elicited no forearm movement. After 7 days of pairing stimulation of the cerebral peduncle with electrical stimulation of the forearm, forearm flexion could be elicited by stimulation of the cerebral peduncle alone. In parallel with the improved performance score, the minimum current to produce 100 percent performance also decreased. The performance was not elicited after a period of several days during which the CS was not paired with the US. Random presentation of the US and CS also failed to produce conditioning. These data rule out non-specific changes in excitability along the conditioned pathway.

Key brain areas and the synaptic mechanism of learning. The site of synaptic change with conditioning could reside in the cortical pathway, in the interpositus pathway, or in subsequent steps that activate the muscle. The probability of firing red nucleus neurons after cortical stimulation increased after conditioning, suggesting that synaptic transmission through cortico-rubral synapses is associated with conditioning.

The cortico-rubral synapses already present may have increased their strengths, or new synapses may have grown. Studies of partial denervation distal to the red nucleus and on cross union of peripheral nerves point to the possibility that new synapse formation may have occurred (see Tsukahara, 1986 for a review). In the adult, destruction of the cerebellar input causes the cortical input to sprout and form new synapses onto proximal regions of the dendrites. Tsukahara and coworkers have also shown that sprouting in the red nucleus can be induced, in the absence of direct lesions, in response to cross-innervation of flexor and extensor nerves of the forelimb (Tsukahara & Fujito, 1976; Tsukahara, Fujito, Oda, & Maeda, 1982; Fujito, Tsukahara, Oda, & Yoshida, 1982).

These data suggested the hypothesis that cortical fibers innervating the distal dendrites of red nucleus cells may have sprouted additional terminals to form synapses along regions of the dendrites more proximal to the cell bodies during the acquisition of the learned response. Indeed, in preliminary experiments Tsukahara and coworkers have reported that, after conditioning, additional cortical synapses have grown onto the cell body of red nucleus neurons. Thus, learning may be mediated by new synaptic growth of a type similar to that seen after partial denervation. The mechanisms initiating growth are unknown but may be similar to those involved in reactive synaptogenesis after injury (see Nieto-Sampedro, & Cotman, 1985, for discussion).

Summary

Sprouting of cortico-rubral synapses appears to serve as the neurobiological mechanism for learning of a conditioned motor response of limbs. Conditioning occurred over 7 days, when it became maximal. Synaptic growth also mediated functional recovery after cerebellar lesions and after crossing of peripheral nerves. These studies illustrate not only remarkable plasticity of the system but also common use of key, centrally placed mechanisms for mediating several adaptive responses. An interesting implication of these studies is not only that learning and damage-induced plasticity share a common mechanism, but also that the mechanisms in one may predict those in the other.

Discovering the basic mechanisms of classical conditioning through invertebrate models

Three models of learning in invertebrates have been studied extensively in the last ten years and have provided a wealth of information concerning the biochemical and cellular mechanisms involved in the storage of experiences. These are: (1) the gill and siphon withdrawal reflex and the tail withdrawal reflex in the sea snail *Aplysia californica;* (2) classical conditioning in *Hermissenda crassicornis;* and (3) associative conditioning in the mollusc *Limax maximus.*

Learning and memory in Aplysia californica

Several defensive reflexes on *Aplysia* exhibit various forms of non-associative learning (habituation and sensitization) which have both short-term (minutes to hours) and long-term (days to weeks) components. While habituation consists of a decreased behavioral response to a noxious stimulus as a result of repeated experience, sensitization involves a non-specific enhancement of the response to a test stimulus following a second aversive stimulus applied to another part of the organism (Kandel & Schwartz, 1982).

The connections between sensory neurons and motor neurons controlling these reflexes have been relatively well described anatomically and exhibit a number of plastic properties including synaptic depression, presynaptic facilitation and long-term increases in synaptic efficacy. These systems present the additional advantage that the whole circuitry can be studied not only in the intact animal but also in isolated preparations. More recently it was shown that these connections can even be investigated in dissociated cell culture conditions (Belardetti, Schacher, Kandel, & Siegelbaum, 1986).

The best understood phenomenon in *Aplysia* is sensitization (Kandel & Schwartz, 1982). A sensitizing stimulus in one part of the animal induces the release of a modulating transmitter that produces presynaptic facilitation of many sensory neurons. Presynaptic facilitation increases neurotransmitter release from these sensory neurons when they are subsequently activated and thus enhance activation of motor neurons and enhanced behavioral response. Recently it has been shown that an elaboration of this mechanism is probably involved in associative learning in *Aplysia*. It is assumed that two sensory pathways make weak subthreshold connections to a common response system and that activity in one sensory pathway (the CS pathway) modifies in response to the facilitatory effect due to the activity in the second pathway (the US pathway) if the appropriate temporal association between the two stimuli is present. This hypothesis was tested by using a classical conditioning procedure in which intracellular activation of individual sensory neurons represented the CS, and shock to the skin the US. Paired presentation of the CS and US resulted in an enhanced postsynaptic potential to CS presentation (Hawkins, Abrams, Carew, & Kandel, 1983).

Learning appears to take place at a defined set of synapses, where the molecular mechanism has been worked out to a degree unprecedented for other systems. It involves an increase in cyclic AMP, the phosphorylation of select proteins and a decrease in potassium currents. The decrease in potassium current increases the duration of the action potential, causing a larger output of neurotransmitter.

Little is known concerning the mechanisms responsible for the long-term effects except that structural changes have been shown to take place in the terminals of the sensory neurons (increased number of active zones; Bailey & Chen, 1983). More recently, Kandel and coworkers have shown that protein synthesis is required to establish the long-term modification of synaptic transmission underlying long-term sensitization (Goelet, Castelucci, Schacher, & Kandel, 1986). It has been proposed that signals that initiate short-term memory can initiate, through common intracellular messengers, both covalent modification of proteins responsible for the short-term effects and also additional steps resulting in the expression of different genes and the formation of lasting traces of experiences.

Learning and memory in Hermissenda

For the sea slug *Hermissenda*, light elicits oriented positive movement and foot lengthening, while rotation, a strong aversive stimulus, elicits "clinging" and foot contraction. Paired presentation of light (CS) and rotation of the animal (US) produces classical conditioning, with several characteristics similar to that observed in vertebrate systems. In *Hermissenda, as in Aplysia,* learning occurs because of the convergence of two sensory pathways on a set of motor neurons responsible for the behavioral response. Analysis of the changes in electrophysiological properties of the sensory neurons responding to light presentation was used to uncover the molecular and cellular mechanisms underlying the learning process (Alkon, 1984).

The biochemical steps are not completely elucidated but there is evidence that the changes are due to the paired activation of a calcium-calmodulin kinase and a calcium-dependent phospholipid-dependent protein kinase (kinase C), and the resulting phosphorylation of specific proteins. It is interesting that similar biophysical and biochemical mechanisms may contribute to neuronal changes observed in rabbit hippocampus following classical conditioning of the nictitating membrane.

Learning and memory in Limax

Limax is a terrestrial mollusc which is a generalist herbivore and employs various mechanisms to optimize its food choices, and in particular learns to avoid plant odors associated with toxicosis (Gelpering, 1975). The learning procedure by which an attractive plant odor is paired with a bitter taste is identical to a typical classical conditioning with the attractant odor being the CS and the bitter taste the US. Following training the CS is repellent, eliciting an avoidance and rejection response. Although the circuitry responsible for the learning as well as the biochemical and cellular mechanisms underlying the changes in synaptic connectivity are far from being well known, this system is interesting because it has been the subject of a formal computer simulation and is possibly one of the first neural networks to be currently transposed into a silicon chip network (Gelperin, Hopfield, & Tank, 1986).

The circuitry which has been proposed to be responsible for the behavior consists of a set of sensory neurons detecting various characteristics of the odors (or tastes) of plants which project to a matrix of interneurons (a cataloger), the outputs of which synapse on two control/motor output networks determining the behavioral response of the animal: eat or flee.

The biochemical and physiological properties of the various neurons participating in the circuit are currently being investigated and there is evidence that traditional transmitters (acetylcholine, dopamine and serotonin) as well as neuroactive peptides are involved in some aspects of the neural control system of feeding. The role of phosphorylation of ion channels in the synaptic changes underlying learning and memory in this system is also currently being investigated. A formal neural model of associative learning has been developed and simulated (LIMAX simulation program), which uses realistic abstractions of real neurons and an algorithm of learning based on Hebbian rules. It is assumed that internal representations of foods are generated and learned by the taste categorizer network and that the associations between the representations and their significance (attractive or repulsive) take place at the level of the control/motor output network.

Correlates of learning in cortical circuitries during development
In the preceding sections, we found that the study of simple systems has yielded a new set of reasonably specific ideas about the ways in which learning is etched into neuronal circuitries. It is appropriate now to consider modifications produced in higher brain regions during developmental learning and to look for links between these and the mechanisms identified in the work on simple systems. Since one of the themes of this review has been learning in humans, we will focus our attention on forebrain and neocortical structures (i.e., those regions that are greatly expanded in the human brain) and consider results from immature animals.

Early learning is an important survival mechanism for the young. Learning is used too in establishing bonds with the parents, adapting the nervous system to particular environments and in general beginning to build the encyclopedia of experience for later life. Nervous system circuitry, once set during development, is relatively permanent. Changes which occur in the adult are relatively subtle compared to the impact that disturbances or the environment can have on the developing nervous system. What role does early learning play in establishing nervous system circuitry? What are the critical variables? And what mechanisms predispose the circuitries to particular changes?

Developmental neurobiology has demonstrated that differential neural activity, including learning, causes the selection of specific neurons and synapses. While early neuronal death in the selection of connections has long been linked to differential neural stimulation, the mechanism by which specific neurons survive has received less attention. It appears that learning may be a selective agent in this process. Such selection processes may help to provide answers to the question of how normal variation in early experience produces individual differences in brain and the expression of behavior.

In early development when early circuitry is forming, learning and environment have an impact on the formation of the brain's networks. Two examples illustrate the impact of early experience on brain structure: (1) early learning in the olfactory system; and (2) experience in development of the visual system.

Early learning in the olfactory system

Early olfactory experience determines one of the many routes by which the normal olfactory brain will develop. Neonatal rodents, like babies, learn to prefer the odor of their mother when the odor is experienced with appropriate tactile stimulation (Leon, 1974; Leon & Moltz, 1971, 1972). Human neonates acquire an attraction for the odor of their mother within the first weeks of life and also can acquire a behavioral preference for other odors following early experience (Balogh & Porter, 1986; MacFarlane, 1975). The numbers of certain groups of cells and their connections in the olfactory bulb permanently increase. NMDA receptors and therefore neural activity appear to mediate this process. This effect is restricted to the first week of life.

Structural correlates of early learning
The nature of the response in the olfactory bulbs of 19-day-old odor-learning or control rat pups to peppermint odor was examined using [^{14}C]2-deoxyglucose (2-DG) autoradiography. This technique reveals spatially specific activation of the olfactory bulb glomerular layer evoked by different odors (Greer, Stewart, Kauer, & Shepherd, 1981; Greer, Stewart, Teicher, & Shepherd, 1982).

The odor-learning pups had 64 percent higher 2-DG uptake in focal areas of the glomerular layer (Coopersmith & Leon, 1984). Neither the level of uptake in the periventricular core nor the uptake in other portions of the glomerular layer differed between groups. This difference was not attributable to differential respiration of the odor (Coopersmith & Leon, 1984) nor trigeminal system activation (Coopersmith, Henderson, & Leon, 1986a). The enhanced 2-DG uptake in the identified glomeruli areas (Coopersmith & Leon, 1984) persisted for at least three months, the longest period examined. To date, this is the largest localized structural change found in the brain that has been associated with learning.

Learning caused an enlargement in glomeruli only during the first week of life. Olfactory experience using the same paradigm given to adults did not evoke a special neurobehavioral response. Indeed, the development of the enhanced glomerular response appears to be restricted to olfactory experience given within the first week postpartum (Woo & Leon, 1986).

The cellular mechanism: a critical role for NMDA receptors
Glutamate receptors of the *N*-methyl-D-aspartate (MNDA) type have been identified in the neonatal bulb and blocking them prevents the development of olfactory preference and the enhanced glomerular response in young rats (Lincoln et al., 1986). The specific NMDA antagonist AP5 blocked the enhanced 2-DG uptake in focal areas of the glomerular layer, as well as the specific neurobehavioral response to early olfactory learning. It appears as if there is an increase in survival of select cell populations in the developing bulb.

Experience in development of the visual system

A minimum level of normal stimulation is also required for the visual brain to develop along its normal path. For example, children may permanently lose vision in one eye if vision is temporarily impaired by eye injury early in life, even if the damage to the eye itself heals completely. The nature of the needed visual stimulation has the formal characteristics of a learning situation. It is an activity-dependent process that produces long-lasting change in cortical structures. Both pre- and postsynaptic activation are necessary in accordance with the predictions of a Hebbian synapse.

Visual stimulation is only effective in organizing the system if attended to or recognized by the brain by means of coincident non-specific arousal. In the mature visual system, inputs from the two eyes terminate in different laminae of the thalamic relay (lateral geniculate). These thalamic inputs terminate in layer V of the visual cortex (the ocular dominance columns). While the afferents are initially comingled, the overlapping connections retract and separate. Suppression of retinal input blocks this segregation. This finding indicates that neural activity is needed for segregation (Archer, Dubin, & Stark, 1982; Mower, Cristen, & Caplan, 1984; Swindale, 1982).

Asymmetry in afferent activation from the two eyes also causes an asymmetry in the segregated columns (Blakemore, Gary, Henderson, Swindale, & Vital-Durand, 1980; Hubel, Wiesel, & LeVay, 1977). Monocular deprivation causes the size of the patches derived from the other eye to expand (LeVay & Stryker, 1979).

Mechanisms underlying visual cortex organization

The changes in segregation patterns depend on particular patterns of afferent activation. The necessary condition is concurrent activation of both the presynaptic and postsynaptic neurons in the system. This requirement is reminiscent of Hebb's (1949) model for synaptic plasticity during learning. Interestingly, it is also the requirement for long-term potentiation.

If the signals from the two eyes simultaneously converge on their target neuron, their dual connection to the neuron is likely to be stabilized. If, however, the two eyes send information that is out of phase, the two inputs are in competition with each other and one pathway is repressed. Signals from the two eyes must be present within 200–400 ms. Otherwise, the binocular disparity imposes a shift in the segregation of the afferents (Altmann, Luhann, Singer, & Greuel, 1985).

Both pre- and postsynaptic activity is necessary. Postsynaptic activation alone is insufficient. Postsynaptic activation of target neurons, even with afferent input, is insufficient to induce the normal pattern of visual system organization. Visual information does not influence cortical organization when kittens are paralyzed or anesthetized (Singer, 1979). Similarly, blocking sensory information from the extraocular muscles prevents the expression of ocular dominance despite the fact that the visual information is generating activity in the afferents (Buisseret & Singer, 1983).

Requirements for concurrent arousing stimuli
Pairing monocular visual stimulation with electrical stimulation of the reticular formation or the intralaminar nucleus of the thalamus can overcome the inability of anesthetized and paralyzed animals to develop ocular dominance (Singer, 1986). Conversely, when lesions of the intralaminar nucleus of the thalamus are made, monocular deprivation does not change the cortical neurons from binocular to monocular (Singer, 1982).

These data suggest that the changes in visual input are effective in organizing the system only if attended to or recognized by the brain by means of coincident non-specific arousal. Thus, only when sensory stimulation is paired with a non-specific, arousing stimulus does cortical plasticity occur. It would be important to determine whether manipulation of the non-specific arousal system would affect other types of early learning. At present, however, no information is available.

Just as with adult learning (Morris et al., 1986), early olfactory learning (Lincoln et al., 1986), and long-term potentiation, NMDA receptor activation also appears to be required for mediating the consequences of early visual experience (Singer, Kleinschmidt, & Bear, 1986). Chronic infusion of AP5 into the visual cortex during the critical period prevents the ocular dominance shift in response to monocular experience.

Summary
These findings indicate that the normal pattern of visual system development depends on a specific coincidence of visual stimulation and arousing stimulation. An abnormal pattern of visual system organization occurs if either aspect of this early experience is not present. The implication of these findings is that the developing brain circuitry registers environmental signals when the non-specific arousal system places significance to the events.

General comments on early learning

Research on the neurobiology of early learning during development is not extensively studied and yet offers great promise. Rather than dealing with the subtle and often inaccessible changes that appear during adult learning, the changes observed following learning during early life appear quite large and accessible. Indeed, it seems that the developmental process may amplify small changes that are made early in life so that they can be observed by the experimenter. There is a clear need for more research.

There are indications that some mechanisms are shared by adults and infants during learning. For example, both glutamate and norepinephrine have been implicated in the mechanisms underlying both adult and neonatal learning (Morris et al., 1986; Lincoln et al., 1986; Sullivan & Leon, 1986a, b; Gold & Zornetzer, 1984). Similar neural structures involved in adult learning also increase their activity during neonatal learning (Kucharski, Browde, & Hall, 1986).

There are several implications of this work. It means that an early learning experience is permanently etched into the circuitry of the CNS. This will bias the type of response to similar situations in the future. In other words, early experiences produce long-lasting changes in neural circuitry which affect subsequent behaviors.

From the preceding sections it is clear that the cellular and molecular substrates of learning are accessible to analysis in several vertebrate and invertebrate systems and that excellent progress is being made. Clearly learning depends on the proper operation of defined circuits which transfer the information and ultimately store it in a form accessible for retrieval. The substrate often appears to involve molecular changes in existing connections, or as more recent data indicate actual formation (turnover) of new synapses.

What are the steps where learning has "weak links?" Neuropsychologists have amply documented the crucial roles played by general body and brain states such as arousal, motivation, attention, etc. Learning does not occur without a prior focusing of attention and without appropriate motivation. Perturbations in the machinery that controls arousal, for example, are not uncommon in children and are often present as a hyperkinetic syndrome. Brain states are also known to exert a powerful influence over the body's endocrine system, and hormone levels in turn have been linked to the strengths of the memory trace.

Many new tools are available to stimulate and capitalize on the advances being made. New imaging techniques will help us bridge the gap between animals and man. Computer networks are being built which simulate real brain networks, allow an examination of their properties and predict where weak "links" exist. In fact, interest in computer models which simulate brain functions may be synergistic to the biological and cognitive sciences.

Summary and conclusion

Over the last five years, results of research on the mechanisms of learning have dramatically expanded the knowledge base. Recent efforts have focused on defining systems for analyzing relatively simple types of learning (sensitization, habituation, and classical conditioning) and for analyzing how physiological activity changes synapses. It is now clear that defined circuits exist for learning, that the site and location of the synaptic change can be localized, and that many specific biochemical mechanisms can be identified.

Invertebrate models are teaching us much about the fundamentals of learning, just as the squid axon taught us much about the fundamentals of action potentials. Most work on invertebrates involved studies on molluscs as models. The mollusc nervous system is simple and well defined, and its circuits can be outlined. The mollusc *Aplysia californica* shows a suprising repertoire of behaviors, including long-term sensitization and classical conditioning. Learning appears to take place at a defined set of synapses, where the molecular mechanism has been described to a degree unprecedented for other systems. It involves an increase in cyclic AMP, the phosphorylation of select proteins, and a decrease in the potassium currents. The decreased potassium current increases the duration of the action potential, which causes a larger output of neurotransmitter. In another mollusc, *Hermissenda*, classical conditioning occurs when a light stimulus is paired with a noxious stimulus, such as rotation of the animal. The mechanism appears to involve an inactivation of calcium-dependent potassium currents, which renders the cell more excitable. In *Limax*, the circuits have been moduled in detail by computer and shown to operate in accordance with the classical rules for conditioning of a mammalian nervous system.

Learning occurs throughout life, from the earliest times after fertilization until the last days of old age. Events learned early in life can dictate later responses. Several exciting advances in model systems have been made for certain types of early learning. Like children, rodent pups learn to recognize key odors early in life, such as those of their mothers. An odor paired with tactile stimulation during a critical period can alter the behavioral response to that odor. The mechanism appears to involve an increase in the size of the neural network in the olfactory bulb, which processes these odors. NMDA receptors and calcium ions appear to be involved in this early change.

While the primary pathways of the nervous system are laid down at the time of birth, many adjustments and calibrations within these pathways occur in the course of development. The visual system is a premier example where, early in the course of development, the two retinal images from each eye have to be matched, calibrated, and segregated in the proper fashion within the visual cortex. Such changes are clearly activity-dependent, and the proper segregation of the cortical wiring does not occur in the absence of normal neural activity. The development of the system also depends on a non-specific arousal stimulus. NMDA receptors appear to be involved as in the developing olfactory system.

In rodents, it has been demonstrated that an enriched environment during rearing makes the structure of the visual cortex richer in the arborization of its neurons and in the number of synapses on each cell. Some of these changes are transient, reversing when the environment becomes less complex. Others appear permanent, indicating that the imprint of the environment remains on the cortex and its potential functional properties. Information in the literature suggests that the primate brain can be similarly influenced by experience. It is likely, but not proven, that each sensory system with its associated cicuitries can be influenced by early environment and experience. These sensory systems appear to go through critical periods of high plasticity, and once past that period the system becomes more fixed. It may be that the key areas involved in cognition have a similar critical period for programming various types of learning or learning sets. However, there is no evidence at present.

Once the nervous system matures, the basic circuitry is set and serves as a substrate for consequent operations. Insults very early in life can sometimes be compensated for, particularly if they are minor. Such a compensation, however, can often detract from other parallel abilities. Learning depends on a combination of different systems, not only for the stimuli that are processed but also for the type of learning. In a broad sense, the learning of skills or procedures is distinguished from that of certain cognitive tasks, so-called declarative or fact memory. The conditioning of a motor response is an excellent example of skill or procedural learning. A component of a complex of motor skills that had been quite well studied is that of learning forearm position. This learning occurs over a time course of a few days and seems to reside within the red nucleus, a key integrative structure where cortical and cerebellar inputs converge. In this nucleus, injury-altered sensory input and conditioning appear to share a common mechanism: the formation of new synapses.

These data are but one example which suggests that the response to injury produced by cell loss shares certain common features and mechanisms with that of adaptive plasticity during learning. More examples are needed. They would enhance this field of study because the information about regenerative plasticity after injury is rapidly increasing. It would seem as if there are common mechanisms which adapt the CNS to recovery from its own internal signals and modify its responses to transfer external experience to memory.

It is increasingly recognized that cognitive learning (facts, episodes) is the type of learning most relevant to the central needs of humans and their intellectual pursuits. Ironically, this type of learning also appears vulnerable to various neuropathological conditions. Cognitive learning losses in Alzheimer's disease patients, for example, far exceed losses of skill learning.

The development of animal models of such data recognition and processing systems is at an early stage, relative to those for classical conditioning. Tasks like the match-to-sample or non-match-to-sample are most commonly employed. Various sensory systems gain access to key components of the data memory system. In rodents, primates, and humans, learning of match-to-sample procedures depends on the function of the amygdala, entorhinal cortex, and hippocampus, which are key components of the limbic memory system. Damage to one or more of these components interferes with the retention of information. A synaptic analog of learning has been identified in these structures and is called long-term potentiation. Stimulation of a pathway at a particular frequency or an association between two pathways causes a long-lasting strengthening of synaptic transmission. At least one form of long-term potentiation appears to involve NMDA receptors and calcium.

Overall, it appears that different types of learning involve different types of record systems and possibly different types, or mixture of types, of cellular processes. Therefore, our present inability to identify a single mechanism for learning may be due to the absence of a ubiquitous mechanism and to the fact that learning, seen in intact animals, involves a constellation of processes, which, taken together across brain systems, refine and adjust responses.

It is important to recognize that learning, according to all models so far analyzed, involves sequences of cellular events and that disturbances of any sequence could impair the acquisition and storage of new information. Neurobiological experiments have served to identify events that are at risk. Such events are candidates for the causes of disabilities. Further progress, coupled with information obtained from the study of other instances of brain dysfunction, will lead to new treatment strategies.

References

Akers, R.F., Lovinger, D.M., Colley, P.A., Linden, D.J., & Routtenberg, A. (1986). Translocation of protein kinase C activity may mediate hippocampal long-term potentiation. *Science, 230,* 587–589.

Alkon, D.L. (1984). Calcium-mediated reduction of ionic currents: A biophysical memory trace. *Science, 226,* 1037–1045.

Altmann, L., Luhmann, H.J., Singer, W., & Greuel, J. (1985). Ocular dominance distribution in the striate cortex of kittens raised with rapidly alternating monocular occlusion. *Neuroscience Letters Supplement, 22,* S353.

Anderson, P., Silfvenius, H., Sundberg, S.H., & Sveen, E. (1980). A comparison of distal and proximal dendritic synapses on CA1 pyramids in guinea pig hippocampal slices in vitro and serotonin release by leupeptin and antipain. *Journal of Physiology, 307,* 273–299.

Archer, S.M., Dubin, M.W., & Stark, L.A. (1982). Abnormal development of kitten retinogeniculate connectivity in the absence of action potentials. *Science, 217,* 743–745.

Bachevalier, J., & Mishkin, M. (1986). Cortical vs. limbic immaturity: Relationship to infantile global amnesian monkeys. *Society for Neuroscience Abstracts, 12,* 22.

Bailey, C.H., & Chen, M. (1983). Morphological basis of long-term habituation and sensitization in *Aplysia. Science, 220,* 91–93.

Balogh, R.D., & Porter, R.H. (1986). Olfactory preferences resulting from mere exposure in human neonates. *Infant Behavior and Development, 9,* 395–401.

Barker, D., & Ip, M.D. (1966). Sprouting and regeneration of mammalian motor axons in normal and deafferented skeletal muscle. *Proceedings of the Royal Society, London, Series B, 163,* 538–556.

Belardetti, R., Schacher, S., Kandel, E.R., & Siegelbaum, S.A. (1986). The growth cones of *Aplysia* sensory neurons: Modulation by serotonin of action potential duration and single potassium channel currents. *Proceedings of the National Academy of Science USA, 83,* 7094–7098.

Benson, D.F., Marsden, C.D., & Meadows, J.C. (1974). The amnesic syndrome of posterior cerebral artery occlusion. *Acta Neurologica Scandinavia, 50,* 133–145.

Blakemore, C., Garey, L.J., Henderson, Z.B., Swindale, N.V., & Vital-Durand, F. (1980). Visual experience can promote rapid axonal reinnervation in monkey visual cortex. *Journal of Physiology, 307,* 26.

Bliss, T.V.P., & Gardner-Medwin, A.T. (1973). Long-lasting potentiation of synaptic transmission in the dentate area of the unanesthetized rabbit following stimulation of the perforant path. *Journal of Physiology (London), 232,* 357–374.

Buisseret, P., & Singer, W. (1983). Proprioceptive signals from extraocular muscles gate experience-dependent modifications of receptive fields in the kitten visual cortex. *Experimental Brain Research, 51,* 443–450.

Burgess, P.R., English, K.B., Horch, K.W., & Stensaas, L.J. (1974). Patterning in the regeneration of type I cutaneous receptors. *Journal of Physiology (London), 236,* 57–87.

Butters, N., & Cermak, L.S. (1980). *Alcoholic Korsakoff's syndrome: An information processing approach to amnesia.* New York: Academic Press.

Cassell, M.D., & Brown, M.W. (1984). The distribution of Timm's stain in the nonsulphide-perfused human hippocampal formation. *Journal of Comparative Neurology, 222,* 461–471.

Chang, F.L.F., & Greenough, W.T. (1984). Transient and enduring morphological conclats of synaptic activity and efficacy change in the rat hippocampal slice. *Brain Research, 309,* 35–46.

Cohen, N.J. (1984). Preserved learning capacity in amnesia: Evidence for multiple memory systems. In L.R. Squire & N. Butters (Eds.), *Neuropsychology of memory.* New York: Guilford Press.

Cohen, N.J., & Squire, L.R. (1980). Preserved learning capacity and retention of pattern analyzing skill in amnesia: Dissociation of knowing how and knowing that. *Science, 210,* 207–209.

Collingridge, B.L., Kehl, S.J., & McLennan, H. (1983). The antagonism of amino-acid-induced excitation of rat hippocampal CA1 neurons in vitro. *Journal of Physiology, 334,* 19–31.

Coopersmith, B.L., Henderson, J., & Leon, M. (1986a). Odor specificity of the enhanced neural response following early odor exposure. *Development Brain Research, 27,* 191–197.

Coopersmith, R., Lee, S., & Leon, M. (1986b). Olfactory bulb responses after odor aversion learning by young rats. *Development Brain Research, 24,* 271–277.

Coopersmith, R., & Leon, M. (1984). Enhanced neural response to familiar olfactory cues. *Science, 224,* 849–851.

Corkin, S. (1968). Acquisition of motor skill after bilateral medial temporal lobe excision. *Neuropsychologia, 6,* 255–265.

Cotman, C.W., & Nieto-Sampedro, M. (1984). Cell biology of synaptic plasticity. *Science, 255,* 1287–1294.

Cotman, C.W., Nieto-Sampedro, M., & Harris, E. (1981). Synapse replacement in the nervous system of adult vertebrates. *Physiological Review, 61,* 684–784.

Disterhoft, J.F., Kwan, H.H., & Low, W.D. (1977). Nictitating membrane conditioning to tone in the immobilized albino rabbit. *Brain Research, 137,* 127–144.

Drachman, D.A., & Adams, R.D. (1962). Herpes simplex and acute-inclusion body encephalitis. *Archives of Neurology, 7,* 45–63.

Dunwiddie, T.V., & Lynch, G.S. (1978). Long-term potentiation and depression of synaptic responses in the rat hippocampus: Localization and frequency dependency. *Journal of Physiology (London), 276,* 353–367.

Eichenbaum, J., Shedlack, K.J., & Eckman, K.W. (1980). Thalamocortical mechanisms in odor-guided behavior. Effects of lesions of the medio dorsal thalamic nucleus and frontal cortex on olfactory discrimination in the rat. *Brain Research, 17,* 255–275.

Eslinger, P.J., & Damasio, A.R. (1986). Preserved motor learning in Alzheimer's disease: Implications for anatomy and behavior. *Journal of Neuroscience, 6,* 3006–3009.

Feldman, J.A. (1981). A connectionist model of visual memory. In G.E. Hinton & J.A. Anderson (Eds.), *Parallel models of associative memory.* Hillsdale, NJ: Erlbaum.

Fujito, Y., Tsukahara, N., Oda, Y., & Yoshida, M. (1982). Formation of functional synapses in the adult cat red nucleus from cerebrum following cross-innervation of forelimb flexor and extensor nerves. II. Analysis of newly-appeared synaptic potentials. *Experimental Brain Research, 45,* 13–18.

Gelperin, A. (1975). Rapid food-aversion learning by a terrestrial mollusk. *Science, 189,* 565–570.

Gelperin, A., Hopfield, J.J., & Tank, D.W. (1986). The logic of *Limax* learning. In A.I. Selverston (Ed.), *Model neural networks and behavior.* New York: Plenum Press.

Goelet, P., Castelucci, V.P., Schacher, S., & Kandel, E.R. (1986). The long and the short-term memory: A molecular framework. *Nature, 322,* 419–422.

Gold, P.E., & Zornezer, S.F. (1984). The mnemon and its juices: Neuromodulation of memory processes. *Behavioral and Neural Biology, 38,* 151–189.

Gormezano, I. (1972). Investigation of defense and reward conditioning in the rabbit. In A. Black & W. Prokasy (Eds.), *Classical conditioning II: Current research and theory.* New York: Appleton-Century-Crofts.

Greenough, W.T., Larson, J.R., & Withers, G.S. (1985). Effects of unilateral and bilateral training in a reaching task on dendritic branching of neurons in the rat motor-sensory forelimb cortex. *Behavioral Neural Biology, 44,* 301–314.

Greer, D.A., Stewart, W.B., Kauer, J.S., & Shepherd, G.M. (1981). Topographical and laminar localization of 2-deoxyglucose uptake in rat olfactory bulb induced by electrical stimulation of olfactory nerves. *Brain Research, 217,* 279–293.

Greer, D.A., Stewart, W.B., Teicher, M.H., & Shepherd, G.M. (1982). Functional development of the olfactory bulb and a unique glomeruli complex in the neonatal rat. *Journal of Neuroscience, 2,* 1744–1759.

Harris, E.W., Ganong, A.H., & Cotman, C.W. (1984). Long-term potentiation in the hippocampus involves activation of N-methyl-D-aspartate receptors. *Brain Research, 323,* 132–137.

Hatton, G.I. (1985). Reversible synapse formation and modulation of cellular relationships in the adult hypothalamus under physiological conditions. In C.W. Cotman (Ed.), *Synaptic plasticity.* New York: Guilford Press.

Hawkins, R.D., Abrams, T.W., Carew. T.J., & Kandel, E.R. (1983). A cellular mechanism of classical conditioning in *Aplysia*: Activity-dependent amplification of presynaptic facilitation. *Science, 219,* 400–405.

Hebb, D.O. (1949). *The organization of behavior.* New York: Wiley.

Hilgard, E.R., & Marquis, D.G. (1940). *Conditioning and learning.* New York: Appleton-Century-Crofts.

Hubel, D.H., Wiesel, T.N., & LeVay, S. (1977). Plasticity of ocular dominance columns in monkey striate cortex. *Philosophical Transactions of the Royal Society of London B, 278,* 377–409.

Kandel, E.R., & Schwartz, J.H. (1982). Molecular biology of learning: Modulation of transmitter release. *Science, 218*, 433–443.

Kaushall, P.J., Zetin, M., & Squire, L.R. (1981). Amnesia: Detailed report of a noted case. *Journal of Nervous and Mental Disease, 169*, 383–389.

Kesslak, J.P., Cotman, C.W., Chui, H.C., Van den Noort, S., Fang, H., Pfeffer, R., & Lynch, G. (1988). Olfactory tests as possible probes for detecting and monitoring Alzheimer's disease. *Neurology and Aging, 9*, 399–403.

King, J.S., Martin, G.F., & Connor, B. (1972). A light red electron microscope study of corticorubral projections in the oppossum. *Didelphis marsupialis virginiana. Brain Research, 38*, 251–265.

Kucharski, D., Browde, J.A., & Hall, W.G. (1986). Relative regional metabolic changes in the brains of neonatal rats during appetitive olfactory learning. *Society for Neuroscience Abstracts, 12*, 751.

Larson, J., & Lynch, G.S. (1986). Synaptic potentiation in hippocampus by patterned stimulation involves two events. *Science, 232*, 985–988.

Larson, J., Wong, D., & Lynch, G. (1986). Patterned stimulation at the theta frequency is optimal for induction of long-term potentiation. *Brain Research, 368*, 7–35.

Lavond, D.G., Hembree, T.L., & Thompson, R.F. (1985). Effect of kainic acid lesions of the cerebellar interpositus nucleus of eyelid conditioning in the rabbit. *Brain Research, 326*, 179–182

Lavond, D.G., Steinmetz, J.E., Yokaitis, M.H., & Thompson, R.F. (1986). Retention of classical conditioning after removal of cerebellar cortex. *Society for Neuroscience Abstracts, 12*, 753.

Lee, K., Schottler, F., Oliver, M., & Lynch, G. (1980). Brief bursts of high frequency stimulation produce two types of structural change in rat hippocampus. *Journal of Neurophysiology, 44*, 247–258.

Leon, M. (1974). Maternal pheromone. *Physiology and Behavior, 13*, 441–453.

Leon, M., & Moltz, H. (1971). Maternal pheromone: Discrimination by preweaning albino rats. *Physiology and Behavior, 7*, 265–267.

Leon, M., & Moltz, H. (1972). The development of the pheromonal bond in the albino rat. *Physiology and Behavior, 8*, 683–686.

LeVay, S., & Stryker, M.P. (1979). Development of ocular dominance columns in the cat. *Society of Neuroscience Symposia, 4*, 83–98.

Lincoln, J.S., Coopersmith, E.W., Harris, E.W., Monaghan, D.T., Cotman, C.W., & Leon, M. (1986). NMDA receptor blockade prevents neural and behavioral consequences of early olfactory experience. *Society for Neuroscience Abstracts, 12*, 124.

Lippe, H.P., Schwegler, H., & Driscoll, P. (1984). Postnatal modification of hippocampal circuitry alters avoidance learning in adult rats. *Science, 225*, 80–82.

Lynch, G. (1986). *Synapses, circuits and the beginnings of memory.* Cambridge, MA: MIT Press.

Lynch, G., & Baudry, M. (1984). The biochemistry of memory: A new and specific hypothesis. *Science, 224*, 1057–1063.

Lynch, G.S., Dunwiddie, T.V., & Gribkoff, V. (1977). Heterosynaptic depression: A postsynaptic correlate of long-term potentiation. *Nature, 266*, 737–739.

Lynch, G., Halpain, S., & Baudry, M. (1982). Effects of high frequency synaptic stimulation on glutamate receptor binding studies with a modified in vitro hippocampal slice preparation. *Brain Research, 244*, 101–111.

Lynch, G., Laron, J., Kelso, S., Barrionuevo, G., & Schottler, F. (1983). Intracellular injections of EGTA block the induction of hippocampal long-term potentiation. *Nature, 305*, 719–721.

MacFarlane, A. (1975). Olfaction in the development of social preferences in the human neonate. *Ciba Foundation Symposium, 33*, 103–117.

Malamut, B.L., Saunders, R.C., & Mishkin, M. (1984). Monkeys with combined amygdala–hippocampal lesions succeed in object discrimination learning despite 24-hour intertrial intervals. *Behavioral Neuroscience, 5*, 759–769.

Mamounas, L.A., Madden, J., Barchas, J.D., & Thompson, R.F. (1983). Microinfusion of bicuculline into dentate/interpositus region abolishes classical conditioning of the well-trained rabbit eyelid response. *Society for Neuroscience Abstracts, 9*, 830.

McCormick, D.A., Clark, G.A., Lavond, D.G., & Thompson, R. (1982a). Initial localization of the memory trace for a basic form of learning. *Proceedings of the National Academy of Science USA, 79*, 2731–2735.

McCormick, D.A., Guyer, P.E., & Thompson, R.F. (1982b). Superior cerebellar penduncle lesions selectively abolish the ipsilateral classically conditioned nictitating membrane/eyelid response of the rabbit. *Brain Research, 244*, 347–350.

McCormick, D.A., & Thompson, R.F. (1984). Responses of the rabbit cerebellum during acquisition and performance of a classically conditioned nictitating membrane eyelid response. *Journal of Neuroscience, 4*, 2811–2822.

McNaughton, B.L., Douglas, R.M., & Goddard, G.V. (1978). Synaptic enhancement in fascia dentata: Cooperativity among inactive afferents. *Brain Research, 157*, 277–293.

Milner, B. (1968). Disorders of memory after brain lesions in man. Preface: Material-specific and generalized memory loss. *Neuropsychologia, 6*, 175–179.

Mishkin, M. (1978). Memory in monkeys severely impaired by combined but not separate removal of amygdala and hippocampus. *Nature, 273*, 297–298.

Morris, R.G.M., Anderson, E., Lynch, G.S., & Baudry, M. (1986). Selective impairment of learning and blockade of long-term potentiation by an N-methyl-D-aspartate receptor antagonist, AP5. *Nature, 319*, 774–776.

Mouly, A.M., Vigouroux, M., & Holley, A. (1985). On the ability of rats to discriminate between microstimulations of the olfactory bulb in different locations. *Behavioral Brain Research, 17*, 45–48.

Mower, G.D., Christen, W.G., & Caplan, C.J. (1984). Absence of ocular dominance columns in binocularly deprived cats. *Investigative Ophthalmology and Visual Science (ARVO abstr.), 25* (Suppl.), 214.

Murakami, F., Katsumaru, H., Saito, K., & Tsukahara, N. (1982). A quantitative study of synaptic reorganization in red nucleus neurons after lesion of the nucleus interpositus of the cat: An electron microscopic study involving intracellular injection of horseradish peroxidase. *Brain Research, 242*, 41–53.

Murray, E.A., & Mishkin, M. (1984). Severe tactual as well as visual memory deficits follow combined removal of the amygdala and hippocampus in monkeys. *Journal of Neuroscience, 4*, 2565–2580.

Nakamura, Y., Mizuno, N., Konishi, A., & Sato, M. (1974). Synaptic reorganization of the red nucleus after chronic deafferentation from cerebellorubral fibers: An electron microscope study in the cat. *Brain Research, 82*, 298–301.

Nieto-Sampedro, M., & Cotman, C.W. (1985). Growth factor induction and temporal order in CNS repair. In C.W. Cotman (Ed.), *Synaptic plasticity*. New York: Guilford Press.

Oda, Y., Kuwa, K., Miyasaka, S., & Tsukahara, N. (1981). Modification of rubral unit activities during classical conditioning in the cat. *Proceedings of Japanese Academy Series B, 57*, 402–405.

Prokasy, W.F., (1972). Developments with the two-phase model applied to human eyelid conditioning. In A. Black & W. Prokasy (Eds.), *Classical conditioning II. Current research and theory*. New York: Appleton-Century-Crofts.

Pysh, J.J., & Weiss, G.M. (1979). Exercise during development induces an increase in Purkinje cell dendritic tree size. *Science, 206*, 230–232.

Rescorla, A., & Wagner, A.R. (1972). A theory of Pavlovian conditioning: Variations in the effectiveness of reinforcement and non-reinforcement. In A. Black & W. Prokasy (Eds.), *Classical conditioning II. Current research and theory*. New York: Appleton-Century-Crofts.

Rose, F.C., & Symonds, C.P. (1960). Persistent memory deficit following encephalitis. *Brain, 83*, 195–212.

Scoville, W.B., & Milner, B. (1957). Loss of recent memory after bilateral hippocampal lesions. *Journal of Neurology, Neurosurgery and Psychiatry, 20*, 11–21.

Siman, R., Baudry, M., & Lynch, G. (1985). Glutamate receptor regulation by proteolysis of the cytoskeletal protein fodrin. *Nature, 315*, 225–227.

Siman, R., Baudry, M., & Lynch, G. (1986). Calcium-activated proteases as possible mediators of synaptic plasticity. In G.M. Edelman, W.M. Cowan, & E. Gall (Eds.), *Dynamic aspects of neocortical functions.* New York: Wiley.

Singer, W. (1979). Central core control of visual cortex functions. In F.O. Schmitt & F.G. Worden (Eds.), *The neurosciences fourth study program.* Cambrigde, MA: MIT Press.

Singer, W. (1982). Central core control of developmental plasticity in the kitten visual cortex. I. Diencephalic lesions. *Experimental Brain Research, 47,* 209–222.

Singer, W. (1986). Activity-dependent self-organization of synaptic connections as a substrate of learning. *The Dahlem Workshop Report: Neural and molecular mechanisms of learning.* Berlin: Springer-Verlag.

Singer, W., Kleinschmidt, A., & Bear, M.F. (1986). Infusion of an NMDA receptor antagonist disrupts ocular dominance plasticity in kitten striate cortex. *Society of Neuroscience Abstracts, 12,* 786.

Slotnick, B.M., & Katz, H.M. (1974). Olfactory learning-set formation in rats. *Science, 185,* 796–798.

Smith, A.M. (1970). The effects of rubral lesions and stimulation on conditioned forelimb flexion responses in the cat. *Physiology and Behavior, 5,* 1121–1126.

Squire, L.R. (1986). Mechanisms of memory. *Science, 232,* 1612–1619.

Squire, L.R., & Moore, R.Y. (1979). Dorsal thalamic lesion in a noted case of chronic memory dysfunction. *Annals of Neurology, 6,* 503–506.

Standing, L. (1973). Learning 10,000 pictures. *Quarterly Journal of Experimental Psychology, 25,* 207–222.

Staubli, U., Fraser, D., Faraday, R., & Lynch, G. (1987). Olfaction and the 'data' memory system in rats. *Behavioral Neuroscience, 101,* 757–765.

Staubli, U., Fraser, D., Kessler, M., & Lynch, G. (1986). Studies on retrograde and anterograde amnesia of olfactory memory after denervation of the hippocampus by entorhinal cortex lesions. *Behavioral and Neural Biology, 46,* 432–444.

Staubli, U., Ivy, G., & Lynch, G. (1985a). Denervation of hippocampus causes rapid forgetting of olfactory memory in rats. *Proceedings of the National Academy of Science USA, 81,* 5885–5887.

Staubli, U., Roman, F., & Lynch, G. (1985b). Selective changes in synaptic responses elicited in a cortical network by behaviorally relevant electrical stimulation. *Society for Neuroscience Abstracts, 11,* 837.

Sullivan, R.M., & Leon, M. (1986a). Early olfactory learning induces an enhanced olfactory bulb response in young rats. *Developmental Brain Research, 27,* 278–282.

Sullivan, R.M., & Leon, M. (1986b). Implications of norepinephrin in olfactory learning in infant rats. *Society for Neuroscience Abstracts, 12,* 124.

Swindale, N.V. (1982). Absence of ocular dominance patches in dark reared cats. *Nature, 290,* 332–333.

Talland, G.A. (1965). *Deranged memory.* New York: Academic Press.

Teuber, H.-L., Milner, B., & Vaughan, H.G. (1968). Persistent anterograde amnesia after stab wound of the basal brain. *Neuropsychologia, 6,* 267–282.

Thompson, R.F., Berger, T.W., Cegavske, C.F., Patterson, M.M., Roemer, R.A., Taylor, T.J., & Young, R.A. (1976). A search for the engram *American Psychologist, 31,* 209–227.

Thompson, R.F., Berger, T.W., & Madden, J. (1983). Cellular processes of learning and memory in the mammalian CNS. *Annual Review of Neuroscience, 6,* 447–491.

Townes-Anderson, E., & Raviola, G. (1978). Degeneration and regeneration of autonomic nerve endings in the anterior part of rhesus monkey ciliary muscle. *Journal of Neurocytology, 7,* 583–600.

Tsukahara, N. (1986). Synaptic plasticity in the red nucleus and its possible behavioral correlates. In C.W. Cotman (Ed.), *Synaptic Plasticity.* New York: Guilford Press.

Tsukahara, N., & Fujito, Y. (1976). Physiological evidence of formation of new synapses from cerebrum in the red nucleus neurons following cross-union of forelimb nerves. *Brain Research, 106,* 184–188.

Tsukahara, N., Fujito, Y., Oda, Y., & Maeda, J. (1982). Formation of functional synapses in adult cat red nucleus from the cerebrum following cross-innervation of forelimb flexor and extensor nerves. I. Appearance of new synaptic potentials. *Experimental Brain Research, 45,* 1–12.

Tsukahara, N., Hultborn, H., & Murakami, F. (1974). Sprouting of cortico-rubral synapses in red nucleus neurons after destruction of the nuclei's interpositus of the cerebellum. *Experimentia, 30,* 57–58.

Tsukahara, N., Hultborn, H., Murakami, F., & Fujito, Y. (1975). Electrophysiological study of formation of new synapses and collateral sprouting in red nucleus neurons after partial denervation. *Journal of Neurophysiology, 38,* 1359–1372.

Tsukahara, N., & Oda, Y. (1981). Appearance of new synaptic potentials at corticorubral synapses after the establishment of classical conditioning. *Proceedings of the Japanese Academy, Series B, 57,* 389–401.

Tsukahara, N., Oda, Y., & Notsu, T. (1981). Classical conditioning mediated by the red nucleus in the cat. *Journal of Neuroscience, 1,* 72–79.

Uylings, H.B.M., Kuypers, K., Diamond, M.C., & Eltman, W.A.M. (1978). Effects of differential environment in plasticity of dendrites of cortical pyramidal neurons in adult rats. *Experimental Neurology, 62,* 658–677.

Victor, M., Adams, R.D., & Collins, G.H. (1971). *The Wernicke–Korsakoff syndrome.* Philadelphia: Davis.

Volpe, B.T., & Hirst, W. (1983). The characterization of an amnesic syndrome following hypoxic ischemia injury. *Archives of Neurology, 40,* 436–440.

Wagner, A.R. (1981). A model of autonomic memory processing in animal behavior. In N. Spear & R. Ritter (Eds.), *Information processing in animals: Memory mechanisms.* Hillsdale, NJ: Erlbaum.

Wenzel, J., & Matthies, H. (1985). Morphological changes in the hippocampal formation accompanying memory formation and long-term potentiation. In N. Weinberger, J. McGaugh, & G. Lynch (Eds.), *Memory systems of the brain.* New York: Guilford Press.

Williams, N., & Pennybacker, J. (1954). Memory disturbances in third ventricle tumors. *Journal of Neurology, Neurosurgery and Psychiatry, 17,* 115–123.

Wilson, D.A., & Leon, M. (1986). Localized changes in olfactory bulb single unit response to learned attractive odors. *Society of Neuroscience Abstracts, 12,* 123.

Wilson, D.A., Sullivan, R.M., & Leon, M. (1985). Odor familiarity alters mitral cell response in the olfactory bulb of neonatal rats. *Developmental Brain Research, 22,* 314–317.

Woo, C.C., & Leon, M. (1986). Temporal characteristics of the enhanced neural response following odor experience in rats. *Society for Neuroscience Abstracts, 12,* 123.

Zola-Morgan, S., Squire, L.R., & Amaral, D.G. (1986). Human amnesia and the medial temporal region: Enduring memory impairment following a bilateral lesion limited to fields CA1 of the hippocampus. *Journal of Neuroscience, 6,* 2950–2967.

Zola-Morgan, S., Squire, L.R., & Mishkin, M. (1982). The neuroanatomy of amnesia: Amygdala–hippocampus versus temporal stem. *Science, 218,* 1337–1339.

Résumé

L'étude de la mémoire est un grand défi, peut-être le plus grand dans les sciences biologiques. La mémoire implique des changements dans une infime fraction d'un ensemble extrêmement vaste d'éléments, une conclusion qui rend formidable la tâche de trouver ces changements en utilisant les technologies courantes. Que peut-on faire pour contourner cet obstacle dans les recherches neurologiques de l'apprentissage? Une voie de réponse devenue particulièrement productive au cours des années récentes est d'étudier les phénomènes d'apprentissage dans des systèmes "modèles" relativement simples. L'idée est d'extraire des principes de base de ces modèles dans lesquels les détails moléculaires et anatomiques peuvent être étudiés, puis de les utiliser en analysant l'apprentissage dans les régions supérieures du cerveau. Nous présentons dans cet article les progrès en cours et les nouveaux concepts dérivés de cette approche sur des modèles animaux simples.

Granstrom, B., 127
Grating, process of, 17
Grating acuity, 146–148
Green, S., 120
Greenough, W. T., 217
Griffith, B. C., 115

Habituation, 225
Halsted, N., 118, 122
Harris, K. S., 115
Head-aim tracking accuracy, bat's, 159
Head-movement artifact, 166
Hebb, D. O., 53, 86
Hebbian assemblies, and representations, 83–85
Hebb synapse, and resonance, 87–88
Heidmann, T., 87, 93
Held, Richard, 17
Henri algorithm, 66
Hermissenda, 226–227
Hippocampus
  and data memory, 211
  and LTP, 213–215
  and memory, 204–205
Hirsh-Pasek, K., 118
Hoffman, H. S., 115
Homeostat, 83–84
Hopfield, J., 85, 88
Hopfield model, 90
Hubel, D., 144
Hyperbolic frequency scale, 194, 195

Image(s)
  fusion of time- and frequency-domain information into, 192–194
  and neural representations, 156
  neural substrate of formation of, 192
Imagery, and perception, 142
Ingvar, D. H., 129
Insects, sonar interception of, 158–165
Intendment, 69
  and knowledge, 70–71
Intention(s)
  and frontal cortex, 96–97
  and inventions, 96
  neural base for, 97
  selectionist test for, 97–98
Intentionality, and context dependence, 97
Interception, stages in, 159
Internal entities, 42

Internal organization, genesis of, 96
Invariance problem, 112, 113–114
Inventions, selectionist test for, 97–98
Invertebrates, as research tool, 225–227
Isomorphism, lack of, 112

Jitter, effect of, 168
Julesz, Bela, 45
Jusczyk, Peter W., 16–17, 117, 118

Kandel, E. R., 12, 226
Kant, I., 69
Katz, J., 117
Kemler Nelson, D. G., 118
Kennedy, L., 118
Key brain regions, and memory, 203
Killeen, P. R., 124
Kluender, K. R., 124
Knowledge
  at categoric levels, 34
  entity-centered, 52–53
  requirement for episodic, 34
Konishi, M., 131
Kosslyn, S. M., 13
Kuhl, P. K., 117, 123, 124

Labilization, 79
Lamarckian associationism, 100
Lamarckian mechanism, 85
Lambertz, G., 118, 122
Language
  innate vs. acquired, 55
  neurobiological understanding of, 5
Larson, J. R., 217
Lassen, N. A., 129
Learning
  in *Aplysia californica*, 225–226
  in cortical circuitries, 228
  definition of, 202
  and differences in brain structure, 218–219
  in *Hermissenda*, 226–227
  in *Limax*, 227
  and LTP, 215–216
  and memory, 51–54
  neural substrates for, 53–54
  neurobiology of, 201–235
  sequence of, 235
  synaptic mechanism of, 224
  See also Early learning